Marie Špiláčková
Enterprise Social Policy as a
of Development of Social Work

Marie Špiláčková

Enterprise Social Policy as a Means of Development of Social Work

Budrich Academic Press GmbH
Opladen • Berlin • Toronto 2020

The book is based on the author's habilitation thesis, which was successfully defended in November 2016 at the Faculty of Social Studies of the University of Ostrava in Czech Republic.

A CIP catalogue record for this book is available from Die Deutsche Bibliothek (The German Library)

© 2020   by Budrich Academic Press, Opladen, Berlin & Toronto
www. budrich-academic-press.de

      ISBN   978-3-96665-022-9
      eISBN   978-3-96665-992-5
      DOI   10.3224/966650229

Das Werk einschließlich aller seiner Teile ist urheberrechtlich geschützt. Jede Verwertung außerhalb der engen Grenzen des Urheberrechtsgesetzes ist ohne Zustimmung des Verlages unzulässig und strafbar. Das gilt insbesondere für Vervielfältigungen, Übersetzungen, Mikroverfilmungen und die Einspeicherung und Verarbeitung in elektronischen Systemen.

Die Deutsche Bibliothek – CIP-Einheitsaufnahme
Ein Titeldatensatz für die Publikation ist bei Der Deutschen Bibliothek erhältlich.

Budrich Academic Press
Stauffenbergstr. 7. D-51379 Leverkusen Opladen, Germany

86 Delma Drive. Toronto, ON M8W 4P6 Canada
www. budrich-academic-press.de

Professional guarantor of the text: prof. PaedDr. Oldřich Chytil, Ph.D., Dr. h.c.
Jacket illustration by Bettina Lehfeldt, Kleinmachnow – www.lehfeldtgraphic.de
Translator - Bc. Petra Lukšová
Editing Máiréad Collins, Belfast, UK
Typesetting by Ulrike Weingärtner, Gründau – info@textakzente.de
Printed in Europe on acid-free paper by Books on Demand GmbH, Norderstedt

Enterprise Social Policy as a Means of Development of Social Work

Marie Špiláčková
Faculty of Social Studies of the University of Ostrava

ABSTRACT

The topic of the treatise is a reconstruction of the development of social work in enterprises implemented as part of enterprise social policy in the territory of Bohemia and Moravia between the years 1876-1989. Since its professional beginnings, social work has been a major actor and instrument of social policy. Social policy created an environment for the establishment of professional social work. In current specialised literature, enterprise social work is described only in fragments, without any link to the content of social policy realised in individual enterprises nor to how it is implemented. This research's methodology used a hermeneutical approach based on historical research, which is a qualitative research strategy approach. The selected research design corresponds to the concept of social and economic history exploring the transformation of societal institutions, communities and structures. Research methods were hermeneutical in approach – classificatory content analysis, oral history methodology and thematic analysis applied to the collected findings. The final result is a synthesis of findings about the constitution of enterprise social work elaborated on scientific foundations. The enterprise social policy of the Vítkovice Ironworks, or the Baťa company or policy implemented through comprehensive programmes of care for workers created a motivating environment for the constitution and development of expert social work.

Keywords:

social work, enterprises, social policy, historical research, Bohemia and Moravia

Dedicated to my teacher, an important figure in Czech social work,
prof. PaedDr. Oldřich Chytil, Ph.D., Dr.h.c.,
on the occasion of his 75th birthday.

Ostrava, July 2020

Table of Contents

INTRODUCTION

The topic of the treatise entitled *Social Policy in Enterprises as a Means of Development of Social Work* is a reconstruction of the development of social work in enterprises[1] implemented as part of enterprise social policy in the territory of Bohemia and Moravia between the years 1876-1989. Since its professional beginnings, social work has been a major actor and instrument of social policy. Social policy created an environment for the establishment of professional social work. In current specialised literature, enterprise social work is described only in fragments, without any link to the content of social policy realised in individual enterprises nor to how it is implemented. Yet, according to Šálková (1980), social work in organisations was an important part of enterprise social policy.

The aim of the treatise is, based on the study of primary sources of written material in particular, to describe and analyse enterprise social policies of selected entities from the territory of Bohemia and Moravia, implemented mainly in the twentieth century, to describe the areas of enterprise social welfare including institutions and social services offered to employees, and to identify the applied methods of social work, with regard to constitution of enterprise social work as one of the areas of social work performance.

The main aim of the treatise was split into sub-objectives pursuing (1) description, analysis and interpretation of implementation of enterprise social policy (a) in Vítkovice Ironworks between 1876-1954, (b) in the Baťa company between 1900-1945 and (c) complex programmes of employee welfare methodologically guided by the Federal Ministry of Labour and Social Affairs of the Czechoslovak Republic in Prague after 1969; (2) identification of the areas of enterprise social care and offered institutions and social services of the selected entities in the defined territory and observed period; (3) description, analysis and interpretation of implementation of enterprise social policy of the selected entities in the defined territory and observed period; (4) identification of the methods of social work in enterprise social policy of the selected entities in the defined territory and observed period; (5) confrontation of social work carried out in enterprises in the context of the prevalent paradigm of social policy.

---

1 Variations in terms: social work in enterprises, enterprise social work, factory social work and social work in organisations can be found in materials of that time period. The mentioned terms are considered synonymous in specialised literature, and I approach this fact in my treatise in the same way.

The selected entities of implemented enterprise social policy are Vítkovice Ironworks, the Baťa company and the state, or more precisely the Federal Ministry of Labour and Social Affairs (hereinafter 'FMLSA'), centrally shielding the social policy of state-owned enterprises starting from the 1970s in terms of methodology. The selection of the entities was made deliberately. Vítkovice Ironworks were already referred to as one of the biggest metallurgical enterprises during the Austro Hungarian empire period, having become famous for its social programme of providing for employees (cf. Ševeček, 2009). In historical literature a substantial development of social policy coincides with P. Kupelwieser starting as the new director general of the Ironworks in 1876. However, an analysis of social work in this enterprise is absent in specialised literature. According to Matějček (1977) and Ševeček (2009), the Baťa company is considered as a successor to the Vítkovice Ironworks, including the employees' social welfare. Therefore, the second chosen enterprise is precisely the Baťa company in Zlín. This selection is also confirmed by a statement by Jemelka et al. (2015) when they describe Vítkovice and Zlín as iconic examples of European factory cities, with Vítkovice in the last decades of the Austro-Hungarian monarchy having the same position as Baťa's Zlín in the interwar Czechoslovakian Republic. However, according to Jemelka et al. (2015), there is still not evidence of common roots between the two. Šústková (2011), too, finds an increased interest by historians in the history of factories, again after a certain decline. She substantiates the revival by viewing the subject through a different lens than was customary in the past, based on new methodological as well as historical-philosophical impulses, and in a political climate which allows historians to express themselves freely, not being bound by a rigid Marxist schematism. The third analysed entity is the state represented by Federal Ministry of Labour and Social Affairs (hereafter FMLSA), because between 1968-1989 it was the sole implementer of enterprise social policy in the Czech territory.

Timewise, historical research in the treatise is delimited in line with the available source base on the topic of the implementation of enterprise social policy of selected entities and constitution of social work, namely by the years 1876 and 1989. The beginning of the analysis is related to the director Kupelwieser's start at the ironworks in Vítkovice and the end in 1989 correlates with democratic changes and the "Velvet Revolution" in Czechoslovakia. The text of the treatise is arranged chronologically in individual topics.

Diagram No. 1 – Definition of the objective of the treatise in terms of time and topic

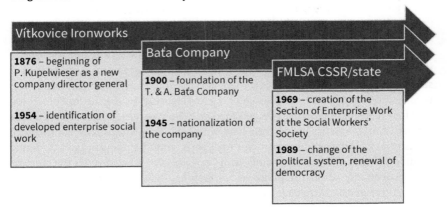

Source: Špiláčková, own construct

Two phenomena of the research subject matters can be deduced from the treatise content. The first subject matter is social work as a practical activity supported by theoretical anchoring and its development implemented in enterprises in the above-mentioned scope. The second phenomenon is the development of enterprise social policy in the same period and territory. Historical discourse mentions social work particularly in connection with changes in social policy.

Research on the history of social work presupposes qualified knowledge of the field, codified in the Czech Republic in the Minimum Standard of Education in Social Work. Research on the history of enterprise social policy does not require this knowledge. Social policy and its branches are a common subject matter of historical science, as stated by Rákosník (2004). The design of the research subject matter implies the basic requirements for the research structure, for the selection of relevant research methods and techniques, as well as the researcher's competence and qualification. The chosen topic requires an interconnection of the social policy discourse, social work and historical discourse. In her study, Davidová Glogarová (2015: 43) emphasises the importance of the, nowadays highly promoted, interdisciplinary approach. The author states that in the context of multidisciplinarity, each scientific discipline comes up with procedures which combine knowledge from related fields. History, like other scientific disciplines, has not only a specific research subject matter, but also methods applied to the given issues.

The study of social work development is predominantly a domain of qualified professionals in the field of social work, using research practices and tools typical of their field, while the historical science is responsible for the study of history in general, naturally, with the relevant methodological apparatus of historical science. This fact is expressed pertinently by Dvořák et al. (2014). Historians are faced with "competitors" in the form of natural scientists, technicians or experts coming from other science disciplines who deal with the history of their own field. As a rule, these specialists are much better qualified in the history of their given field, because they really understand it, unlike historians who are able to describe the history of a field and its researchers, but less so the development of the field as such, because they simply do not understand it. Among other things, this process is confirmed by awarded professorships e.g. in Germany, where the first professorship for the history of physics was awarded in 2014, whereas professorships for the history of mathematics are already commonplace. They are usually not awarded to historians, as we would expect, but to experts from the relevant field. A similar opinion is found in Zwettler, Vaculík, and Čapka (1996) who consider the boundaries between individual disciplines as overlapping. Individual scientific disciplines support one another in many ways. History as a science deals with the activities of people as social beings. It has numerous and close relations to other disciplines like no other. For their work, historians need to use their auxiliary knowledge typical of the individual fields whose history they are studying. According to Hlavačka and Řepa (2014), historians' consideration, respect and humility for the research results of related social disciplines, which help to enhance the vividness of the historical image and enrich the methodological apparatus of historical science, play an increasingly important role.

When implementing historical research, social workers may experience deficiencies in the methodology of historical science and a lack of orientation in historical discourse. Similarly, historians may be uncertain about the professional definition of social work and its practical implementation when working with a client, family, group or community.

It follows that an ideal researcher should be a social worker and a historian in one person. An ideal research strategy should be historical research whose methodology of could be applied to the source base, the subject matter as well as the object of the field or scientific discipline of social work. Being aware of this fact and the potential risks, I have become a competitor of historians. I have elaborated the topic of enterprise social work using professional knowledge of social work, with the assistance of historical research tools.

In accordance with the hermeneutic background, methodology of the empirical part of the treatise is based on historical research which is an approach of qualitative research strategy. The chosen research design corresponds to the concept of social and economic history exploring the transformation of social institutions, communities and structures. Research methods are represented by the hermeneutic-classificatory content analysis according to Plichtová (1996), the oral history method used as a triangulation method and the thematic analysis applied to the collected findings.

Scientific methods of data collection were used to achieve the goal of the treatise. The treatise builds on a combination of theoretical and descriptive approach to the content analysis method according to Plichtová (1996). The theoretical approach consists in the data collection technique, while the descriptive approach is a way of analysing the obtained data. Deductively, basic theoretical categories were created from the findings published in the available literature of primary and secondary character, to which sub-categories were inductively created afterwards. The obtained findings were subsequently subjected to a thematic analysis in accordance with Foucault's genealogical method. Thematic analysis plays a role of 'secondary analysis'. The result is contextual themes aimed at achieving the set goal of the treatise.

Validity of the findings ascertained within the methodological triangulation of the content analysis of primary documents is supported by the memories of witnesses and direct participants of the implemented social policy in selected entities. For this purpose, the technique of semi-standardised interviews was used. The interviews were carried out with: (1) a married couple (the Heczkos) who spent their personal as well as work life in Jubilejní kolonie in Ostrava as employees of the Vítkovice Ironworks; (2) Mrs. Štěpánka Vitásková, she was a member of the 'Young Woman'movement from the Baťa company and a worker at a shoemaking workshop in Zlín; (3) Ing. Anežka Červenáková, a graduate of the University of Social Sciences in Brno, a teaching staff member and a teacher of personnel social work at the Secondary School of Social and Legal Studies in Prague and at the same time an active enterprise social worker in the factory of Tesla Hloubětín; (4) Ing. Helena Šálková who occupied the position of a factory social worker at the Company of heavy current electrical engineering (in Czech name Závody silnoproudé elektrotechniky Elektropřístroje n.p.) enterprise in Praha-Modřany for thirteen years (1952-1965), was a founding member of the Enterprise Social Work Section of the Social Workers', and later a methodologist with FMLSA at the Department of Working Conditions in Comprehensive Care for Employees in the years 1968-1992.

The research subject matter were documents held in the State District Archives of Zlín-Klečůvka, in the Archives of Vítkovice jsc in Ostrava-Vítkovice and the Ostrava City Archives, journals of 'Sociální pracovnice (Social Worker)' and 'Sociální revue (Social Review)' held in the Prague City Archives, materials from personal archives of the contemporaries and research respondents, as well as specialised primary and secondary literature relevant to the treatise topic available in the libraries of the Research Institute for Labour and Social Affairs in Prague, the library of the University of Ostrava and the Moravian-Silesian Research Library in Ostrava.

The topic was not chosen randomly. Researchers' interest in exploring the history of social policy has dropped considerably since 1989. Given the long tradition of its research in the past, Rákosník (2004) proposes to rehabilitate this research subject matter and incorporate it again as a relevant topic in the social history of modern times. Hilger (1996), too, describes a growing importance of enterprise social policy as part of the incentive system in an industrial enterprise.

Considering that social policy is a very broad topic and overlaps various areas of society, Rákosník (2004) admits a plurality of methodological approaches which can be utilised to enrich our knowledge of past events.

This book does not aim at creating a comprehensive treatise on the history of enterprise social policy and enterprise social work in Bohemia and Moravia, but at partially contributing to understanding the social work development, thus motivating or inspiring researchers to further ensue work.

Definition of the terms used, such as social policy, enterprise social policy, care for the poor, social care, social work and enterprise social work with a view to the historical context is found in the first chapter called *Terminological Definition of Terms*.

The second chapter entitled *Social Policy in Vítkovice Ironworks* deals with the constitution of enterprise social policy and social work from 1876 to 1954.

The content of the third chapter with the title *Social Policy of the Baťa Company* is a comprehensive social analysis of the Baťa company between the years 1900 and 1945.

Description and analysis of enterprise care for employees methodologically led by the Federal Ministry of Labour and Social Affairs of the Czechoslovak Socialist Republic between 1969 and 1989 is presented to readers in the fourth chapter entitled *Social Work as an Element of Enterprise Social Policy Methodologically Led by the FMLSA CSR*.

In line with the historical research methodology, chapter five, entitled *Triangulation of Historical Research*, follows. It contains thematic selections from four interviews conducted in an effort to support and supplement the findings ascertained from both primary and secondary sources.

The sixth and last chapter summarises the final research phase, which is the *Research Evaluation*. Its integral part consists of answering the research questions and describing the accomplishment of the goal of the treatise.

A list of used literature, archival aids, primary sources, used symbols, diagrams, figures and tables follow the conclusion. With a view to identifiability of the source materials and preservation of the historical context, the original terms linked to archival sources appear in the treatise. This applies especially to the materials for topics relating to the Vítkovice Ironworks and the Baťa company.

There is still interest in studying history in society. Research results (Šubrt, Vinopal et al., 2013) show that in the Czech Republic, people give weight to history and the knowledge it carries and that most people consider the past a source of important findings. That is why history is important in terms of contemporary Czech society.

The prevailing approach of people to history is largely influenced by their age, gender and education. Women, slightly more often than men, sense historical legacy and the necessity of passing it on. By contrast, men are more often present- and future-oriented. Differences in age are even stronger. As people get older, they increasingly tend to incline to the position of positive affirmation. Younger people tend to hold opinions of historical nihilism. Education seems to have the greatest influence on these opinions. The higher an education a person receives, the greater the likelihood that a person will side with supporters of the necessity to know history is growing as a form of cultural heritage and a legacy for future generations, as something we can learn from for our future (Šubrt, Vinopal et al., 2013).

The public always judges history through the prism of the context of a given period and it primarily highlights historical phenomena and events symbolising a certain current ideal or value which that time's society has become attached to. At present, in terms of importance in Czech history, the period of the First Republic is positively evaluated, for instance. (Šubrt, Vinopal et al., 2013).

Like each scientific discipline, social work has its history. By knowing the history, the context and the factors which influenced it, and its implications, it is possible to understand the causal factors affecting the presenct and to a large extent the future as well (Oláh et al., 2009). This corresponds to an understanding of history based on the concept of causal relationship. The present is the necessary result of previous developments. According to this concept, the patterns of historical development are encoded and, therefore, also an opportunity to take a look into the future. History is not a unit step function, but a necessary part of the process (Šubrt, 2010).

According to Foucault (2002), discontinuity holds a key position in historical disciplines. It has become one of the fundamental elements of historical analysis. Discontinuity is a stigma of time fragmentation and it is historians' task to oust it from history. The new emerging history should reveal something which has been hidden, neglected or even carefully, consciously, maliciously distorted and obscured (Foucault, 2005).

Social work is perceived as an independent profession, an academic discipline and a transdisciplinary practical science (Göppner, Hämäläinen, 2004). Given the threefold perspective of social work, the rationale behind the need to explore historical facts also differs. It consists in exploring the process, the causal relationship along the line of past – present – future. Description of historical facts and their interpretation play an important role in the concept of social work, while being an essential part of the programme of social work science as stated and further elaborated by Špiláčková (2016).

Knowledge of social work history has the potential to act as a source of identity for social workers in relation to their profession and, at the same time, it is a prerequisite for its preservation and cultivation. Abbott, Adler (1989) and Reisch

(1988) also consider the study of social work history as important for strengthening the identity of social workers and anchoring the core values and targets of the profession. The past is especially important for our collective identity. It provides arguments and incentives for group self-identification and cohesion. The past reinforces this identity through the consciousness of a shared destiny, brings evidence to assess the current state, and is a prerequisite for finding and shaping a common future (Šubrt, 2013). Czech social work has still been waiting for a comprehensive elaboration of its history (Špiláčková, 2016).

1. TERMINOLOGICAL DEFINITION OF TERMS

The phenomenon of help is an essential element of humanism, a measure of human solidarity. It does not find itself in a vacuum, but is anchored as well as solved within the social-political system, in the functioning of economic structures, in culture and in the entire intellectual potential of society. However, society evolves, changes and has its own time determinacy. Therefore, the phenomenon of help is historically graded, too. It means that the subject and entity of help change, and the forms, causes and criteria are changing in response to emerging problems (Brnula, Kusin, 2013). Help is, according to Brnula and Kusin (2013), a historical-social phenomenon which can be analysed using two complementary and conditional aspects. The first is a historical-analytical aspect, chronologically identifying various stages of a society's development, its socio-political, economic and cultural background which affects the efforts of individuals, groups and institutions to help the needy. The second aspect is descriptive-factual, reflecting the first aspect from a philosophical point of view, while at the same time identifying the phenomenon of help as a completely free act typical of humankind, which is, however, determined by the historical context.

Historical discourse does mention social work, in particular in connection with changes in social policy. Since its professional beginnings, social work has been an important tool of social policy. Hlavačka and Cibulka (2013) refer to professionalisation and etatization, but also the bureaucratisation of social work as a significant instrument of society in addressing poverty. Apart from social work, instruments such as philanthropy, charity, foundations, alms, supportive social institutions, as well as a state practice, called *postrk, involving forcibly relocating a person (vagrants, beggars, prostitutes) to a municipality where they were required to stay*. Thus, the role of family, church, state and trade unions all contributed to tackling poverty (Hlavačka, Cibulka, 2013). Care for the poor in the Bohemian lands was a duty of municipalities based on the domicile law. It represented one of the few agendas of municipal self-governments where the municipalities cooperated closely with the engaged public, e.g. women who participated in the public life of the community in the form of philanthropy (Pokludová, 2013). Starting from the end of the 18th century, models of care for the socially needy inhabitants envisaging a cooperation between state and local government authorities, public and private sectors, were becoming increasingly popular. In the field of social care, women's organisations attained a remarkably significant position from a gender perspective. Diversification in systems of care for the poor gave rise to various types of social and health facilities. The practice of eliminating poverty, including the policies regarding poverty, were a fundamental indicator for European societies on their way towards social modernisation. Instrumentalisation of the past may remind contemporaries of the functioning of past models for tackling various social problems, but also draw their attention to the possibilities of coping with the pressing social problems of today and to their contextualisation in the economic, cultural and social environment (Hlavačka, Cibulka, 2013).

At the beginning of the 20th century, the development of social opinions in Czechoslovakia copied the German and Austrian patterns. After the World War I, social spending was rising in these countries, which was closely related to political circumstances, such as the collapse of monarchies and the emergence of republican regimes with influential social democratic parties (Rákosník, Tomeš et al., 2012). In 1921 the Minister of Welfare, Dr. J. Gruber, positively evaluated the social policy of the Czechoslovak Republic. He wrote that in certain ways we were at the forefront of social policy of the European and American continent and far beyond the international conventions. For example, he highlighted enterprise socialisation (Gruber, 1921). Social measures significantly influenced both the form and content of the social work practice which was in the territory of Bohemia and Moravia in many respects similar to other European countries.

With regard to the topic of this treatise, it is necessary to further focus on the historical development and content variability of the relevant terms such as social policy, social policy of organisations, care for the poor, social care, social work and enterprise social work.

1.1 Social Policy versus Social Policy of Organisations

The concept of social policy changes depending on how the practice in society changes its function, content and scope (Šálková, Tomeš, 1983). The term is well-known to everyone, but each generation understands and uses it differently.

Albín Bráf (1851-1912) is considered the founder of the 'Czech School of Social Policy'. Since the beginnings of its activity, the Czech school has had a history of more than a hundred years. His followers are represented by his students grouped around the Social Institute of the Czechoslovak Republic, namely prof. Josef Gruber, prof. Karel Engliš, prof. Josef Macek, JUDr. Evžen Štern, prof. Emil Schoenbaum and JUDr. Osvald Stein (Kotous et al., 2014).

It is evident from Bráf's writings that he regarded social policy as part of economic policy, where social policy is identified with a system of measures, particularly in the area of employment, wage development and social security. According to Bráf, the aim of social policy is a successful development of society and protection against social upheavals. Bráf defines social policy as "using public power by means of legislation and administration for the benefit of those social classes which have been constrained or endangered in the conditions of their being and prosperity by the process of life following the lines of legal frameworks valid so far" (Kotous, Munková, Peřina, 2003: 32). According to Kotous et al. (2014), the roots of social-political institutes often date back far into the past when the historical development was highly complex and closely linked with the development of social conflicts. Therefore, the emergence of social policy in the territory of Bohemia and Moravia cannot be bound or dated to a specific historical event.

Hlavačka, Cibulka et al. (2015) establish social policy as a transformed care for the poor.

Albín Bráf's pupils and successors built on his definition discussed above. K. Engliš (1916: 9) understood social policy in general as a practical endeavour to "cultivate and transform a social whole as ideally as possible". He understood the social whole as a segment of society which stands in the shadow of a common legal order, i.e. society of the population within the same state. Here, Engliš talks about social policy in the widest sense of the word, about social policy which includes all policies aimed at strengthening and enhancing the social whole – hence a policy seeking to increase the production of productive forces, to increase the health conditions and cultural level. Macek (1923) considers Engliš's definition as too broad and, in some respects, he accepts its interpretation as a completely anti-social.

In the narrower and inherent sense, social policy, according to Engliš (1916: 19), takes care that "the fruits of material and spiritual culture are divided into the different layers of the social whole as fairly and therefore as evenly as possible".

An ideal society for him was one "which preserves and economically multiplies its energies, as quickly as possible but permanently fulfils its task of deepening and intensifying the life of possibly all its members towards the ideal of a healthy, educated and moral human" (Engliš, 1992: 77). It follows from this definition that Engliš (1992) did not place special emphasis on the quantity but on the quality of life. People should not only have enough food and other consumer goods, but also have the opportunity for further education and cultural development. He determined the social ideal of life, health and culture of the whole society was described as a so-called supreme good which is a manifestation of the will to live within the social whole.

According to Engliš (1916), social policy disregards individuals and is only concerned with entire groups, layers, classes whose status and destiny is not indifferent to the state and development of the social whole. Basically, it was a levelling policy which balances social discrepancies and as such, it pays attention to the layers and classes of the weaker, oppressed, less wealthy, to those who carry the greater part of the burden of work within society, while obtaining less than the average share of the fruits of material and spiritual culture. Social policy strives to enhance these layers.

Working conditions of labourers were regulated in the Trade Licence Code which was amended on 15th March 1883[2]. Here, the employer-employee relationship was also officially regulated for the first time. Based on an amendment from 1883, only one ministerial decree was created, characterising the factory as a "manufacturing plant in which about 20 labourers worked in enclosed spaces and were accommodated outside their workplace, where machines were used in some degree of division of labour, where the owner did not participate in the manual labour and paid an appropriate amount of taxes" (Efmertová, 1998: 165). Trade licence inspectors supervised observation of the Trade Licence Code. The Trade Licence Code was further amended several times. The individual amendments regulated e.g. a day off, work safety, funds established at individual industrial plants and others. By enacting a compulsory accident and sickness insurance, social reforms in Austria-Hungary developed (Efmertová, 1998).

Engliš (1916: 20) points out that acts of mercy do not belong to social policy: "The driving force behind social policy is not mercy, but justice and social purposefulness". Tomáš Baťa had the same assumption.

Engliš (1916) considers the role of the state to be crucial for social policy. Apart from the state, which is the supreme body of social policy, its agent may also be lower body within the state which enforces government policy – of both local (provinces, districts, municipalities) and interest nature (communities, chambers of commerce and trade licence). Voluntary and self-help associations for the vulnerable also belong to these arms of the state . The fundamental role of the state has found its image in the agent view of social policy. Engliš (1992) divides social policy by the agent, i.e. based on the nature of the state which implements it. Engliš (in Kotous et al., 2014) distinguishes between general and special social policy. General social policy was about dividing the fruits and the burden of labour based on the principles of personal solidarity. Special social policy was a policy for certain classes, such as middle classes, labourers, the poor and consumers.

According to Macek (1923, 1925), social policy should remedy the shortcomings and injustices arising from the ruling social order. In a narrower sense, Macek understood social policy as one of the fields of state policy; in the narrowest sense of the word, as an effort of help to improve the conditions of the labourer population as much as possible (Rákosník, Tomeš, 2012).

In 1930 Arnošt Bláha presented a contribution at the Masaryk Sociological Society dealing with the sociological aspect of the social situation of the labourers' group. In his text he encouraged implementation of scientific research into the life of labourers as for work and their family life. Bláha states that the labourers' satisfaction does not only result from the fulfilment of material needs, but also from

---

2   The amendment to the Trade Licence Code No. 39 of the Code of 15th March 1883 expanded and deepened the Emperor's Patent No. 227/1859.

fulfilment of intellectual needs. Labourers do not only want wages and insurance, they want culture and entertainment, too. Social dissatisfaction of labourers arises from failing to fulfil one of these goals: "The welfare of the whole is conditioned by the welfare of all its parts. The life of a group and the life of a whole is not autotelic, it only makes sense in the context of a higher relationship frame, higher moral superiority" (Bláha, 1931: 315). In Bláha's words we can recognise the necessity of meeting the needs of those working through available means, e.g. through employers.

Contemporary publications on social policy are generally influenced by authors from the first half of the 20th century, for instance M. Potůček (1995), I. Tomeš 2010), and V. Krebs (2007).

Social policy represents a unity of three elements:

a) Normative determinants – they represent a necessary value basis of social policy, always resting upon a certain idea of the proper social order, as follows from Engliš's definition.
b) Economic determinants – they represent the limit of socio-political activities; a certain amount of wealth in society allows redistribution and donation of funds for selected targets.
c) Socio-structural determinants – each social policy is based on the currently existing social structure of society, following the 'Merton' definition of social structure as "an organized set of social relationships in which members of society or group are involved in different ways" (Rákosník, Tomeš, 2012: 12-13).

According to Rákosník and Tomeš (2012) social policy can be summarised as a systematic and targeted effort to maintain or transform the vertical and horizontal social structure of society.

Social policy of the socialist state was conceived as a policy of living standards, lifestyle and personal development. It was part of the targeted control of society. The main implementer of targets in the area of growth in both material and cultural level of the population and its social security was the state, along with social, socialist, economic and other organisations (Šálková, 1981). Průcha (1983) defines the target of social policy in a narrower sense as creation of life and social securities for working people.

In accordance with the sociological definition, an industrial plant consisted in a social group characterised by standing among small groups, such as family, and large groups, such as the nation, the state. An industrial enterprise was described as a social system in which signs of problems, interests and conflicts typical of society-wide, national or national aspects were reflected on a smaller scale (Zapletalová, Zapletal, 1972).

Zapletalová, Zapletal (1972) considered external relationships to be vital in determining the social system/enterprise. The first relationship is enterprise and society/type of social order. The second relationship is enterprise and the geographical location of the enterprise. Both relationships influence the course of processes in the social system of the enterprise.

According to Sova (1978), social policy incorporated the policy of the standard of living. In this sense, according to Šálková (1981), the main target of social policy was to create equal living conditions for the development of personality of all members of society. Through the policy of the standard of living, social policy:

a) increased living standards of social groups not participating in the distribution of work (children, students, disabled and sick people, pensioners).
b) established and ensured social securities (employment, working conditions, housing, health care, upbringing and education, pricing policy, social welfare).
c) provided aid to a part of the population finding itself in difficult life situations (young people in need of special care, persons with reduced working capacity, etc.) (Sova, 1978).

The main bearer of responsibility for implementing social policy was still the state, as well as social and economic organisations, as well as enterprises, cooperatives, and institutes. Šálková (1981) talks about the three pillars of complementary activities, aimed at optimal arrangement of human needs and universal development and realisation of a person in society.

According to Šálková and Tomeš (1983), enterprise social policy in the period of CSSR organically satisfied the social needs of workers through a system of social facilities and services, professionally qualified people and funds, organised to carry out social activities for the benefit of workers and their family members. This system represented enterprise care for workers.

The above implies that social policy is of great importance in enterprises. We cannot avoid contemplation on the positive influence of historical roots in applying social policy in enterprises such as Baťa Zlín or Vítkovice Ironworks. However, if we look at the description of the historical development of social policy in organisations in the Ministry materials of that time, the origins can be found only after the year 1945, put in place by the leading party and a result of the process of nationalisation of enterprises.

Rákosník (2004) outlines another view on the usage of the term social policy in connection with implementation in enterprises. He writes that when the Krupp enterprise provided social benefits to its workers, it cannot be perceived as social policy. Policy is tied to a public space, while the employment relationship is a relationship under private law. He admits an exception to the use of social policy in enterprises in the case of Marxists, because only in the doctrine of base and superstructure, can one speak in this sense of bourgeoisie policy outside the sphere of a political system. Subsequently, activities which become the subject of state or derived norm-making can form social policy, which also applies to enterprises and organisations.

Hilger (in Jemelka et al., 2015) observed a growing importance of social policy as part of the incentive system in the business organisation of the German iron and steel industry starting from the mid-19th century, in the process of transitioning from ownership to managerial business. The proprietary system allowed better identification with the business entity. Social policy was a motivational and compensatory element. The second managerial type of business was more anonymous and social policy functioned as a financial compensation in the form of wages and their extraordinary components.

Šálková (1973) mentioned three mutually harmonising pillars of social policy in the socialist era, specifically: (1) state social policy, (2) social policy of social organisations, and (3) enterprise social policy. All three pillars contained complementary activities aimed at solving human problems in an optimal way.

The broadest legal standards for enterprise social policy were the Labour Code No. 65/1965 Coll., Act No. 121/1975 Coll. on Social Security, including related regulations, Government Resolution of CSSR No. 66/1973, Government Resolution No. 139/1975, Guidelines on Compilation of Comprehensive Care Programmes for Workers for the Years 1976-1980, Government Resolution of CSSR No. 59/1980 passing principles for improving the planned control of screening, personnel and social governance and Act on the State-Owned Enterprise No. 88/1988 Coll.

Tomeš (2013) states that in the years 1969-1972, labour productivity dropped significantly in connection with a decline in work discipline and as a result of political events. To reinforce work discipline, the Labour Code No. 153/1969 Coll. was amended, amending and supplementing the existing Labour Code. In the explanatory memorandum, the authors complained about an unsatisfactory state of work discipline, adversely affecting the development of national economy. The Labour Code was meant to become a more effective tool for strengthening work discipline and state discipline at all governance levels and for empowering the authority of senior staff. This was, besides tax adjustment, a way to reinforce centralisation.

Enterprise social policy was based on state plans of a directive nature and it was anchored in legislation as well. It represented continuous and purposeful care for employees in terms of ensuring their justified social needs. It focused on health and safety at work, on factory catering, recreation of workers, children's recreation in pioneer summer camps of the trade union movement, enterprise kindergartens and nurseries, housing policy in enterprises, issues of work environment and living conditions, and wage policy (Kutta et al., 1980a; Kutta et al., 1980b); social responsibility of the state moved smoothly to enterprises and organizations.

Hilger (1996) was concerned with a precise definition of the term enterprise social policy in connection with researching social policy of leading German enterprises. According to the author, enterprise social policy encompasses a wide range of contents, distinguishing among the following main groups: pension security, cash benefits, facilities for employees, support from the employer in the field of housing and education. According to Preller, writing in 1953 (in Hilger, 1996: 26), in addition to material benefits, enterprise social policy also includes "social, organizational, psychological and sociological measures established by a particular enterprise". However, this term has not been clearly defined yet. According to Herbert Hax (in Hilger, 1996: 26), in a very broad sense, it entails a summary of all enterprise measures designed to improve the situation of employees in industrial society beyond payment of work remuneration, to eliminate certain disadvantages and shortcomings at the workplace as well as outside the enterprise, and in particular, to contribute to securing against certain life and work risks.

1.2   Care for the Poor versus Social Care

Two terms are described in historical discourse: care for the poor and support of the poor. Care for the poor in Bohemia was related, not only to a short-term change to the means of the poor, by contributions in cash and in kind, but also included providing accomodation in an institution for the poor lasting several years. Support was understood as temporary aid with funds. The care was provided by the administrative bodies, while charity (support) was usually performed by private persons or private institutions (associations). The difference between care and support consisted in the fact that the care for the poor was mostly linked to closed institutions (Hlavačka, 2015).

Systems of care for the poor, managed solely by municipalities or parishes, were developing from early modern times. The Habsburg monarchy had had care for the poor since the sixteenth century. The care was linked to the residents' home affiliation. The home municipality was obliged to take care of its socially needy citizens. Care for the poor was anchored in legislation, especially in the imperial-royal Act on Home Law. The region of Bohemia was governed by the Law on the Poor No. 59 of 1868 (Rákosník, 2010).

Traditionally, care for the poor included measures to provide the most necessary nutrition, shelter, clothing and other essential needs for residents who suffer from both culpable and non-culpable poverty. At the turn of the 19th and 20th century, care for the poor (called *chudinství*) and care for working people turned into social policy with preventive and pedagogical-defensive goals. Social policy was abandoning repressive tools of action such as the forced relocation of citizens (noted above '*Postrk*') and the coercion of these same people to work in particular jobs, while paying more attention to the active creation of jobs and upbringing of poor youth (Hlavačka, Cibulka et al. 2015).

At the turn of the 19th and 20th century, the notion of care for the poor was replaced by the term public care. According to Hlavačka (2015), public care was not only meant to alleviate poverty by improving the economic situation for the poor, but also to promote public care by legislative measures and mainly to create new jobs. According to Krakeš and Krakešová (1934), public social welfare was carried out exclusively in poorhouses throughout the nineteenth century. Tomeš (2010) states that social care replaced the older term care for the poor and it was used to refer to all public social agendas combined. Social care as an institute of social protection of the population is significantly older than social insurance (Rákosník, 2010).

Jurnečková (1935) points out the absence of the term social care in the valid legal order of the Czechoslovak Republic in 1935. The laws of that time identified some tasks from this field under the umbrella of health policy, care for the poor or charitable institutions. In connection with changes in society, with modern economic life and the growth of industrial cities, various forms of poverty and deficiencies were emerging. And in the spirit of the new needs, not only a new concept of social care came into being, but new social work came into existence, too. According to Šilhánová (1992), before World War II voluntary care along with public care formed integral parts of social assistance which were tied to each other and interconnected.

A practical institutional highlight of Czech (Czechoslovak) social practice was the creation of the Ministry of Social Welfare, and the founding of the Social Institute of the Czechoslovak Republic and its press body, Social Review. A symbolic and ultimately practical achievement was the construction of the exemplary Masaryk Homes in Prague-Krč in the late 20th century (Hlavačka, 2015: 101).

After 1945, the notion of social care was associated in the contemporary literature with a capitalist notion of "caring" for the socially weak. Kraus (1948: 9) declares social care "merely a somewhat more organized degree of charity". Minister Šoltész already emphasised the inferiority of social care within the concept of social policy in his speech on 4th December, 1945, when he proclaimed that it would no longer be just about social welfare, but about protection of work and creative power which is the most important component in the national creation of goods and values. (Rákosník, 2010). This is also reflected in the social plan of the first five-year plan. Kraus (1948) wrote there that social services during the five-year plan would primarily focus on preserving and developing the physical and mental abilities of all working people, in a planned distribution of labour force, on achieving the greatest possible effect of the labour force mobilisation, and further more caring for citizens who, through no fault of their own, cannot actively participate in an economic activity. Overall, social services will contribute to raising the standard of living of the population.

In the years 1945-48, there was no conceptual change in social care. Basically, social care only replaced care for the poor on the terminological level. In this sense, the executive body changed, replaced by national, local or district committees. The principle of home law persisted because the municipality to which the citizen belonged had a subsidiary duty to provide for them from public funds, unless the person was protected e.g. from their own resources or through charity. Home Law was repealed by Act No. 174/1948 Coll. When entitlement to maintenance arose, the municipality where the person concerned had a residence or place of stay was obliged to take care of it (Rákosník, 2010).

After 1945, factory social service was established based on the instructions of the then Ministry of Labour and Social Care. Factory social service was conceived as a new, higher form of social care, free from charitable elements (Šálková, 1981). Its task was, according to Šálková (1981), to focus on a gradual fulfilment of social needs of workers in the interest of their full employment, to prevent difficulties and phenomena which would hinder the ability of a person to work, and to induce satisfaction at work.

For this purpose, social-political departments were created in nationalised enterprises, whereas social-political deputies and, in big enterprises, directors for social affairs were entrusted with their management. Within these departments, also social workers pursued their activities. This institutional development was supported by the bodies of the Revolutionary Trade Union Movement (hereinafter 'RTUM'). This is evidenced by the RTUM Bulletin from 1947 in which a directive entitled "Main Principles for the Activities of Social-Political Directors and Social Clerks" was published. Another tool for developing the care of organiaations of their employees was collective agreements. In some companies, collective agreements were concluded already in 1922 (Šálková, 1981). The development of social policy in enterprises was significantly influenced by a resolution of the Board of the Central Committee of the Communist Party of Czechoslovakia: "Resolution of the Board of the Central Committee of the Communist Party of Czechoslovakia on Screening and Personnel Work" of 6th November 1970, which commanded organiaations to develop comprehensive care for employees, including socio-legal counselling and care for groups of workers. This legitimiaed the main tendency of transferring social costs to state-owned enterprises and including them in production costs, thus shifting the social responsibility for social services.

In the 1950s, attention was concentrated on three areas of benefit and service recipients:

1) War invalids and survivors/victims of war– who were usually socially needy. The method of protection consisted in a maintenance principle from the state budget. It was a form of social solidarity.
2) Social welfare – included special protection of people with specific needs, as well as safety net benefits for those who found themselves in difficult living conditions due to a lack of subsistence means.
3) Social pension – by its nature, it was a benefit of the social safety net. The recipients' social neediness was tested thoroughly (Rákosník, 2010).

A different understanding of social care in Czechoslovakia in the 1950s is found in the Explanatory Memorandum to the Social Security Act of 1956 which includes the following definition: "Social care is primarily understood as placement of people with reduced working capacity, provision for disabled and elderly persons in social care institutions and granting of specials benefits to citizens in need" (Rákosník, 2010).

There was no statutory regulation of social care between 1948-56. A new tool of social care was a social pension anchored in the Act on National Insurance. Thanks to it, social protection became universal. A condition for its granting was level of need and reaching the age of 65 years. It was only an optional benefit and not claimable like old age pension. Social pension consistently appeared in further legislation propositions of social security from the years 1956, 1964, 1975 and 1988 (Rákosník, 2010).

Apart from the social pension, another component of social welfare at the time was individual support provided by National Committees and care institutions for persons with special needs. National Committees were not sufficiently adapted for performing social care. Ruling authorities were reflected in the manner of social care performance. Sources suggest that criteria other than the social ones also found their way into the evaluation criteria (Rákosník, 2010).

National Committees implemented two forms of care: individual and specialised. Individual care consisted of subsidiary assistance to needy citizens from the means of National Committees. It represented additional protection in cases where the citizen for various reasons did not have enough means of subsistence. One of the special forms was common catering for pensioners. In 1956, the existing trend in opinions on social care began to turn. It gradually began to be rehabilitated as a standard part of a comprehensive system for social protection of the population. It was statutorily regulated in the Act on Social Security No. 55/1956 Coll. (Rákosník, 2010).

Hodek (1978) demonstrates the demand for introducing care for workers through Marx's ideas from Part Three of Capital. Accomplishment of the socialist model of "labour humanisation", which was meant to support the self-realisation of workers, presupposed changes in the social structure (elimination of private property), changes in the division of labour and the creation of opportunities for a universal development of workers. Through an objective development, individuals should be prepared to participate in democratic control. And this situation required active preparation for social control, as predicted by K. Marx.

According to Hodek (1978), in the era of socialism, care for people had to include two approaches: (a) approach towards a person as an object of attention, i.e. care for his problems and interests, (b) approach towards a person as an evolving agent. In this sense, the system concept of care for workers in an enterprise did not consist only in protecting against negative consequences and improving the living conditions. Hodek emphasised that workers would become agents of progress, agents of convergence of the advantages of socialism with the achievements of capitalism. There he saw differences from the "human relations" and "social planning" models presented in the then so-called Western capitalist world. The interconnection of achievements from Eastern and Western social systems presented by Hodek in 1978 in the Sociological Journal corresponds to the theory of convergence, whose dominant period was the 1960s.

1.3   Social Care versus Enterprise Social Work

The content of social work and its methods evolved following the specific social needs of citizens in social care and social policy. It is complicated to define the notion of social work because it has various aspects, in the practice of social care, the term applies to many different things (Novotná, Schimmerlingová, 1992).

Mary Richmond (1942: 112) defined social work as follows: "Social case work consists of those procedures which develop personality by deliberately guiding a person to adaptation to another person and their social environment."

According to Klíma (1931), the notions of social care and social work were in the same broad sense considered synonymous. Lund (1935) talks about the relationship of social work and social care as follows: "Professional social work means work in the field of social care based on special knowledge, derived from thinking and experience, and developed by the creative power and skills of those who perform it. ... These two new areas – of which the larger movement is social care and the second area is professional social work, converge in social organizations" (Lund, 1935: 74).

Professor In. A. Bláha defined social work at the Congress of Social and Health Work in the Czechoslovak Republic in 1928 entitled "Education and Social Work". He understood social work as "a specialized activity, seeking to eliminate or remedy social deficiencies" (Klíma, 1931: 31).

Social confidants/Volunteer counsellors', were a function of the wider public intended to help people in need. They worked at Baťa's factories, and provided a definition of social work as well. At the conference of enlightenment and social confidants of shops held in Prague on 12th October 1944, the following was presented: "The whole of social work rests on the principle of the doctrine of social establishment based on social ownership. This doctrine is called social and in principle it says that people should share both the sorrows and pleasures which they encounter, help one another and come to an accommodation with one another. Social work is of ancient origin. Historians found it in ancient times in all cultural nations. Even in the Bible, in the Old Testament, a willing opening of hands for the poor and destitute in the country is ordered, and the New Testament states that it is the duty of one to bear the burden of others" (SDAZ, Zlín, Prodejní v ČSR X, inv. No. 87).

According to Šmýd (1972), social work was terminologically defined as a set of activities whose purpose was a direct effort immediately acting on a person or their family to maintain their relationship with society, their closest environment, education, work, etc. Social work was characterised as a social-diagnostic, counselling and educational work, providing social services in specific cases. A similar view is found in Tomeš (1996) who states that social work is perceived as a social service for the benefit of people in social distress.

Practically implemented social care was in practice as early as 1923 at the Czechoslovak State Railways, where lay supervisors functioned.

The topic of "Social Services in Industry" was listed as an official professional section of the International Conference on Social Services in Paris, which was held as part of the "Fourteen Days of International Social Welfare" from 1st to 13th July 1928. For instance, Marie Krakešová, Helena Radlinska and others gave a speech at the congress (Kotek, 1928).

According to Hromada (1942), the activity of social workers in industrial plants abroad was not new either. Social workers known as Fabrikspflegerin, Sozialbeamtin and Sozialbetriebsarbeiterin had functioned in many German factories since 1904. The basis for their social-health activities in industrial plants was formed by two important circumstances: (1) a massive development in occupational medicine and all its components, and especially (2) practical implementation and deepening of social and social-health care for workers' health and well-being. In this respect, social workers in industrial plants represented another successful step in labourers' social care. As for the employment relationship, factory social workers were employees of the given factory. They were hired to care for the social and health aspects of the factory workers and their families.

The activity of factory social workers was divided into two parts: (a) the health and social component and (b) the occupational-health component. In the social component, according to Hromada (1942), they were independent forces, primarily relying on the factory management when carrying out their tasks. In the occupational-health component, they were auxiliary forces for the company physician. The social part of their work covered activities inside the factory and outside the factory in the workers' families. Social workers gave advice regarding socio-legal protection of labourers such as insurance, rent issues, compensation for occupational diseases, health care, guardianship, etc. They helped to write various applications concerning social-health care, placement in sanatoriums, hospitals, health spas. In some cases, factory social workers acted as an intermediary between workers and official places (Hromada, 1942).

Activities outside the factory included visits in families. According to Hromada (1942), it was an important part of their work. A stimulus for a visit could in some cases be of an economic nature, sometimes it was an educative stimulus, e.g. in the case of families with children with disabilities. They could give practical advice to these families and refer the families to professional counselling centres or relevant educational institutions. Other tasks of family visits included: health reasons (illness in the family, childbirth, post-natal care, infant care), decontamination of families with tuberculosis, guiding of women to cleanliness and household care, assessment of the necessity of sending a child to a sanatorium, elimination of social injustices and others. Visits to families were also of a profound psychological significance. For an ill labourer, a visit by the factory social worker meant a practical evidence that they were not excluded from the factory work community, that the factory depends on them and is trying to assist them at the times of illness, too.

Hromada (1942) points out the fact that with such an extensive set of duties, social workers may have faced a lot of difficulties, because they were in a double position. Firstly, they were the labourers' confidants and at the same time the confidants of the factory management. Due to a lack of understanding and little awareness of their work content, some regarded factory social workers as a supervisory factory body. According to Hromada, the same doubts were also encountered in other countries. However, these were mostly initial doubts which were eliminated with time and by the goal-directed actions of workers in practice.

At the beginning of October 1942, a total of 1966 factory social workers and 327 helpers worked in Czechoslovakia. They were mainly employed in arms factories and in factories with largely female staff. At the same time, there were 499 in training courses to become factory social workers (Factory Social Workers, 1943).

After World War II, significant efforts to establish factory social services conceived as an enterprise social institution were noticeable. The task was to satisfy the social needs of workers in organisations with a view to preventing phenomena which would hinder their work performance. The Revolutionary Trade Union Movement contributed to the introduction of factory social services. Activities were carried out by social workers who often functioned as social clerks (Berka, Šálková, Tomeš, 1987).

Higher secondary vocational schools responded to the need for professionally prepared social workers for work in factories, too. In 1947, the first year of the future four-year Social and Health School and the second year of education for social workers were experimentally established at the Higher Secondary Vocational School for Women's Occupations in Ostrava. By reading the records of school-leaving examinations we can find that in the second year, the students completed compulsory practical course in Vítkovice Ironworks in the field of factory care. Thematically selected school-leaving examination questions were "Organisation of Social Policy in Nationalized Enterprises", "Care for Workers in People's Democracy" or "Care for Labourers' Housing and Catering" (AMO, Higher School of Health Care in Vítkovice, NAD 490, cart. 6, inv. No. 125).

Care for factory employees was part of the social plan and corresponded to the idea of a countrywide social policy, according to Dr. Purkyňová (1946) from the Institute of Human Labour in an article included in the Social Worker journal in the first post-war volume. The diagram shows classification of factory social workers in the countrywide social policy system.

Diagram No. 2 – Countrywide Social Policy

Nationwide policy	Ministry of Social Welfare (division IV, VI)	Labour Protection Offices (Social Dept., Labour Protection Dept.)	Enterprise management • enterprise social worker
	Central Trade Union Council (Social-Political Board)	Regional Trade Union Councils (Social-Political Boards)	RTUM of Works Council • social clerk of RTUM of Works Council

Source: Purkyňová, 1947: 2

The first task of enterprise social care was to ensure social work "dealing with care for socially needy individuals and with care of collective nature, too" (Purkyňová, 1946: 76).

In the diagram below, Purkyňová (1947) shows the organisational classification of factory social workers in an enterprise structure.

Diagram No. 3 – Organisational Structure of Large Enterprises

Social-Political Enterprise Directorate	Personnel Department	Disposition Section
		Educational and Training Section
		Legal Section
		Pay and Wages Section
	Social Department	**Social Care Section – enterprise social worker**
		Section of Cultural and Recreational Care
	Department of Hygiene and Safety at Work	Company Physician
		Section of Safety at Work
	Secretary's Office	

Source: Purkyňová, 1947: 1

Both organisational charts matched the needs of large enterprises. The organisation was easier in smaller enterprises. The charts prevented misunderstandings in the definition of activities between a factory social worker and a social clerk of the Works Council. Purkyňová pointed out the need for synergies between these functions (Purkyňová, 1947).

In 1947, Purkyňová, presents, in the pages of the Social Worker journal, factory social care as a new establishment, without traditions, only in the early days of its inception and development. We find other professional texts on factory social work only after 1968 by the author H. Šálková.

After 1969, enterprise social work was carried out in line with an organisational social plan or programme from its own resources. Only in some cases were resources of the Trade Union Movement or National Committees used. Basic tasks were subsequently reflected in collective agreements between the organisation management and the relevant Trade Union body. Social workers were entitled to conduct appropriate investigations with workers both at the workplace and in the place of residence as directed by the organisation management (Šálková, 1971). Social activities carried out by social workers were targeted at members of working collectives and their families. Enterprise social work was part of the enterprise social policy. Social work in an enterprise is understood as a concretisation of enterprise social/personal policy.

Based on the plan of the division of Social Workers' Society for 1969 (Šálková, 2016), enterprise practice was included in agricultural and industrial plants and other manufacturing and non-manufacturing organisations, regardless of the size and structure of their base unit. The main goal of social workers in enterprise practice was to prevent and solve the social problems of people in conjunction with their environment. Through group and individual social work, organisations offered professional assistance to their employees, especially in preventing adverse life situations or eliminating their consequences (Šálková, 1989).

1.4   Selected Examples of European Enterprise Social Policy

Enterprise social policy was not a realm of large organizations only. Numerous examples can be found in articles of that time in the professional journal of Social Worker, in primary literature, in conference agendas or abroad. Organisers of the social work course, too, were aware of the necessity to include the field of social policy in the education of social workers, as evidenced by a mention in the journal. The question of social policy and social care appeared as a separate lecture by Dr. L. Winter entitled "Social Policy and Social Care of the Present Time" as part of a social work course organised by the Higher School of Social Welfare and the Organisation of Social Workers in Easter week 1935 under the chairmanship of Dr. Alice G. Masaryková (Social Work Course, 1934; Social Work Course, 1935: 80).

Literature from the 1970s reviewing the history of the topic, mentions the development of social work in organisations the year 1945 and later years as the inception. This statement can be easily disproved by findings, for instance, from the articles on the beginnings of factory social work in Czechoslovak State Railways in the 1930s, or actions in the social sphere of the large metallurgical enterprises of Třinec Iron and Steel Works, and others. The examples below illustrate the scope of enterprise policies in the territory of the then republic, as well as abroad, outside the analysed enterprises. In practice, many more can be found.

1.4.1 Czechoslovak State Railways

The social insurance system in the Habsburg monarchy and in the Czechoslovak Republic had two forms: state and enterprise. The first signs of securing employees against injury, illness or old age can be traced back to the Middle Ages in mining brotherhoods. The first railway company in the Habsburg monarchy which established a pension institution was the Emperor Ferdinand Northern Railway. Shareholders voted for establishing a pension institution in 1844 (Bek, 2015).

One of the institutes complementing the social system of the Northern Railway company (Pension Society and Sickness Fund) was the "Emperor Ferdinand Jubilee Shelter", set up in Valtice in 1898 to mark the 50th anniversary of Emperor Franz Joseph I acceding to the throne. A foundation focusing on care for children of employees of the state railways was established ten years later (Bek, 2015).

The first mentions of setting up so-called factory social work in Czechoslovakia can be found already at the beginning of the 20th century. In the Social Review journal from 1923, we can read about social care at the Czechoslovak State Railways. The security system for employees of the Czechoslovak State Railways (hereinafter 'CzSR') was functioning between 1919-1938. By participating in this system, the employees obtained a guarantee of security in old age, in case of accident and illness (Bek, 2015).

Social welfare provided by the CzSR included a sickness fund, own accident insurance, a pension fund, care for children, care for students, provision of benefits, loans, and housing care. In 1921, it was provided to 175 000 employees of the Czechoslovak State Railways. So-called lay supervision was introduced as part of the sickness fund. The task of these lay supervisors was to visit the ill at home and check whether they were really at home. Furthermore, they had the same task as social workers, namely the obligation to "point to cases of striking misery and propose contributions" (Sociální péče čsl. státních drah, 1923: 299).

In the area of housing care, the activity of employees' building railway cooperatives was supported by interest-free advances on pay from resources of the state railways and from Zahradník's fund. After at least 10 years of service, employees leaving due to disability or age, as well as employees' survivors, were given so-called grace donations. These were permanent monthly subsidies if these people were no longer entitled to a pension or injury annuity. In care for children, the sickness fund and its support fund, and the railway administration itself, too, participated by sending children to holiday camps to recover. Every year, 500 children set out for these stays (Sociální péče čsl. státních drah, 1923).

The training of lay supervisors took place in Prague in the form of two-week courses. The financial costs of social care at the Czechoslovak State Railways were primarily covered by the "Zahradník's Social Care Fund of Czechoslovak State Railways", founded in mid-1919 and named after the First Minister of Railways. It was kept as a special self-help fund for railway employees. Its purpose was to provide financial support, reimbursement of medical expenses, provide scholarships for employees' children, contributions to bridal trousseau for daughters, cheaper interest-bearing loans, and pay for children's holiday camps. It was subsidised solely by voluntary contributions from employees and donations. As of 31st December 1921, the fund had CSK 1,071,694 in its account. A version of the social fund was later also used as a model by the Ministry of Post Office (Sociální péče čsl. státních drah, 1923).

1.4.2 Třinec Iron and Steel Works

Třinec Iron and Steel Works were founded in 1839. In 1906 it became part of the newly created Austrian Mining and Metallurgical Company. By doing so, the ironworks were given the opportunity to increase its investments, to modernise and expand the plant. Together with Vítkovice Ironworks and the Prague Iron Company, Třinec Iron and Steel Works formed a triplet of the most important steelworks in the territory of Bohemia, Moravia and Silesia (Efmertová, 1998).

According to Zahradník (1969), Třinec Iron and Steel Works can be proud of a very chequered history. The years 1906-1938 are considered as the most significant period of the ironworks. The years following the Munich Agreement brought big changes for the factory, reflected in its overall status. Stanislav Zahradník described the social aspect of the development of Třinec Iron and Steel Works in this period very extensively based on primary sources.

Specific social care was not described in archival sources. However, activities of a social nature, or activities for the benefit of workers, can be traced from Zahradník's texts. They are included in social security. Health care for labourers was ensured in a factory hospital, opened after 1897. Pulmonary tuberculosis, stomach diseases and pneumonia were among the most common diseases of Třinec labourers. The so-called fraternal treasury established in 1842 fulfilled the role of social insurance. In 1906 it was renamed Fraternal Treasury of the Austrian Mining and Metallurgical Company in Těšín. The task of the treasury was to provide support to its members and their family members at times of illness, to pay out subsidies in case of death and work premium to people unfit for work, widows and orphans. All Třinec labourers were compulsory members of the treasury. There were two components within the treasury: sickness and premium.

The sickness fund provided its members with support in case of illness, injury, death of a family member, whereas labourers' wives and children under 14 were entitled to free medical care including medication for six weeks of illness. Another task of the sickness fund was to check the ill people, provide support to its members in extraordinary cases, grant support to schools, contribute to live music in the factory. The sickness fund receipts consisted of workers' membership contributions (1.5% of earnings), employer contributions in the same amount as labourers, labourers' fines, donations and interest on deposited capital, especially from the reserve fund (Zahradník, 1969: 53).

The commission fund provided a pension (commission) to its members who became incapable of work due to old age or injury, as well as to treasury members' widows and orphans. The receipts consisted of membership contributions and employer contributions, marital taxes, interest and various donations. The employer paid a contribution to the treasury equal to the amount of all members' contributions. The employer also paid contributions for apprentices (Zahradník, 1969: 53).

The factory hospital in Třinec was funded by the sickness fund, too. Apart from the field of social security, we find other activities in favour of labourers. In 1907, a factory school of Třinec Iron and Steel Works was established to ensure the necessary education to young labourers. In the 1870s, the factory built two labourer settlements for its employees – Borek and Olza. In the following years, factory flats for labourers and clerks, new houses and sleeping quarters for both single and married labourers from more distant places were added. Třinec labourers living in factory flats commonly rented a piece of land from the ironworks to grow the most necessary crops. This also enabled them to keep domestic animals. Leasing of the land to the workers was important for the management in the sense that it tied the workers to the factory. With the support of Třinec Iron and Steel Works, a Catholic church was built, three factory pubs and a factory cooperative store (foodstuff and consumer items) were founded, the factory management established factory music, a male choir, the Labourers' House Association and others (Zahradník, 1969).

1.4.3 Swedish Factory Inspectors

Vostřebalová (1933) brings information about Swedish factory inspectors on the pages of the Social Worker journal. Annual reports of the Swedish Social School (Social Politiska Institutet) show what a large percentage of female graduates was employed as social workers in factories and business ventures. Vostřebalová clarifies the term "inspector" with a view to its correct understanding. It was not a trade inspection in our sense of the word, but performance of social work. Each worker was an employee of one enterprise. There, she was entrusted with the care of labourers' education, health and welfare. She was considered an expert, she presented her proposals directly to the directorate, managed courses with great independence, founded nurseries, organised holiday camps. Her organizational skills and higher education were also reflected in her financial evaluation. A senior factory inspector enjoyed a very good social status as well.

1.4.4 Social and Health Care for Labourers in France

During World War I, women were massively recruited in France, especially in arms factories, in order to compensate for the missing workforce as men were mobilized for the army. However, the working conditions were incompatible with childcare. The Ministry of Labour feared a decline in the birth rate, which would be a major threat in times of war. Therefore, France sent a working group to England to gain experience from centres where female work prevailed. In England, there were the positions of "ladies superintendents" and "lady welfare supervisor". France aimed at creating a similar system of social services which already existed in England. Social services in enterprises were created in France following the example of England in 1917 (Toulotte, 2014).

Providing social and health care at the workplace was enacted as an obligatory duty by an act of 28th July 1942. Organizations employing more than 50 employees were bound to ensure health care, and organizations with more than 250 employees had also to proide social care. Supervision of the act implementation was carried out by an authority – Regional Compensationn Fund – (called *Caise de Compensation de la Region*) – managed by social workers. The authority employed about 300 social workers. The task of this authority was to care for labourers' families, to retrain and relocate the sick and invalided, and to provide immediate help in incidental difficulties. Certified social workers were selected for this work who additionally attended evening classes with lectures in the field of labour and social legislation. Subsequently they received a diploma named Diploma of Work Counsellor – (called *Diplom de conseillere du travail*) (Roháčková, 1947).

As a specific example of a social service in a French enterprise, Roháčková (1947) presents the example of a Parisian factory with 800 employees, which she personally visited. Social services were completely independent of health services there. They only had common card files where social workers could supplement the medical history. The service consisted of dealing with the records of "Caise de Compensation" and "Assurance Sociale", as well as placing the employees' children in sanatoriums and recreational camps, providing scholarships to apprentices, care for the factory library, assisting nursing mothers and pregnant women, supervising nurseries and supervising the hygiene practice in the factory kitchen (Roháčková, 1947).

1.4.5 Social Entrepreneur from Switzerland

At a meeting of the Social Institute of Czechoslovakia in December 1924, Dr. Štern presented a paper on the work of a Swiss entrepreneur, Theodor Tobler, in the social field. The entrepreneur also presented his experience at the International Social Policy Congress in Prague. Štern described the factory owner as a practical entrepreneur, a social entrepreneur. Tobler held the view that it is necessary to make social reforms during economic crises, seeing them as a necessity and a suitable means to increase intellectual ability, to improve undermined confidence in state and labourers' interest in the economic development of factories, hence improving the labourers' performance and the competitive ability of the plant, during times of unemployment, poverty and embitterment. He promoted keeping the eight-hour working time, the employees of his firm had a share in the plant profit, he voluntarily introduced old-age and disability insurance. He set up a sickness fund, flat settlements, and organised language courses. There was also a cafeteria and a factory library in the plant and he introduced paid holidays (1 week of vacation after two years, 3 weeks after 12 years), provided two nurses to support families, and both Saturday and Sunday were free from work (Štern, 1925).

As long as the business was small, Tobler maintained personal contact with all his employees. When the company expanded and had 800 employees, a special clerk, a so-called social secretary, started to handle personal affairs. It was a 50-year-old esteemed and experienced gentleman who had been working as a secretary for twenty years. Tobler said about the task of the social secretary: "You know, people must not be shouted at, it is necessary to deal with them sensibly, to educate them, while being accommodating to them and giving advice to them" (Štern, 1925: 4). The main task of the secretary was to ensure discipline in the factory.

2. SOCIAL POLICY OF VÍTKOVICE IRONWORKS

Vítkovice Ironworks had been building various social facilities almost since they came into existence. Already in the 1830s the factory built the first houses for officials and some skilled labourers. Later a was Czech school was established, a factory canteen was built, and an own grocery store was operated. In the 1840s, a fraternal treasury existed within the enterprise, providing support during illness to permanent labourers. In the second half of the seventies, in connection with the new director general, P. Kupelwieser (1843-1919), a qualitatively new entrepreneurial strategy was applied in the plant management. According to Ševeček (2009), it signified a beginning of a well-thought out employee and social policy resting on scientific foundations. The Vítkovice phenomenon is given as a typical example of a corporate town (Jemelka et al., 2015).

The social system for employees of Vítkovice Ironworks, but also of private and state railways and mining companies, was, in Austria, considered a structured form of assistance which did not call the premise of primary individual assurance of existence by self-help into question. Employees were described as disciplined and skilled labourers. The aid initially focused only on support in cases of inability to work and injury (Hlavačka, 2015: 37).

The extensive social programme[3] included construction of: hospitals and health care facilities, crèches, kindergartens, an institution for orphans and older labourers without family, factory kitchens, canteens, and construction of the so-called New Vítkovice (called Nové Vítkovice). Thanks to the social programme, the ironworks became in many ways a pioneering enterprise in the field of modern business methods not only in the Czech lands, but also in the entire Habsburg monarchy (Ševeček, 2009).

The social system of Vítkovice Ironworks was viewed in the 20th and at the beginning of the 21st century, in accordance with the development of the Czech and Czech-German historiography, not only at the level of development of the historical methodology of social and economic history, but also at the level of political changes which took place there. This is visible in the positive evaluations by "company" historians Wattolika and Drapala, who exhibited the social feelings of the enterprise owners and management (Šústková, 2011).

---

3 The term "social programme" appears in secondary sources. However, it is not a classic structured plan. I was not able to find any in primary documents. I took the term over as a synonym for the notion "activities of social nature".

In the uniqueness of New Vítkovice, a new society was born, which, with all its imperfection, meant a significant assertion of a new modern lifestyle and style. Nové Vítkovice was also affected by heavy work, dissatisfaction of employees with the enterprise policy and working conditions in the ironworks. There were conflicts between the labourers and the enterprise interests there, too. Abandoned and orphaned children, old and helpless people, hunger, disease and hopelessness were also all there. However, there were many more satisfied people with a secure future and fewer worries than was common at that time (Matěj, Korbelářová, Levá, 1992: 53).

2.1 Brief History of Vítkovice Ironworks with the Beginnings of Social Policy

Considering the topic, we cannot avoid a factual description of the key events in the ironworks. The Vítkovice Ironworks (or 'VI') was one of the largest metallurgical enterprises in Austria-Hungary. The launch of the construction of the Vítkovice Ironworks, the so-called Rudolph's Smelter, was finally agreed in 1828 and by April 1829 building, directed by the Olomouc Archbishop Rudolph, began. The director of the Frýdlant Ironworks, Franz Kleinpeter, was entrusted with top management. In 1835, the ironworks were leased by the company of Viennese entrepreneurs. The company was named Vítkovice Mining and Iron Corporation (hereinafter 'VMIC') (Myška, 1960; Matějček, Vytiska, 1978). In the 1830s Vítkovice was a small village with about 157 inhabitants (Myška, 1960).

The construction and industrial activities of VI significantly influenced the economic and social development not only in the municipality but also in the neighbouring municipalities (Pokludová, 2001). The relationship of Nové Vítkovice as a town and factory was fully controlled by one production entity, which controlled all areas of public and private life in a directive way (Jemelka et al., 2015).

At the end of the first half of the 19th century, about 1200 labourers worked in the factory. One third came from the districts or surroundings of present-day Ostrava, mostly from Zábřeh, Krmelín, Přívoz, Hrabůvka, Nová and Stará Ves, Kunčice and others. Only 3% of the factory workers were directly from Vítkovice. Many labourers were from Hlučín, from Prussian Silesia and from Austrian Galicia. In the 1860s and 70s, the influx of new, unskilled labourers from the agricultural areas of Austrian Galicia increased. The ironworks management increasingly focused on cheap labour forces. In part the increase was due to factories approaching incoming labour and allocating small pieces of land to them. An "own" house and "own" piece of land were a great attraction for many people. In this way, the enterprise committed them to the factory and demanded their obedience as workers (Matějček, Vytiska, 1978). In 1831, the enterprise built six dwelling houses for labourers and a one-storey house for officials. Housing construction also continued in the years to come, but it was far from maintaining the pace with the growth of the ironworks and the influx of new labourers and their families. Single labourers used common dormitories called barracks. They were mostly set up in old, unused premises and extensions (Myška, 1960).

Myška (1960) considers late 1830s as the beginning of the industrial revolution in the Moravian and Silesian iron industry. VI gradually educated their own experts, but they still lured specialists away from other factories with higher wages and various benefits. Around the middle of the century, the share of Slavs in the ironworks management began to decline. The office staff was exclusively German. There were a lot of foreigners among senior executives, especially citizens of the German Reich (Matějček, Vytiska, 1978).

In April 1843, a contract was ratified under which VI with all appurtenances became property of S. M. Rothschild for a total of 346,000 guldens (Myška, 1960).

Several factors influenced the labourers' social status. One of them was the labourers' education. In 1844, Rothschild opened a school for children of ironworks employees in Vítkovice so that employees' children did not have to go to a remote parish school in Moravská Ostrava. At the time of its opening, it was attended by 67 boys and girls. The language of education was German. Myška (1960: 97) mentions Rothschild's motives for establishing a school. They were: upbringing of future skilled labourers, an important tool for influencing the labourers, a successful mode of Germanisation, and a way to impact the minds of the growing generation of labourers.

In 1843, the Fraternal Treasury, managed by the plant, was first mentioned in VI. Workers, initially only the skilled ones, paid contributions to it and received support during illness for a certain period of time. But it was far from the average wage. In 1860s, the daily amount was one third of the average wage. For a larger family, a breadwinner becoming ill meant disaster. In 1844 the factory built a hospital for ill labourers, extended in 1864. The then owners could not afford better care for the labourers, despite their millions of earnings. Based on the Trade Licence Code of 1859, the enterprise was obliged to take care of labourers who had suffered an accident and could not continue to work. However, according to Matějček and Vytiska (1978), it was not the case in practice in Vítkovice at that time.

Myška (1960) discusses Rothschild's motivation to establish various social facilities. He states that bourgeois historians, in their efforts to celebrate the entrepreneur's charity, as a rule highlighted the merits of the social uplift of labourers and the care of labourers, for example the historiographer of the Rothschild family Egon Eugen Caesar Conte Corti. The second reason behind the motivation was a clear function of increasing the entrepreneur's profits[4], by returning the money

---

4 It should be noted, that the author produced this work, by order of VI.

paid to the labourers as wages back into the treasury through institutions such as the factory pub, shop etc. By setting up a school, factory flats, a hospital, introduction of medical care, establishment of the fraternal treasury, and later a pension institution, the entrepreneur did not only influence the labourers' minds, but attached hundreds of labourers to him and made them dependent on him. The labourers were aware (and were continually reminded) of the fact that their children went to the entrepreneur's school, that they were treated in the entrepreneur's hospital, that they lived in homes he provided, etc. According to Myška (1960: 98, 141), this awareness along with the awareness that every violation of the working order is associated with dismissal, acted as a brake on the development of the labourers' movement. He presents these institutions as another form of exploitation.

In the first half of 1870s, the situation of VI was really dismal. The production facilities were outdated, the labourers were not skilled enough and the products were of poor quality. The ironworks dismissed labourers as a result of lack of work and they were forced to seek employment elsewhere. It was a sad situation (From History, 1940). In 1873, Vítkovice Mining and Iron Corporation owned by the Rothschilds and Gutmanns was created, starting from 1876 with 50/50 ownership. The company management pursued a single goal: of getting the enterprise to the forefront of economic prosperity in Europe. This required a new type of manager, open to new technical and technological innovations, able to estimate the market needs, but also "a tough boss" in relation to subordinates (Myška, 2007).

On the initiative of the Gutmanns, a new director was appointed to uplift the ironworks. Starting from 1876, a new history of VI was written under the leadership of a thirty-three-year-old director, Ing. Paul Kupelwieser, who had experience in working in ironworks in Graz where he met with an outstanding expert Englishman Hall, as well as experience from trips to Rhineland, Westphalia and Belgium (Myška, 2007). He had the reputation of being a young but capable and ambitious metallurgist and organiser who could uplift the stagnant ironworks to a high level again (Matěj, Korbelářová, Levá, 1992). Before his start, Vítkovice suffered a considerable loss due to an economic crisis. The factor was not well manged and only 800 out of 2400 labourers remained (Myška, 2007). In the following years, the new director assigned tasks for a unified regulatory plan of Nové Vítkovice. The authors Myška (1960) and Šústková (2011) state that the new director was, in terms of his social security reform, merely a continuator of the established system. The owners' earlier employment policy promoted elements of social system inconsistently and with varying intensity. On the contrary, Barcuch and Rohlová (2001) attribute the unified plan of Nové Vítkovice from the 1870s to the prestigious reasons of director Kupelwieser. Another motivation for his actions was a lack of housing, poor facilities and the impossibility of continuing the existing chaotic building development.

Nové Vítkovice represented an unprecedented building achievement in the Central European context of the late 19th century, combining the unity of architectural and technical design, while exceeding the requirements of the common standard of living at that time (Matěj, Korbelářová, Levá, 1992).

Matěj, Korbelářová and Tejzr (2014) refer to the urbanistic complex of Nové Vítkovice as a modern-type satellite town. Red bricks became a dominant feature of Vítkovice, used uniformly on important buildings such as the church, town hall, school facilities, hospitals, residential buildings up to production halls and utility premises. A consistent use of the same building material demonstrated an ideological unity and belonging to the enterprise (Matěj, Korbelářová, Levá, 1992).

The extent to which the ironworks contributed to the construction development of Vítkovice was also enabled and facilitated by the fact that starting from the 1950s, the local politics of Vítkovice was partly, and from the 1870s completely, dominated by the ironworks. From the early 1870s, from two-thirds up to three-quarters of all members and substitute members of the municipal council regularly came from the ranks of the VI managers and officials. They were regularly appointed as mayors, councillors and committee chairmen. This allowed enforcement of the enterprise interests in the local politics in a significant way (Barcuch, Rohlová, 2001; Kladiwa, 2007). Matěj, Korbelářová and Tejzr (2014) state that the acquisition of substantial influence in the municipal decision-making was a result of the purposeful personnel policy of VI, also with a contribution from the then electoral system.

The ironworks needed a supportive environment for their employees, therefore they took care of the social, health and educational conditions of their employees. According to Kladiwa (2007), on that account, the ironworks' owners expected absolute commitment and a political and national population mindset which corresponded to the aims of German liberalism.

Despite all his successes, which raised the enterprise again to the leading position among the industrial enterprises of the monarchy, Kupelwieser left in 1893. This was due to disagreements with the enterprise owners who did not want to make further investments in the enterprise. At that time, the Rothschilds ceased to be interested in direct industrial production and shifted to other areas of expanding their property. From Kupelwieser's departure until 1918, the enterprise continued to focus on arms production, especially production of armour plates for the navy (Myška, Zářický et al., 2007).

In the year 1900, the contemporary newspaper 'Spirit of the Time' drew attention to the state of health of the VI labourers. Despite the positively evaluated social policy of the ironworks, the authors of the article described negative aspects influencing the health of the VI employees. These included: frequent sickness of the labourers, high injury rate, mainly due to burns, the negative environment of Vítkovice, poor quality food sold in the factory market and finally, the insufficient capacity of the Vítkovice hospital (Vítkovice and Labourers 1900).

By 1908, Vítkovice had developed into a town with an area of 435 hectares, while the area of VI was about 510 hectares (Barcuch, Rohlová, 2001). Due to the geographical location of Vítkovice the company could and, according to Matějček (1977) it was forced, to employ labour forces, especially unskilled, from the relatively backward areas of north-eastern Moravia, the Beskids, from Austrian Galicia (increasingly so after 1900) and even from Hungary and the Balkans. As for the social and professional origin of the labourers, more than half of them had a background in agriculture. Due to the workers from these areas having comparably lower living standard expectations, the company management was able to maintain a significant wage differentiation and to implement a specific social policy (Matějček, 1977).

At the end of 1918, the Habsburg monarchy disappeared from the map of Europe and new states began to form on its ruins. VI were still in the hands of the original owners, of the Rothschild and Gutmann family. In the new political situation, the ironworks had to struggle for new orders much harder than previously (Palát, 1989).

After the Protectorate of Bohemia and Moravia was established, the Ostrava industry became part of the imperial economic sphere, which from the beginning was subject to the needs of war production. In 1939, the Rothschilds together with the Gutmanns were trying to sell the whole enterprise to an English company Metal Industries Investments Ltd., but the sale failed as England joined the war. At the beginning of the war, the ironworks were formally an independent enterprise, but in fact they were controlled by an imperial German company Reichswerke AG for Erzbergbau and Eisenhütten H. Göring, headed by the Nazi Prime Minister Herman Göring, who gradually took over all the management bodies of the ironworks. In 1942, VI officially became part of Göring's company, with unlimited decision-making about the entire property management (Matějček, Vytiska, 1978).

Throughout the war, the VI and the whole industrial area of Ostrava were of strategic importance for Nazi Germany, which increased even further after losing the industrial Ruhr region and the industrial base in Upper Silesia at the end of the war. In this situation, great hopes were placed in the Ostrava agglomeration and Ostrava was strongly defended. Yet the ironworks, as well as the city centre, were liberated on 30th April 1945 (Matějček, Vytiska, 1978).

After the World War II, Vítkovice was affected by demolition of some of the bombed-out residential buildings in the centre. The most serious degradation of Vítkovice occurred during the 1970s and 1980s (Matěj, Korbelářová, Tejzr, 2014).

2.1.1 Paul Kupelwieser's Style of Company Management

The evaluation of Kupelwieser's work in Vítkovice carried out one century later by authors Matěj, Korbelářová and Levá (1992) suggests that his abilities, but above all his general knowledge, orientation and foresight, far outstripped his time and significant improved the economically significant – but socially more than provincial – region of Ostrava. The era of his management activity is the beginning of what we today call the Vítkovice phenomenon. The CEOs who followed Kupelwieser were simply further developing his concept (Šústková, 2011).

Kupelwieser was one of those who understood that restoring an enterprise's prosperity and, in the long run ensuring it a leading position in the metallurgy branch, does not only mean putting considerable sums into renovation of the traditional production, but also looking for new production possibilities, introducing modern technologies, and primarily that it is necessary to invest "in people", while changing the attitude of the enterprise (both management and owners) to the employees. Kupelwieser never built on philanthropy, but he understood the connection between universally well-secured employees and their families, and the workforce quality reflected in the ultimate enterprise outcomes (Matěj, Korbelářová, Levá, 1992: 9). This is in line with Šústková's (2011) statement, seeing in the forefront of this endeavour above all a rational entrepreneurial consideration and an effort for social reconciliation, whose manifestations and limits are always influenced by the time of their existence.

After becoming the director general, he decided to enforce strategic production, which resulted in a significant share of VI in the arms industry of the monarchy. This logically led to the need for having not only professional and efficient but also mentally and socially balanced employees, without any significant social problems, loyal to the enterprise and its management in all respects (Matěj, Korbelářová, Levá, 1992). According to Šústková (2011), these achievements created a sense of uniqueness and special belonging among the employees, which, however, at that time greatly complicated the development of the workers' and trade unions movement.

2.2   Social System of Vítkovice Ironworks

At the beginning of the 20th century, the social system had almost been created. The ironworks management granted a number of benefits to its employees. All social measures formed an integral part of the tactics applied to the labourers. Social achievements positively influenced the labourers' standard of living and encouraged their interest in working at the enterprise. According to Matějček and Vytiska (1978), the Vítkovice Mining and Iron Corporation carried out a flexible and well-thought-out social policy which was universally worthwhile. The social system was being built up until approximately 1910, later it was modified only a little as Matějček (1977) notes.

The first steps of the reforms concentrated on the labour and wage field. The labour organization was changed, qualification requirements were set, and employee's work-morale profile was emphasised (Matěj, Korbelářová, Levá, 1992).

The VI social system paid increased attention to technicians, foremen, supervisors and skilled labourers. Differentiation was reflected in remuneration and other social benefits, too (Jiřík, 2001).

Employee housing care was one of the most important sections of the VI social programme, mainly because of the enormous influx of workforce into the ironworks (Jiřík, 2001).

Table No. 1 – Numbers of employees accommodated in VI facilities in the years 1886-1944 (in %)

Year	In factory flats	In barracks and tenements	Total number of accommodated people
1886	10,3	22,8	33,1
1914	12,6	40,3	52,9
1930	18,4	32,0	50,4
1944	12,2	17,9	30,1

Source: Jiřík, 2001: 323

The number of the flats built is not the only basis to assess the housing care provided, but also their overall standard, layout and design, equipment quality, etc. Jiřík (2001) writes that the residential and housing stock of VI was of a high standard because most settlements, officials' houses and villas are still serving their purpose to this day.

In 1926, according to archival sources, VI was spread over an area of 8 km². Vítkovice merged with Velká Ostrava and became a city of thirty thousand residents. At that time, the ironworks were employing twenty thousand labourers, two thousand officials and another ten thousand labourers were working in coal mines and coking plants belonging to VI. Care for employees was provided to a much greater extent than required by the applicable legislation (AV, Vítkovice, VMIC 11, inv. No. 1610, reg. No. 302).

Starting from 1919, the VMIC management regularly sent a well-developed report to the District Youth Care in Moravská Ostrava with statistical data on health and social facilities which the plant set up for the benefit of the labourers. The report always had 8 annexes and contained a description and statistical data of the following facilities: VMIC Orphanage Foundation, Shelter for Convalescents, Counselling Centres for Skin and the Sexually Diseased, Infant Counselling Centres, Tuberculosis Counselling Centres, children's homes Shelters (called *Dětské útulny*), the Wilhelm Gutmann Almshouse Foundation and Apprentice Shelters

(AV, Vítkovice, VMIC 11, inv. No. 1610, reg. No. 302). The social system was continuously supplemented as new social facilities were established.

In 1937, VI had a total of 18,533 workers and 2,240 officials. The company director, Dr. Herain, was entrusted with execution of social policy, with the help of several senior officials who were responsible for wage policy, assignment wages, time wages, legal affairs, housing affairs, reception office and safety. Furthermore, Herain was in charge of the sickness insurance company, pension institution, care giving institution, factory hospital and apprenticeship. Social care was led by inspector Langfort with six other employees (AV, Vítkovice, Vítkovice 1946-1954, inv. No. 901, reg. No. 153).

In the archival documents, it is possible to draw information on the topic from a preserved study on labour and social policy of VI, which was probably written in 1937 in German by Dr. Rudolf Schwenger. The author introduces the enterprise social policy of VI, consisting of measures and institutions of ironworks, aimed at the welfare of employees and their family members. The enterprise social policy stemmed from the fact that the plant is not only a production site where goods are produced, but also a social community/collective. As such, it also had its social roles. Over time, the enterprise social responsibility towards employees developed into large a number of measures and facilities to meet almost all employees' needs and, above all, to cover the gaps which threatened their standard of living, be it sickness, poverty, old age or other "blows of fate". Precisely in this respect, the enterprise social policy of Vítkovice was extraordinarily developed and comprehensive. For example, up to the peak of the economic crisis, voluntary social spending grew from 13.3% in 1925 to 25.6% in 1932. Therefore, the author argued that despite declining employment, social security was not restricted but remained almost unchanged (AV, Vítkovice, VMIC 17, inv. No. 6099, reg. No. 1405).

A high level of the VI enterprise social policy is also evidenced by a comparison of voluntary social spending in VI and in large German ironworks, the Krupp Works and the Gutehoffnungshütte. It is surprising to conclude that the Krupp Works, known in the world and literature for a high level of social benefits, considerably lagged behind Vítkovice regarding the volume of effective social spending. Welfare benefits of the Gutehoffnungshütte were much lower again, which is remarkable, as this enterprise along with the Krupp Works is the oldest one and has the broadest enterprise social security in the West German iron and steel big industry (AV, Vítkovice, VMIC 17, inv. No. 6099, reg. No. 1405).

Schwenger (AV, Vítkovice, VMIC 17, inv. No. 6099, reg. No. 1405) noted an explanation as to why VI invested in measures and institutions to increase workers' purchasing power. There was a widespread belief in employee circles that the ideal relationship between an enterprise and employees is limited to the performance/reward relationship. According to the author, the sole aim of the labourers' movement was to achieve the highest possible wage. "If this attitude is correct, can the improvement of the labourers' living situation be achieved only by way of increasing wages as such?" Schwenger answered in the negative. Experience from Czechoslovakia and other countries showed that higher wages were regularly consumed by increased prices on vital products. Thus, a general wage increase caused a reduction in the value of money. It was not only this aspect which prompted the VI management to create an extensive and comprehensive system of enterprise social care over decades (AV, Vítkovice, VMIC 17, inv. No. 6099, reg. No. 1405).

A great social importance of the measures consisted in their acting as "wage supplements". The labourers' needs varied widely within the same wage range, depending on the family size, age, or with regard to special reasons such as illness, distress, etc. Wages could generally not allow for these differences in the labourers' needs. If only because the statutory social benefits were merely sufficient for a negligible compensation. Here, enterprise social facilities and measures came in useful. Enterprise social policy was meant to make labourers invulnerable in times of crisis and to provide them with the greatest possible existential security. According to Schwenger, the social policy of Vítkovice also needs to be viewed from another angle, as these social services represented a way of profit sharing for workers at the same time. The extensive and comprehensive social system of VI enabled a part of the company's revenue, instead of its more or less purposeless dissipation, to be kept together and used to ensure a high degree of social impact by providing employees with economic relief as well as an increase in the social, health and cultural standard of living. Such an increase in the standard of living was achieved to a much greater extent by means of the social system rather than by a mechanical division among individuals in the form of wage increases (AV, Vítkovice, VMIC 17, inv. No. 6099, reg. No. 1405).

Contemporary materials suggest that social services, institutions and measures meant an indirect wage premium for labourers (AV, Vítkovice, VMIC 17, inv. No. 6099, reg. No. 1405).

Social policy in 1948 was aimed at increasing labour productivity: "Better, higher and cheaper production than under capitalism." The main factor in the production was still people, therefore care for people was intensified. Work effort was supported by wage policy, i.e. by adequate classification into wage classes, wage increase based on performance within time tasks and performance bonuses (AV, Vítkovice, Vítkovice 1946-1954, inv. No. 1082, reg. No. 167).

Matějček (1977) discusses the conditions for establishment of a comprehensive social system in Vítkovice. One of the conditions, according to the author, was the huge economic and social influence of the owners and sufficient capital for such solutions which other enterprises could not afford. Another condition was a periodic workforce shortage. During the crisis, workers were made redundant, wages were reduced, while the boom period led to rising wage demands. A huge workforce fluctuation which remained until the First World War is mentioned, too.

Matějček (1977) argues that this was partly because physically strong single young people with relatively high wages were not economically forced into permanent employment at one workplace. The fluctuation was accounted for by economic and family circumstances. It was more advantageous for entrepreneurs to slightly increase wages than to risk strikes, which could have catastrophic economic consequences with regard to the metallurgical operation. Along with the adjustment of the wage system, after Kupelwieser took office, the fraternal treasury was reformed. Greater loyalty to the factory and high work performance were appreciated. The old-age insurance retained two elements despite the number of subsequent changes: (1) advantages for Vítkovice Ironworks labourers over other branches and (2) dependence of the old-age annuity on the wage level. Another advantage of VI as compared to other enterprises was the composition of the labourers, who mostly, at that time, came from still underdeveloped areas where they did not come into contact with the social movement and were therefore more malleable and easily controlled (Matějček, 1977).

2.2.1 Activity of the Social Department after 1945

After 1945, the name of the social department[5] changed rapidly, as did its inclusion in the plant divisions. It went through various titles, including social group, staff care and social section, up to the final name of social department in the employee division. By way of illustration, I explain the genesis of the department's name in the footnotes. Due to the identification of individual facts in different documents, the text became very confusing.[6]

In October 1945, a "social care" group – "social group"[7] – was formed. The head of the social group was Albert Kučera. It consisted of the departments listed below.

---

5   Variation of the term 'Department of Social Care'.
6   The summary report "Social Activities in Our Ironworks in 1945" of 29th December 1945 states that the Social Department takes care of an active and positive condition of employees (AV, Vítkovice, VMIC n.a., inv. No. 423, reg. No. 29). In the Activity Report for the Year 1946 of 21st April 1947, the section is referred to as the Department of Personnel Care (AV, Vítkovice, Vítkovice 1946-1954, inv. No. 1070, reg. No. 167). The Department of Personnel Care had its seat in Kotkova Street in 1947. It was headed by the clerk in charge Bohumil Hruboň (AV, Vítkovice, Vítkovice 1946-1954, inv. No. 1684, reg. No. 218). In 1947, the divisions of activities headed in 1937 by the Director Dr. Herain fell under the responsibility of the Social-Political Department, later the Employee Department (AV, Vítkovice, Vítkovice 1946-1954, inv. No. 901, reg. No. 153). The Employee Department, shielding all social affairs, was headed by the Deputy Company Director Albert Kučera (AV, Vítkovice, Vítkovice 1946-1954, inv. No. 1684, reg. No. 218).
7   In archival materials of VI both terms appear as synonyms.

Table No. 2 – Composition of the group of VI social care in 1945

Department name	Department content	Clerk in charge
Social department	1. Housing culture of employees, labour hygiene, funds and foundations (care for survivors of employees, orphanage, almshouse, study contributions	Mr. Valoš Stojeba
	2. Care for active employees, recreational stay of employees, holiday stays of children, shelters, crèches and cooking facilities, counselling for mothers and children	Mr. Boh. Hruboň
Convalescent homes	1. Management of convalescent homes: Rožnov, Villa Maryčka – St. Hamry, Zubří, holiday settlements in Ostravice, recreational camp Hukvaldy	Mr. Jan Horník
Supplying	2. Canteens, marketplace, factory hotel	
Safety	Safety department	Mr. Ant. Smékal
Dept. No. 94	Education of apprentices	Mr. Josef Lazar
K	Kindergartens	Mrs. Drah. Entlová
Dept. S	Sports and physical education	MUDr. Neuwirt
Broadcasting	Factory broadcasting	
Dept. No. 38 and 38/V	Large farm estate Rožnov	Mr. Jos. Toman
	Large farm estate Vratimov	Mr. Lud. Vavrečka

Source: AV, Vítkovice, VMIC n.a., inv. No. 184, reg. No. 23

In a report of the Social-Political Department of 1946, social activities of the former ironworks owners were compared to "throwing a gnawed bone to employees" (AV, Vítkovice, VMIC n.a., inv. No. 423, reg. No. 29).

The number of employees was reflected in statistics which accompanied information on the functioning and use of individual social facilities. Therefore, reports from the Social Department did not work without the total number of employees at the time of their elaboration. For example, the Report on Social Facilities of the Mining and Iron Corporation dated 13th December 1945 states in its introductions the total number of employees: a) there were 19,737 men and 2,563 women as blue-collar workers, b) 2,321 men and 423 women as white-collar workers, c) pensioners of the Maintenance Institute (694 regulatory pensioners, 1427 disabled pensioners, 193 old-age pensioners, 1189 widows and 459 orphans) (AV, Vítkovice, VMIC n.a., inv. No. 423, reg. No. 29).

In 1947, employees who were finding themselves in need or financial distress through no fault of their own were granted the following types of aid upon a written request:

a) Extraordinary aid in long-term illness
b) Aid in distress through no fault of one's own
c) Contributions to cover hospital or spa treatments
d) Contributions for dental interventions
e) Aid for employees transitioning to pension as a result of invalidity or long-term illness
f) Study contributions
g) Allowances for the purchase of layette for new-born babies
h) Extraordinary aid in case of fatal injury
i) Aid in distress provided by the Czech Social Assistance to former employees of VI (AV, Vítkovice, Vítkovice 1946-1954, inv. No. 1684, reg. No. 218).

Assistance a)-e) was granted to all employees after examining their legitimacy and social needfulness. The amount was decided by the social division of the factory council at regular monthly meetings. Study contributions were provided to employees who had worked for 7 years in the factory, or at least one of their parents for 15 years. The amount of study contributions ranged between 250-1000 CSK. The scholarship was awarded on condition that the applicant had good results during their study period and that they were employed in the plant for at least 5 years after finishing their studies. Contribution for the purchase of layette was paid out in the amount of 2000 CSK to an employee who had been at the enterprise for at least one year (AV, Vítkovice, Vítkovice 1946-1954, inv. No. 1684, reg. No. 218).

Other employee benefits on top of the net wage included: the possibility of doing laundry in the factory laundry room, allocation of fuel (coke, coal and wood) for remuneration, allocation of allowance in kind for employees having 4 or more children, jubilee gifts to employees working in the factory for 25-40 years up to a maximum of 1000 CSK, maintenance allowance for employees (family members) performing military service (AV, Vítkovice, Vítkovice 1946-1954, inv. No. 1684, reg. No. 218).

The social wage[8] was granted to all those who suffered damage to health due to an accident or after at least fifteen years of employment and were recognised by the company physician as 35% disabled and no longer able to carry out their pre-

---

8 It was not possible to find an explanation of the content of the notion "social wage" in archival documents.

vious job. The compensatory wage was set at 15.40 CZK per hour (AV, Vítkovice, Vítkovice 1946-1954, inv. No. 1684, reg. No. 218).

For employees who could not commute daily, there were accommodation facilities in barracks and for retired employees the so-called almshouses. The economic administration supplied foodstuff and agricultural products from large farm estates to factory catering facilities. Care for mental and physical health was supported through a sports stadium, an outdoor swimming pool and a chess club. At the beginning of 1948, a self-help support fund was established to provide for funeral expenses (AV, Vítkovice, Vítkovice 1946-1954, inv. No. 1684, reg. No. 218).

In 1949, the agenda of the Economic and Social Department was divided as follows:

1. Economic management – its function consisted in supplying and catering of employees and their family members: wholesale, retail – marketplace, factory hotel, factory canteens, recreational centres.
2. Field and forest management – farmland, large farm estates
3. Housing care and facility management
4. Health care – factor hospital, 8 factory outpatient departments and 4 emergency stations
5. Social insurance – pension institution, general care giving institution
6. Social division
   a) fund and foundations management,
   b) care for employees and their family members,
   c) nursery and shelter with kindergarten for children of mothers employed in the national enterprise,
   d) recreational care,
   e) enterprise social care and hygiene at work,
   f) charitable care,
   g) social research, statistics and planning.

The Social Department managed a total of 3 statutory funds, 3 employee funds, 4 national enterprise funds, 2 statutory foundations and a network of enterprise social workers[9] at workplaces within the plant operation (AV, Vítkovice, Vítkovice 1946-1954, inv. No. 898, reg. No. 153). The head of the Social Department was architect Valentin Stojeba (AV, Vítkovice, Vítkovice 1946-1954, inv. No. 900, reg. No. 153).

---

9 The terms of 'social worker' and 'health-social worker' are synonymously varied in archival documents of VI without any justification for their use.

The central movement decided to change the name of the "Social-Political Department" to "Employee Department". The national enterprise received a new structure. The company management consisted of four departments:

1. Technical department
2. Business department
3. Administrative department
4. Employee department (AV, Vítkovice, Vítkovice 1946-1954, inv. No. 898, reg. No. 153).

The Employment Department consisted of seven groups. The third group was a group of social affairs which included the department of social care. Its work content was management of social funds, care for social, administrative and non-administrative aspects of employees, elaboration of statistics for social surveys, participation with the works council in granting various contributions, organisation of recreation, care for children convalescent homes etc. (AV, Vítkovice, Vítkovice 1946-1954, inv. No. 898, reg. No. 153).

The Social Department of the Klement Gottwald Vítkovice Ironworks (hereinafter 'KGVI') issued, with an approval of the supplying section of the works council, vouchers for textile goods, etc. The largest number of vouchers, i.e. more than nineteen thousand was issued for blue crepe work pants and almost seventeen thousand vouchers for work shoes with leather soles. Further vouchers were supplied for work coats, socks, head scarves, walking shoes, rubber boots, blouses, bicycle tyres, inner tubes, complete bikes, motorcycle inner tubes and tyres, watches, alarm clocks, tins boxes, bedroom furniture, Christmas soap boxes and others. In total, over two-hundred thousand vouchers were issued. The report shows that there was an issuse~~the most difficult~~ situation regarding the number of vouchers for watches, with only 111 of these handed out (AV, Vítkovice, RTUM 1945-54, inv. No. 53, reg. No. 14).

Another beneficial action for employees was the purchase of radio receivers in instalments. An agreement on a fee for the radio receiver was concluded between an employee and a plant representative and it was withdrawn from the employee's wages in 12 monthly instalments along with a 0.5% monthly loan. The contract also included the guarantor's signature. Between 18th January 1948 and 5th June 1948, a total of 1,147 radios were issued (AV, Vítkovice, RTUM 1945-54, inv. No. 78, reg. No. 15).

The Social Section held regular meetings once a month (in 1948 once in 14 days) for joint consultations between social workers and social clerks. It follows from the minutes of the meeting of 21st December 1949 that the most pressing problems were employee absence and fluctuation (AV, Vítkovice, RTUM 1945-54, inv. No. 53, reg. No. 14).

Social workers were recommended to keep themselves from being emotionally engaged in their engagement with workers and to try and objectively explain and convince employees that if they did not fulfil their duties and did not perform the assigned tasks, then they could not demand things from the company which the company does not grant to everyone (AV, Vítkovice, RTUM 1945-54, inv. No. 53, reg. No. 14).

In April 1948, the Ministry of Social Welfare (Department of Social and Health Protection of Work) sent out Interim Work Instructions for Enterprise Social Workers. The letter also included a four-page questionnaire, which the Ministry requested to be revised, supplemented or amended. It was intended for social research (AV, Vítkovice, RTUM 1945-54, inv. No. 53, reg. No. 14).

In 1953 the Social Department provided information about the activities carried out in the previous year. The report was divided into three types of facilities:

- Sh – social-economic facilities
- Ss – social care
- Sv – nourishment (AV, Vítkovice, Vítkovice 1946-1954, inv. No. 1078, reg. No. 167).

Socio-economic facilities included factory accomodation, labourers' homes, bachelor lodging houses etc. Social care included the care of children in nurseries, kindergartens, shelters, children's homes, convalescent homes and holiday sanatoriums. As for adults, there were activities of hygiene at work, i.e. construction of new changing rooms, washrooms, etc. In the area of nourishment, night-time shops and lunch deliveries directly to the workplace were introduced in work operations with hot conditions (AV, Vítkovice, Vítkovice 1946-1954, inv. No. 1078, reg. No. 167).

Content of Social Care

According to documents from 1947, the task of social care was to act in such a way as to create conditions for increasing the standard of living and satisfaction of employees and their family members in the plant with respect to the national social-political plan, and thus create conditions for increasing labour productivity. Social workers were included in workplaces and their activities fit in terms of organisational aspects into the general activity of the plant and meant a deepening of one of the administrative divisions, namely the enterprise social services (AV, Vítkovice, Vítkovice 1946-1954, inv. No. 1684, reg. No. 218).

An enterprise social worker was a professional employee of the plant, just as a company physician or safety technician with whom socials workers cooperated as closely as possible (AV, Vítkovice, Vítkovice 1946-1954, inv. No. 1684, reg. No. 218).

For each social case – employee of VI – a file in the filing cabinet was created. In VI, state-owned enterprise, the records of labourers were kept by the "labourers' personnel department" and the records of clerks by the "clerks' personnel department" (AV, Vítkovice, Vítkovice 1946-1954, inv. No. 1087, reg. No. 168).

The Activity Report for 1946 evidences the content of "general" social care. It is divided into the following components: supportive care, cooperation with social-health institutions, institutional placement, housing care, curative care, clothing events, kindergartens, shelter for children of employed women, workwear repair shop, factory tours, cooperation with occupational medicine, meetings, family investigations – clerical interventions and publicity (AV, Vítkovice, Vítkovice 1946-1954, inv. No. 1070, reg. No. 167).

In 1946, one professionally educated social worker worked in VI with the help of 2 administrative forces who in their free time attended a course for assistant social workers, sby the Provincial National Committee, in order to acquire the most important theoretical knowledge and thus to assert themselves better in practice. In July 1946, a third administrative force was assigned to the department and in December, a second qualified socio-health worker was hired (AV, Vítkovice, Vítkovice 1946-1954, inv. No. 1070, reg. No. 167). Based on a statement by the VI management, this number was sufficient for a state-owned enterprise in 1946 (AV, Vítkovice, Vítkovice 1946-1954, inv. No. 1087, reg. No. 168).

As part of supportive care, the social department processed 1,147 applications for aid in 1946. The largest number were applications for sickness aid, followed by one-off 'poverty aid'. The social department of VI developed cooperation with the Czechoslovak Red Cross, the District Youth Care, the Masaryk League against Tuberculosis, the Social Assistance, the Charity, the Municipal Social Care Authority, the Provincial Holiday and Convalescent Care, the Ludmila Association, the Labour Protection Office and other social-health institutions (AV, Vítkovice, Vítkovice 1946-1954, inv. No. 1070, reg. No. 167).

In 1946, as part of housing care, the social worker made 18 visits to families in order to ascertain the housing conditions. When visiting factory accomodation, she noted the cleanliness of the individual flats, the correct use of the residential space, etc. Special attention was required for visits to the common quarters of men and women because they were outdated, insufficiently equipped and did not meet the requirements of appropriate housing. Social workers focused on ensuring that women did not dry the linen in the rooms and that the rooms were adequately ventilated. In the past, the issues to be solved included personal disputes between women in the women's section, delousing actions, the need to install showers instead of a bath and bidet for women (AV, Vítkovice, Vítkovice 1946-1954, inv. No. 1070, reg. No. 167).

The social department was also involved in institutional placement. In 1946, three mothers with infants and one child without a mother were placed in the

Masaryk Institute for Mothers and Infants in Zábřeh, 6 children were placed in children's homes, 2 over-age employees of the plant in the municipal almshouse, and 5 mothers were provided with placement in the convalescent home in Čeladná. As part of the curative care, 608 children of the plant employees spent their holidays in Ostravice and in Komorní Lhotka (AV, Vítkovice, Vítkovice 1946-1954, inv. No. 1070, reg. No. 167).

As for other activities of the social department, clothing events can be mentioned. The department organised and carried out the distribution of 360 pieces of clothing to the needy family members of the plant employees, donated by the American Red Cross through the Czechoslovak Red Cross. On the occasion of the distribution of Christmas presents, the CZRC also donated 36 pieces of clothing and apparel to 34 children from factory kindergartens. Before donating, social workers carried out an investigation into the situation of the proposed children (AV, Vítkovice, Vítkovice 1946-1954, inv. No. 1070, reg. No. 167).

In kindergartens, the social worker supervised the social-health aspects of ten factory kindergartens with more than 800 children, organised clothing and catering events together with the school administration. She cooperated in radiographic imaging of children and prepared curative events based on the examinations results. She strived for better equipment of rooms in terms of hygiene and for obtaining new premises for inappropriately placed kindergartens in Místecká Street and Prokopa Velikého Street (AV, Vítkovice, Vítkovice 1946-1954, inv. No. 1070, reg. No. 167).

The social worker further performed activities within the Shelter for Children of Employed Mothers. She decided on the admission of children, set the amount of the nursing fee and supervised the shelter operation and the staff who she also hired. On the basis of investigations of the family situation, she determined the amount of the daily nursing fee in individual cases. She supervised the nutrition of children, especially adjusted the menu, organised medical examinations of children, irradiation with mountain sun, serving fish oil, distribution of Christmas gifts and others (AV, Vítkovice, Vítkovice 1946-1954, inv. No. 1070, reg. No. 167).

Until October 1946, a workwear repair shop functioned within the social department. It employed 6 seamstresses who repaired and sewed 4,297 pieces of apparel and factory clothing between January and October 1946. For the next period, uniting the repair shop with the laundry was envisaged. The social worker sought to establish a special laundry for workwear and private clothing of labourers accommodated in the barracks. Thanks to an intervention by the Women's Commission of RTUM, provisional washing of white clothing for all factory employees was implemented. Washing of workwear remained unresolved until the end of 1946 (AV, Vítkovice, Vítkovice 1946-1954, inv. No. 1070, reg. No. 167).

By cooperation with occupational medicine, the social worker tried to improve the hygienic conditions at workplaces, in workshops, dressing rooms, washrooms and toilets, canteens, etc. She participated in inspections of all plant facilities, based on which an investment plan for individual departments was complied, and her task was to supervise its implementation. As part of the plant inspections, the social worker also noted the personal cleanliness of the employees, especially with regard to the occurrence of lice. The cooperation with occupational medicine consisted of referring cases which required social assistance or advice. In 39 cases the social worker negotiated a change of work in the plant for social-health or solely social reasons (AV, Vítkovice, Vítkovice 1946-1954, inv. No. 1070, reg. No. 167).

The seriousness of cooperation with occupational medicine is also evidenced by the social worker's participation in a one-week course on occupational medicine organised by the Ministry of Social Welfare in May 1946 in Čeperka and in September 1946 in Bílá. The social worker also maintained a consistent cooperation with the recruitment department, especially in the recruitment of apprentices (AV, Vítkovice, Vítkovice 1946-1954, inv. No. 1070, reg. No. 167).

Female jobseekers turned to the social department for help in finding suitable workplaces in the factory. An integral part of the work was participation in meetings of social sections, RTUM meetings and other discussions outside the factory (AV, Vítkovice, Vítkovice 1946-1954, inv. No. 1070, reg. No. 167).

Social workers carried out investigations in families, so-called clerical interventions. In 1946, 202 visits to families, 29 visits within the plant, 26 visits to authorities, 13 investigations and 270 visits were made (AV, Vítkovice, Vítkovice 1946-1954, inv. No. 1070, reg. No. 167).

Enterprise social-health services published news both in the daily press and in the factory magazine. On 18th July 1946, the enterprise social worker of VI, along with several other representatives of public social-health care, was accepted by Mrs. Hana Benešová during the President's visit to the Ostrava region. On this occasion, she provided information about enterprise social and health work (AV, Vítkovice, Vítkovice 1946-1954, inv. No. 1070, reg. No. 167).

Publicity took place during visits from abroad, too. In 1946, VI was visited by Belgian social workers who were interested to see the social and health facilities of the factory. The social worker was involved mainly in individual work, however, she also implemented educational lectures from the social-health field and publicity through radio and press. The topics of the lectures were general hygiene, pregnancy, childcare, and venereal diseases. She tried to encourage, particularly young female, workers to attend cooking, sewing and educational courses (AV, Vítkovice, Vítkovice 1946-1954, inv. No. 1070, reg. No. 167).

Incorporating the "disabled" back to work seemed to be problematic. The department encountered a great misunderstanding of the plants whose managers were reluctant to employ the factory "disabled" or less capable employees of other departments. 2,772 persons who had been disabled contacted the department with a request to change their job (AV, Vítkovice, Vítkovice 1946-1954, inv. No. 1070, reg. No. 167).

Enterprise social work in VI was conducted professionally and at an appropriate level, as evidenced by an excursion of students of the Masaryk State School of Health and Social Care from Prague in 1947 and also by a transfer of experience to a social worker from the Škoda Works, who asked to be sent the system of work organisation of socials workers in VI (AV, Vítkovice, Vítkovice 1946-1954, inv. No. 1087, reg. No. 168).

In 1947, the number of social workers increased. 3 professionally trained social-health workers (Miss Růžena Toulová, Mrs. Jana Rubáčková and Miss Ladislava Pielová) and 3 helpers – course attenders (Miss Anna Juřicová, Miss Vlasta Tomšíková and Miss Jana Quisová) were working in VI. According to a statement by VI, addressed to the District Labour Protection Office in Ostrava, this number was sufficient for the national enterprise (AV, Vítkovice, Vítkovice 1946-1954, inv. No. 1087, reg. No. 168).

As reported in the minutes of the social section meeting from 1948, VI social workers obtained year-round tickets for local railways (AV, Vítkovice, RTUM 1945-54, inv. No. 53, reg. No. 14).

The minutes of the meeting of the social section of 20th December 1948 describe a lack of enterprise social workers. Efforts to solve this situation and thus to deepen the social service were made by establishing contact with competent employees in all operations who cooperated with local social workers in social care (AV, Vítkovice, RTUM 1945-54, inv. No. 53, reg. No. 14).

The report of the Social Group of VI from January 1948 shows that in 1947 the company spent more than 58 million CSK on maintenance and operation of social facilities, including voluntary subsidies and pension supplements. Given the total number of employees of thirty-two thousand, the share of social payments per employee amounted to 1,817 CSK (AV, Vítkovice, Vítkovice 1946-1954, inv. No. 1072, reg. No. 167).

The 5 LP programme (five-year plan) also included socially important constructions and investments such as: construction of 600 housing units per year, modification of the existing inappropriate and primitive flats, construction of a boarding school, an apprentice school and apprentice workshops, adaptation of the existing barracks, construction of a 300-bed lodging house, building of children's facilities to accommodate a nursery, a shelter for preschool and schoolchildren, kindergartens and experimental workshops for children, building of necessary changing rooms and washrooms, introduction of air-conditioning in workrooms, health-friendly heating in all rooms, noise reduction, adjustment of the existing eating houses and canteens, construction of new workshops to employ "disabled" persons and to retrain people for a more demanded line of work, construction of a dental clinic, an obstetrics and gynaecology department, an outpatient clinic, modification of the existing convalescent centre in Stará Bělá, construction of a boarding house for nurses, construction of a new marketplace, a recreation centre in Prostřední Bečva, adaptation of recreation centres for children, construction of a swimming pool and playgrounds and construction of a new almshouse (AV, Vítkovice, Vítkovice 1946-1954, inv. No. 1115, reg. No. 169).

In April 1949, a radio report on enterprise social work was produced. The KGVI nominated Miss Mokrošová, a social worker, to appear in the report. In the correspondence between the Czechoslovak Steelworks and KGVI a section of the report text was preserved. Specifically, it says:

The enterprise social worker Miss Marie Mokrošová prepared the following on the topic of work as a social worker: "Talking about the work and health of a working person before the Second World War means talking about poverty, a bad and unhealthy environment both at the workplace and in workers' dwellings, premature mortality, about crippling, alcoholism … simply about moral and physical suffering of workers and their families. … The new era has brought a new view of work. Work must not be a burden to man. It must not be conceived as a fatal punishment either, but as a necessity and life foundation of every individual. Therefore, workers must have a suitable environment to perform their work, an environment which makes their stay more enjoyable, encourages, attracts and carries them along to a work strain with maximum efficiency, to a work strain where they can create a piece of quality work with love and dedication, beneficial to the nation and society" (AV, Vítkovice, Vítkovice 1946-1954, inv. No. 1087, reg. No. 168).

Activity of the Social Section of the Works Council after 1949

The task of the social section was to make life more pleasant for all employees who were affected by various accidents while fulfilling their job duties. The Activity Report of the Social Section for 1949 states that the Social Section only helps those "who deserve it as they were afflicted by a disease or another accident in their employment, or by family members' misfortune" (AV, Vítkovice, RTUM 1945-54, inv. No. 53, reg. No. 14).

In 1949, the department handled a total of 1870 applications, with the highest percent of applications being for illness support. In addition to this number of applications, hundreds of information interviews and interventions in various matters were conducted, as well as many visits to factories, convalescent homes, health-social institutions, authorities, etc. From the resulting numbers, the department deduced conscientious work and assistance in line with the employees' social conditions and the economic possibilities of the enterprise (AV, Vítkovice, RTUM 1945-54, inv. No. 53, reg. No. 14).

Social workers operated directly in individual plants to be as close as possible to the individual workplaces, so that every employee could have the help at hand

and did not have to go far to deal with their affairs. The endeavour of social work was to eliminate all the defects of all employees so that they could carry out their production tasks without any worries, not being burdened with family or other problems and being able to devote themselves fully only to their work (AV, Vítkovice, RTUM 1945-54, inv. No. 53, reg. No. 14).

It follows from the report shows that this activity proved successful, as practice had shown. The success of the social section was evident in establishing cultural rooms in labourers' homes, equipping beds with mattresses, improving catering in factory canteens, establishing bathrooms and sanitary and health measures, improving nursing in factory outpatient departments and in the factory hospital, better education of staff in behaviour towards patients, possibilities of respite in the convalescent home in Stará Bělá, and treatment of overworked employees, opening new crèches in September 1949, and other benefits. Even the most pressing housing issue was not neglected. Over the last 5 years prior to the report, more flats had been built than in the previous 30 years (AV, Vítkovice, RTUM 1945-54, inv. No. 53, reg. No. 14).

Tasks of Social Workers

In a paper from 1947 entitled "How does the state-owned enterprise Vítkovice Ironworks care for its employees and what social benefits does it provide to its employees?", the main tasks of social workers at the plant are summarised (AV, Vítkovice, Vítkovice 1946-1954, inv. No. 1684, reg. No. 218).

1. Cooperating initiatively in organising enterprise catering, caring for its rationalising and improvement, educating on nutrition.
2. Taking care of improving the housing standard, cooperation with construction experts at implementing the factory housing programme, while allowing for the social aspect. Initiative monitoring of the operation of factory flats, both family and collective ones, of youth homes, as well as housing of employees outside the factory flats and educating to a housing culture.
3. Taking care of working women, especially during maternity, taking care of the social conditions of their work in factories, as well as the living conditions in their homes, organising neighbourhood aid events and voluntary enterprise social service. Facilitating the educational duties of mothers by taking care of the placement of their children in social and educational institutions and facilities, both factory and non-factory ones. Supervising well operated factory children's facilities – nurseries, kindergartens, shelters, after-school clubs and other facilities. Initiatively organising and facilitating the housekeeping duties of employees and employees' wives by organising mass purchases, washing laundry, repairing clothes and laundry, setting up factory laundries and supervising a proper operation of these facilities.

4. Taking care of juvenile workers in social terms, especially of their housing, nutrition, recreation, physical and mental health, cooperating in their guidance, education and thus supporting their social interests.
5. Taking care of the employees' children, organising or cooperating short and long-term recreation, monitoring social and socio-health as well as educational conditions.
6. Organising and taking care of recreation of adult employees and their families.
7. Ensuring social kept considerations in the workforce distribution, recruitment, transfer or dismissal.
8. Taking care of workers with reduced working capacity, cooperating in their appropriate work inclusion in both subjective and objective terms, and permanently protecting the social interest of theirs and their families, cooperating in the agenda of social wages and salaries.
9. Carrying out individual care for employees and their family members, investigating social justification of their applications and social assistance of all kinds, and giving reports to relevant officials.
10. Cooperating with the works council, trade union organisation, cooperating in re-education of those who had broken the law, establishing and managing the social file of employees. Providing first aid in case of accidents in the absence of a physician or relevant medical staff.

In order to facilitate performance of all the above tasks, the enterprise was divided into 4 areas. Each area was staffed by two to three permanent social workers with the assistance of members of work councils and confidants, who were specially trained for these purposes. Social workers had the following office hours: for the first shift always from 2-3 p.m., for the second shift from 1-2 p.m. and for the third shift from 1-3 p.m. (AV, Vítkovice, Vítkovice 1946-1954, inv. No. 1684, reg. No. 218).

Arch. Stojeba reminded everyone at a meeting of the Social Section in December 1949 that the activities of social agents need to function as a catalyst in the work process. They must evoke a continuous acceleration of positive creative forces and diminish or abolish all negative forces which could undermine, hamper or threaten productive work (AV, Vítkovice, RTUM 1945-54, inv. No. 53, reg. No. 14).

In-service Training Courses for Enterprise Social-Health Workers

In 1946, the Institute of National Health in Ostrava informed VI about the preparation of a course for enterprise social clerks, confidants and social confidants in associations. It consisted of at least 40 lecture hours of 45 minutes, held twice a week in the evening in the lecture hall of the Ostrava School of Mining. The course fee was 200 CSK (AV, Vítkovice, Vítkovice 1946-1954, inv. No. 1087, reg. No. 168).

Course programme:

- Ethical introduction to socio-health work.
- Overview of facilities and institutions for social-health care and services. Organization of voluntary and public socio-health care and services.
- Chapters from civil law, criminal law and labour law.
- Labour protection authorities.
- Social policy, trade unions, works councils.
- Chapters from health science, social medicine, occupational medicine (environmental and work hygiene), physical education and recreation.
- Public instruction and publicity.
- Specific comments on individual work sections (AV, Vítkovice, Vítkovice 1946-1954, inv. No. 1087, reg. No. 168).

Further training was organised a year later. The Central Council of Trade Unions in cooperation with the Ministry of Social Welfare organised two-month in-service training courses for social-health workers. The Ministry of Social Welfare justified the necessity of their holding by providing uniform professionally led social-health care in enterprises. The courses took place from 26th May to 25th June 1947 in the form of boarding training. The costs per person for 4 weeks including tuition, accommodation and meals amounted to 2500 CSK. The course capacity was 120 people. Information about the course was sent to Czechoslovak metallurgical plants by the Economic Group of the Iron Industry (AV, Vítkovice, Vítkovice 1946-1954, inv. No. 1087, reg. No. 168).

Social Research in Metallurgy

On 21st March 1949, Jiří Čepelák, head of the Social Research Department of the Czechoslovak Institute of Labour, addressed the chairman of the enterprise trade union group in a letter with a request for cooperation of KGVI on social research conducted in metallurgy. 300 questionnaires were sent to the ironworks, which were distributed to confidants in individual plants. The questionnaire had 2 parts, the first part was called "My life and work", the second part "Life in our workshop". Unfortunately, I was not able to find the latter part in the archives. It follows from the comments on the questionnaires completion that the first part was filled by the labourers themselves, while the second part was written only by confidants for the labourers in the workshop they represented (AV, Vítkovice, RTUM 1945-54, inv. No. 189, reg. No. 26).

The research results should be used for planning in the economy. The confidants should emphasise this fact to the labourers as one of the motivations for participation (AV, Vítkovice, RTUM 1945-54, inv. No. 189, reg. No. 26).

2.2.2 Schooling and Care for Children and Youth

The social activities of VI also included care for pre-school and school children and apprentices. The importance of bringing up children, especially from poorer social strata, was at the forefront of the ironworks interest. For this reason, social facilities were built, among which the children's shelter, orphanage, nurseries and kindergartens, schools of general education and an apprentice school with workshops played a vital role.

The plant financed almost all schools in the village. By doing so, the enterprise could select teachers in line with its needs and could introduce German as the language of instruction. Czech was the language of communication. Gradually, the following schools were established:

- 1893 – German Secondary Modern Boys' School
- 1894 – II. German Boys' School of General Education and II. German Girls' School of General Education on the corner of today's streets Ocelářská and Šalounova
- 1897 – *Emperor Franz Joseph Czech School of General Education* – free Czech School of General Education of five classes in today's Zengrova street (Myška, 1960; Matějček, Vytiska, 1978).

As the village grew, schools were expanding quickly. In addition to the apprentice school, which was attended by 507 pupils in 1907, the ironworks had a factory school at the level of a technical secondary school where middle-level technical cadres were being educated. The language of instruction was still German (Matějček, Vytiska, 1978).

In 1911, the ironworks had these facilities for children of school and pre-school:

- Orphanage with 137 children
- Nursery for 30 children
- Holiday home in Staré Hamry established in 1910 for 108 children a year
- Holiday settlement for 70 children in Horní Čeladná established in 1903 (Matějček, Vytiska, 1978: 63).

In the following years, the social facilities for children and youth expanded. In 1930, the capacity of the orphanage was 200 children and 12 kindergartens were opened (AV, Vítkovice, VMIC 11, inv. No. 1610, reg. No. 302).

An important part of childcare was recreational holiday care for school children. After the Second World War, children used to go to the company convalescent home at "Mazák" – Ostravice and to the children's sanatorium České srdce in

Komorní Lhotka near Český Těšín (AV, Vítkovice, VMIC 11, inv. No. 1636, reg. No. 309).

In 1949, four convalescent homes were used for children's recreation. Apart from Mazák and Komorní Lhotka, children went to Štramberk and Hutisko. A total of 814 children were sent to company convalescent homes in 1949, which meant meeting the annual plan at 101,7% (AV, Vítkovice, RTUM 1945-54, inv. No. 53, reg. No. 14).

The Orphanage Foundation of Vítkovice Mining and Iron Corporation

In 1898, VMIC established an independent foundation called The Orphan Foundation of VMIC. It served to educate and provide shelter, nourishment and clothing to orphaned children of labourers and clerks of the corporation, aged 6-14. The orphanage was placed in a one-storeyed building with fixtures and equipment which could accommodate 75 boys and 75 girls. The orphanage was finally completed in 1912. It consisted of a separate group of buildings with a large inner courtyard, including a playground and school garden beds. Nearly all rooms were equipped with central heating (AV, Vítkovice, VMIC 11, inv. No. 1636, reg. No. 309).

Supervision was provided by four nurses led by one superior. Housework was provided by three helpers and caretaker. The children were under constant medical supervision. In 1936, there were 50 children in the orphanage, of which 48 were Czech and 2 of German nationality. Depending on their nationality, the children attended the corresponding basic, secondary and vocational schools (AV, Vítkovice, VMIC 11, inv. No. 1636, reg. No. 309).

Children's Shelter – Nurseries and Kindergartens

In 1893, Pavel Kupelwieser, at that time already a former general director, established a foundation for a children's shelter which was subsequently built in 1896 in Moravská Ostrava in Prokopa Velikého Street. Its purpose was to support female factory employees who were the main breadwinners and had to care for and bring up children from the age of 1-6 years. Children under 3 years of age were looked after by a nurse and an assistant nurse, other children older than 3 years were looked after by a babysitter in a shelter. The main activity was games. The capacity was 40 places, but it was often exceeded. In 1930 there were 49 children in the shelter. The condition for admission was children aged 1-6 whose mothers were widows of a factory employee and who were employed throughout the day. The care and supervision were provided free of charge, all costs were covered by VMIC (AV, Vítkovice, VMIC 11, inv. No. 1636, reg. No. 309).

Table No. 3 – Capacity of nurseries of Vítkovice Ironworks between 1919-1925

Year	Number of children	Costs per child in CSK
1919	57	245
1920	68	407
1921	34	1021
1922	46	651
1923	59	459
1924	63	467
1925	67	490

Source: AV, Vítkovice, VMIC 11, inv. No. 1623, reg. No. 304

In materials from 1936 we encounter a new notion of kindergarten. There were 526 children in kindergartens this year. Ten kindergartens were in Vítkovice, one in Hulváky and one in Hrabůvka. In 1937, there were 13 teachers working in kindergartens led by two inspectors. Kindergartens were supervised by state school authorities (AV, Vítkovice, VMIC 11, inv. No. 1636, reg. No. 309).

The VI archival materials of 1945 refer to maintenance of 10 kindergartens and one shelter for children of employed mothers, providing children with all-day care and meals. Kindergartens were managed by one inspector and 18 teachers. The shelter was managed by a professionally trained babysitter, led by a social worker of the ironworks. 31 children were placed in the children's shelter, for which the mothers paid a contribution of 5-10 CSK. 756 children were registered in kindergartens in 1945. Seven kindergartens and the shelter were situated in the VI own buildings, one kindergarten was located in the building of a school of general education and two were in private buildings. Washrooms and changing rooms were newly established in three kindergartens. Installation of central heating was planned in the following years (AV, Vítkovice, VMIC n.a., inv. No. 423, reg. No. 29).

The Annual Report of the Social Department for 1946 states that the shelter for children of employed mothers of Vítkovice Ironworks, state-owned enterprise, was an institutional facility which allowed working women to place their children for the time of their gainful employment (AV, Vítkovice, Vítkovice 1946-1954, inv. No. 1070, reg. No. 167).

Children aged 2-14 were admitted to the shelter, which was a change from the original age of the children admitted. The operation was adapted to the needs of working mothers, and therefore it was open from 5.30 a.m. to 4 p.m. The entrusted children were divided into 3 departments – toddlers, preschool children and school children. Applications were accepted by the enterprise social-health worker. The mothers brought their children in the morning and handed them over to the administrator or babysitter. During the day, the children were given breakfast, a morning snack, lunch and an afternoon snack. The school children went to school after breakfast, taking the snack with them. After school, they came back to the shelter, where they did their homework and waited for their mothers to return from work. The mothers were obliged to hand over 50% of the ration cards for food belonging to the child to the shelter administrator. Once every 14 days, each child underwent a medical examination by a company physician. The administrator was responsible for running the shelter. Possible complaints were communicated to the Social Department of VI (AV, Vítkovice, Vítkovice 1946-1954., inv. No. 1070, reg. No. 167).

The shelter was owned and financed by the state-owned enterprise of VI. Based on their earnings and social conditions, parents were still required to contribute in the range of 5-10 CSK a day to partially cover the costs. Supervision of the shelter operation fell under the responsibility of the Social Department. Direct supervision was performed by the social-health worker. On average, there were 20 children a day in the shelter in 1946 (AV, Vítkovice, Vítkovice 1946-1954, inv. No. 1070, reg. No. 167).

In 1947, a new nursery for 70-80 infants and toddlers were under construction near the Vítkovice Square and the town orchard. Both the shelter and the nursery were under constant medical supervision of the head physician of the children's department of the factory hospital MUDr. Lukeš (AV, Vítkovice, Vítkovice 1946-1954, inv. No. 1684, reg. No. 218).

Shelter for Apprentices, Education of Apprentices

The apprentices were provided with meals and accommodation free of charge. The building also included workshops. On average, 156 apprentices a day were accommodated in the shelter in 1929 (AV, Vítkovice, VMIC 11, inv. No. 1610, reg. No. 302). After World War II, archival documents refer to the need to renew the apprenticeships, most employees or apprentices having been arrested or fled after the wary due to their German nationality. During this time there was no filing cabinet, no records and administration, no learning contracts. As of 1st September 1945, 700 new apprentices were admitted (AV, Vítkovice, VMIC n.a., inv. No. 423, reg. No. 29).

Table No. 4 – Numbers of apprentices as of 31.12.1945 by classes

Class	Number of apprentices
1st year	584
2nd year	227
3rd year	302

Source: AV, Vítkovice, VMIC n.a., inv. No. 423, reg. No. 29

In terms of nationality, there were 841 apprentices of Czech nationality and 272 Slovaks. A total of 305 apprentices were accommodated in apprenticeship homes. At the beginning of 1945/46, there were 1,239 pupils and 79 teachers in 42 classes of the apprentice school. The apprentice workshops were in a very bad condition after World War II. None of the machines could be put into operation. The foremen and apprentices carried out the cleaning work and the most necessary repairs (AV, Vítkovice, VMIC n.a., inv. No. 423, reg. No. 29).

In the social field, archival materials (Report on the Activities of the Social Group dated 19th October 1946) mention assistance especially to apprentices living in apprentice homes. VI paid their apprentices extra in their first year in addition to their education allowance of 330 CSK, because of this amount, 130 CSK was paid as pocket money and the rest did not cover meals and accommodation. (AV, Vítkovice, VMIC n.a., inv. No. 423, reg. No. 29).

The ironworks did not pay any wages to the apprentices in the second and third years, even though they were working in productive operations. The ironworks calculated that the apprentices performed about 150,000 working hours per month. If the hours were multiplied by the average labourer's earnings, then the cost of apprentice education decreased significantly. That is why the VI management within a two-year plan proposed to set up central apprentice workshops and leave the apprentices of the second year working productively. It was assumed that this would make the apprenticeship department fully self-sufficient (AV, Vítkovice, VMIC n.a., inv. No. 423, reg. No. 29).

The ironworks administration provided the apprentices with shoes and clothes from its own resources. For the apprentices who had to spend the Christmas holidays in 1945 at the boarding school, a Christmas Eve dinner was organised with the participation of national administrators (AV, Vítkovice, VMIC n.a., inv. No. 423, reg. No. 29).

2.2.3 Housing Care

Ironworks took special care of housing conditions. Archival materials point out to purposeful housing care, pursuing the effort to provide good and cheap flats (AV, Vítkovice, VMIC 11, inv. No. 1610, reg. No. 302). Since the foundation of Vítkovice Mining Corporation, there had been a chronic housing shortage in the locality. Therefore, the workers were interested in factory flats with relatively low rent. However, these were not available to everyone, as the differentiation between individual categories of workers was also reflected in housing care. There was a strict distinction among flats for officials, foremen and labourers (Jiřík, 2001).

In 1886, the plant had 139 flats for supervisors and foremen, 39 flats for single officials, and 452 labourers' family flats. Ironworkers, who had their houses in settlements, raised poultry and other small animals and cultivated small pieces of land. The character of life was mostly similar to that of a village. Settlements of blocks of houses built around the year 1900 had already an urban character. In the early 1920s, construction of the so-called Jubilee Settlement for labourers in Hrabůvka began. The construction of the settlement with 95 houses containing 602 flats was completed in 1931 (Matějček, Vytiska, 1978).

VI started construction of factory flats before the First World War. They allocated them to skilled and efficient workers who the ironworks were interested to maintain. In 1921, the Mining Housing Administration took care of 424 buildings with 521 flats for officials and 1840 flats for labourers (Matějček, Vytiska, 1978).

The ironworks distinguished two types of officials' flats. Meritorious officials, technicians and foremen were provided free of charge with so-called flats with benefits in kind, including fuel heating and lighting. For example, in 1933, out of 3,645 factory flats, 523 were flats with benefits in kind. Other officials lived in factory officials' flats or private flats rented by the ironworks. Labourers' houses were built for 4 to 15 or even more families (with the exception of some settlements). The lack of space in these houses was further exacerbated by the large number of members in labourers' families and accommodation of subtenants (Jiřík, 2001).

Rent was a significant item in the labourers' budgets. In factory flats it was regulated so as to be lower than in private houses. It did not amount to more than 15% of the average labourers' or officials' earnings.

Table No. 5 – Rents in 1907 and 1931 vs wages

	Monthly rent	Monthly rent for a room, kitchen and fixtures	Monthly rent for a bed in barracks	**Average wages per shift**
1907	3-6 CSK	8-13 CSK	2-2,4 CSK	unskilled labourers – 2,6 CSK
				craftsmen – 3,8 CSK
				ironworkers 5-7 CSK
	Monthly rent for one room	**Monthly rent for one room and a cabinet**	**Monthly rent for two rooms and a cabinet**	**Average labourers' wage per eight-hour shift**
1931	60-180 CSK	150 CSK	325 CSK	41,52 CSK

Source: Jiřík, 2001: 325-327, modified

A tenancy agreement was agreed with the users of factory flats, which could be cancelled by the VI management with 14 days' notice. The notice period was reduced to only three days when the user left their workplace arbitrarily. The notice of termination could not be appealed. A turnaround on this occurred thanks to the Decree of the Ministry of Justice and the Ministry of Social Welfare No. 21/1918 of the Reich Tenant Protection Law, based on which a tenancy agreement could only be cancelled after a proper justification and approval by the competent district court. The ironworks' owners could no longer 'kick out' dismissed labourers, pensioners and widows from a flat without the provision of substitute accomodation (Jiřík, 2001).

So-called labourers' homes or barracks were built for non-resident employees commuting from more distant locations. They were located in Vítkovice, Ostrava and Kunčice. The accommodation was of a collective nature (AV, Vítkovice, Vítkovice 1946-1954, inv. No. 1684, reg. No. 218). The oldest barracks date from 1882 (two brick buildings for 300 people), another was built in 1885 and two more in 1888. The first barracks were very primitive with large sleeping halls and insufficient sanitary facilities. In 1886, the plant had 12 barracks for 1,387 labourers (Matějček, Vytiska, 1978). At the beginning of the 20th century, the standard was rising, and even double and single rooms were set up for higher-ranking labourers. According to archive materials, the barracks were comfortably furnished, i.e. there were also showers (AV, Vítkovice, VMIC 11, inv. No. 1610, reg. No. 302). The poorly equipped wooden huts were used mainly for the accommodation of seasonal workers, prisoners of war during World War I and forced workers during World War II (Jiřík, 2001).

In 1938 Vítkovice Mining Corporation had 606 houses with 3,678 flats. In 1938, monthly rent in labourers' flats for a room with a kitchen amounted to 100-120 CSK, for a two-room flat from CZK 100-130. The rent in officials' flats ranged between 240-400 CSK per month. These flats were naturally more spacious and more comfortably equipped (Matějček and Vytiska, 1978). Modern officials' apartments consisted of 2-3 rooms, a kitchen, bathroom, hall, pantry and fixtures. Labourers' flats had only 1-2 rooms, a kitchen, hall, pantry and fixtures (AV, Vítkovice, VMIC 11, inv. No. 1610, reg. No. 302).

After 1945, reflections on rebuilding the factory hotel built in 1887 into Community House, also used to educate employees, appeared (AV, Vítkovice, VMIC n.a., inv. No. 423, reg. No. 29).

After 1945, housing care became a part of the social group activities. At the end of 1943, VI owned a total of 4,114 flats in the cadastral area of the municipality of Velká Ostrava, 477 flats in Fryštát and 35 flats in Rožnov pod Radhoštěm. 1737 flats in total were damaged or completely destroyed by the events of World War II. 1332 flats were gradually repaired. After repairs were completed, the total loss of VI flats amounted to 52 flats. Construction of 600 housing units in the Hrabová cadastre was planned within the two-year period (AV, Vítkovice, VMIC n.a., inv. No. 423, reg. No. 29).

In 1946, 4,229 employees were accommodated in labourers' homes, in a total of 7 buildings (AV, Vítkovice, VMIC n.a., inv. No. 423, reg. No. 29).

At the end of 1946, the total number of houses managed by the housing department reached 714 houses with 4,138 flats. The distribution of the individual institutions to which the houses belonged is shown in the following table.

Table No. 6 – Situation of factory houses in 1946

	Number of houses	Number of flats
Pension Institution	258	2054
Maintenance Institute	6	38
Vítkovice Ironworks	450	2046
Total	714	4138

Source: AV, Vítkovice, Vítkovice 1946-1954, inv. No. 1070, reg. No. 167

In 1946, 4,200 beds were occupied in tenements and labourers' homes. On 1st January 1946, the Building Cooperative was incorporated into the VI. Thus, the number of houses newly increased by 103 houses with 479 flats (AV, Vítkovice, Vítkovice 1946-1954, inv. No. 1070, reg. No. 167).

Apart from that, the housing department of VI maintained houses of the chemical pPlants in Ostrava, Kotouč Stone Quarry and Studénka-Štramberk Railway in its register. The housing care in VI was of a high standard. As Jiřík (2001) writes, in Czechoslovakia we would hardly find another industrial enterprise which provided accommodation for almost a half of its employees, as VI did.

In 1947, an auxiliary component – the so-called housing section – was created as part of the housing care to facilitate the management of its tasks. It consisted of three members of the works council, two representatives of the housing department, a social-health worker and a housing care clerk (AV, Vítkovice, Vítkovice 1946-1954, inv. No. 1070, reg. No. 167).

The following initiatives pertained to housing care:

1. Determining the need, type and destination of new residential buildings.
2. Deciding on buying buildings.
3. Deciding on the need to adapt buildings and repair existing buildings.
4. Allocating flats to employees and terminating rental contracts.
5. Adjustment of rent.
6. Purchase of land for residential buildings.
7. Economical management and care of housing hygiene (AV, Vítkovice, Vítkovice 1946-1954, inv. No. 1070, reg. No. 167).

Between 1947 and 1948, 600 new housing units in the Jubilee Settlement, Ruská Street and Mlýnská Street were intended to be built within the two-year period (AV, Vítkovice, Vítkovice 1946-1954, inv. No. 1070, reg. No. 167).

After World War II, labourers' homes had a total capacity of 4,914 beds. Monthly rent in labourers' homes amounted to 25-60 CSK. Lodging houses with single and double rooms were built for single employees in a limited number of 184 beds (AV, Vítkovice, Vítkovice 1946-1954, inv. No. 1684, reg. No. 218).

The cost of managing and maintaining the residential houses highly exceeded the rental income. According to Jiřík (2001), the ironworks' owners continually had to pay extra for the construction, maintenance of the home property and housing care. Even so, the housing care of VI for its employees was a model for other industrial enterprises and ranked among the best. Jiřík (2001: 327) hereby disproves Marx's proposition that "the faster capitalist accumulation, the worse the condition of labourers' dwellings". The opposite was true in VI.

2.2.4   Health Care, Convalescence

The Vítkovice Mining Corporation also built its own medical facilities. The factory hospital had been in operation since the time of the Habsburg monarchy. A high accident rate as well as an immense sickness rate among the ironworks labourers forced the Vítkovice Mining Corporation management to establish the so-called Knappschaftspital – Mining Brotherhood Hospital in one of the residential buildings in 1840. This hospital was the first inpatient facility not only in the Ostrava region, but also in the entire Austrian monarchy. The staff consisted of two doctors/ surgeons or barber surgeons, servants and female medical orderlies looking after the sick at night. The relatives brought food to the sick, or if the patient had money, he could send a servant to make a purchase. The diagnostics of the hospital were rather infamous. Based on the memories of later director P. Kupelwieser, only two diseases were distinguished: headache and abdominal pain (Matějček, Vytiska, 1978; Palát, 1989).

A new factory hospital was built in 1853. In 1890, the factory hospital was reconstructed and equipped with up-to-date equipment. Two years later, a ward for infectious diseases was added to it. Director P. Kupelwieser paid particular attention to the hospital, therefore he also engaged a doctor in the hospital. (Matějček, Vytiska, 1978) In 1878, the first university-educated doctor MUDr. Maximilián Munk was put in post (Kladiwa, Pokludová, Kafková, 2009; Palát, 1989).

Great attention was paid to the employees' health. Despite the positively described social policy of VI, the labourers were often ill or injured. A description of the state of health can be found, for example, in the contemporary newspaper "Spirit of Time" from the year 1900. "Mass injuries, illnesses and deaths are a daily occurrence. About 14,000 labourers are working in Vítkovice, of which 17,297 fell ill in 1899. How is this possible? It shows that some labourers become ill twice or even three times a year" (Vítkovice and Labourers, 1900: 1). The capacity of the Vítkovice Hospital was insufficient for the increasing number of patients, reflected in the same article: "And just as we are writing these lines, the Vítkovice Hospital is overcrowded, and there is a large number of patients lying even in flats as they could not get a place in the hospital. Poor labourers fall under the current heat like flies" (Vítkovice and Labourers, 1900: 1).

Every new employee was required to undergo an initial check-up in order to ascertain their health condition. "It is worthy of note that before a labourer is accepted into work, they must submit to a strict medical examination to see if they are completely healthy. This shows how much the labourers' health gets damaged in the Vítkovice plant, moreover, considering that 4085 labourers and female labourers were injured in 1899. Most injuries can be attributed to burns" (Vítkovice and Labourers, 1900: 1).

The health condition of employees was negatively affected by the environment in Vítkovice, too: "A considerable cause of the diseases of Vítkovice labourers is that apart from the constant clouds of smoke and evolving harmful gases, the municipality itself is very impure. In winter, spring and autumn it is muddy to drown, and in summer dusty to suffocate. All the water in the wells is, pursuant to a medical opinion, poisoned by faeces which flow both in the streets and in the houses on the ground, and since there is no sewerage system, they will soak into the ground and into the wells, so that those who drink the water of Vítkovice, will certainly fall ill" (Vítkovice and Labourers, 1900: 1).

In the summer of 1908, the neighbouring village of Zábřeh na Odrou turned to Vítkovice with a proposal to build a joint infectious diseases hospital. The hospital was opened in August 1912, but its opening was accompanied by disputes over the management of the institute and the bilingual designation with its Czech name in the first place. Vítkovice preferred the German designation arguing that German was the official language of the more significant Vítkovice. After two years, the final verdict was an agreement that the operating costs would be borne by both municipalities equally, and that there would be an equality of German and Czech at the hospital. (Kladiwa, Pokludová, Kafková, 2009).

In the interwar period, the hospital was furnished with the latest equipment and a well-organised rescue service. After 1918, the hospital had 300 beds and five specialised outpatient departments. In order to better monitor the labourers' health condition, outpatient clinics with daily surgery hours were established in each plant (AV, Vítkovice, VMIC 11, inv. No. 1610, reg. No. 302).

In nearby Zábřeh nad Odrou (today's city district of Ostrava), there was a hospital for infectious diseases with 58 beds and a shelter for convalescent people was located in Stará Bělá. A convalescent home was set up for officials where they could spend their vacation in the Beskydy Mountains, providing a full pension for around

18 CSK per day for approximately 100 employees (AV, Vítkovice, VMIC 11, inv. No. 1610, reg. No. 302).

In the interwar period, the medical facilities were expanded to include an institute for mothers and infants, a dental institute, a factory outpatient department in a new housing estate in Hrabůvka, and an outpatient department for children's internal diseases. In 1932, free medical examinations were introduced for employees' children, initially only up to 14 years of age, later also for older youth (Matějček a Vytiska, 1978).

A set of 16 houses in Rožnov pod Radhoštěm was built for officials and retired workers, and for workers who, in the opinion of the enterprise management, contributed to the enterprise development, an old-age house with six pavilions in which 74 families could be accommodated. Also, a summer settlement was built in Ostravice in the Beskydy Mountains, where children took turns for free three-week holiday recreations (Matějček and Vytiska, 1978).

Spacious labourers' bathrooms in all plants, a spa for officials with a large indoor swimming pool and a summer swimming pool served medical purposes as well. It was possible to do sports at a large sports centre with two football pitches, several tennis courts and a cycling track (AV, Vítkovice, VMIC 11, inv. No. 1610, reg. No. 302).

At the end of 1945, the factory hospital consisted of 12 departments: surgical, gynaecological and obstetric, internal, paediatric, eye, throat, dermal, physiotherapy, dental, X-ray, occupational medicine and convalescent. There were 542 beds in the hospital, 38 in the convalescent ward. A team of 35 doctors took care of the patients. The nursing staff consisted of nuns and other personnel totalling 104 persons. The Mining Corporation contributed with more than 8 million CSK to the hospital operation (AV, Vítkovice, VMIC n.a., inv. No. 423, reg. No. 29).

Psycho-Technical Laboratory – Injury Prevention

As a special branch of socio-political activity, a psycho-technical research station was set up (archive document from 1926), which allowed each worker and apprentice to work in a place which best corresponded to their capabilities and abilities. This resulted in a reduced accident rate, as VI were not satisfied with addressing the consequences of injuries merely by medical treatment or accident insurance (AV, Vítkovice, VMIC 11, inv. No. 1610, reg. No. 302).

Shelter for Convalescents

A convalescent home was founded in Stará Bělá in 1899. The owner was VMIC. The shelter had 33 beds in 11 rooms, steam central heating, running hot and cold water in all rooms and electric lighting. The rooms were equipped with iron beds and bedside tables. The shelter included a surgery room with a state telephone, two bathrooms with showers, a laundry, a large park with a lounger space with 12 sun loungers. One radio receiver, a skittle alley and other games served to entertain the convalescent people (AV, Vítkovice, VMIC 11, inv. No. 1610, reg. No. 302).

The purpose of the facility was to provide recovery to members of the Vítkovice Ironworks Works Health Insurance Fund from serious illnesses, including family members, except children. The capacity of 33 places was mostly fully occupied. The shelter was in operation all year. Employment in VI was a condition for admission. The enterprise health insurance fund paid the boarding fees for its members in full, for their family members only partially, requiring a payment of 10 CSK extra per day (AV, Vítkovice, VMIC 11, inv. No. 1610, reg. No. 302).

Table No. 7 – Number of diners in the shelter for convalescents between 1928-1930

Year	Number of diners
1928	332
1929	353
1930	321

Source: AV, Vítkovice, VMIC 11, inv. No. 1610, reg. No. 302

Counselling Centre for Skin and Venereal Diseases

The counselling centre was set up under the guidance of VMIC as part of the factory hospital in Vítkovice in 1919. It was aimed at specific treatment and counselling of members of the factory sickness fund suffering from venereal diseases and their family members. Male patients were admitted by the Department of Dermatology and Venereal Diseases at the factory hospital with a capacity of 23 beds. In 1930, the department was occupied at 50% capacity. The counselling and treatment were provided free of charge, employment in VI was a condition for admission (AV, Vítkovice, VMIC 11, inv. No. 1610, reg. No. 302).

Table No. 8 – Number of medical treatments provided in the Counselling Centre for Skin and Venereal Diseases between 1928-1930

Year	Number of treatments
1928	13777
1929	13491
1930	14762

Source: AV, Vítkovice, VMIC 11, inv. No. 1610, reg. No. 302

Counselling Centre for Infants

The Counselling Centre for Infants was established in 1921 as part of the factory hospital in Vítkovice. The owner was VMIC, too. The purpose was to provide counselling for infants from the VI members' circle. An infant ward with 16 beds at the Institute for the Care of Mothers and Infants served for admission. In January 1930, 10 beds were occupied at the department. Employment in VI was a condition for admission. Members of the enterprise sickness fund paid a boarding fee of 5 CSK for infants (AV, Vítkovice, VMIC 11, inv. No. 1610, reg. No. 302).

Table No. 9 – Number of infants treated in the Counselling Centre for mothers and Infants between 1928-1930

Year	Number of treated infants	Number of consultations
1928	609	3243
1929	560	3352
1930	710	4308

Source: AV, Vítkovice, VMIC 11, inv. No. 1610, reg. No. 302

Treatment Centre for Tuberculosis (TB)

The treatment centre was established in 1919 as a part of the "outpatient clinic" of the 1st internal department at the factory hospital. The purpose was to provide specific treatment for members of the enterprise sickness fund and their family members with TB. Treatment was provided free of charge as part of belonging to VI (AV, Vítkovice, VMIC 11, inv. No. 1610, reg. No. 302).

Wilhelm Gutmann Almshouse Foundation

For Christmas in 1907, Rudolf Gutmann, owner of a mining company, established a foundation in memory of his late father, Wilhelm Gutmann. The purpose of the foundation was to provide free flats to old deserving labourers of VI and of the

Vítkovice Coal Mines, who became incapable of work for any reason after at least 25 years of continuous employment (AV, Vítkovice, VMIC 11, inv. No. 1636, reg. No. 309).

Table No. 10 – Number of flats for veteran labourers of VMIC between 1930-1937

	1930	1937
Number of almshouses	5	7
Capacity – number of flats	60	93

Source: AV, Vítkovice, VMIC 11, inv. No. 1636, reg. No. 309

In 1930, all places were occupied. Based on the foundation charter, the maintenance costs should be covered from the reserve fund revenue. However, as the revenue was not sufficient for the costs, the deficit was covered by VMIC (AV, Vítkovice, VMIC 11, inv. No. 1610, reg. No. 302).

The individual almshouses in Vítkovice were single-storey buildings with flats, consisting mostly of a kitchen, two rooms and a covered built-on gallery. Each pavilion had a washroom and a bathroom with hot water, a laundry room and a mangle room, cellars and attics were the norm. Each flat was assigned a flower bed and courtyard with small gardens (AV, Vítkovice, VMIC 11, inv. No. 1636, reg. No. 309).

In 1947, there were two homes for veteran employees in operation. The so-called almshouses, intended for employees who had worked in the company for 35 years or more, were located in Vítkovice and in the pensioners' settlement in Rožnov pod Radhoštěm. The stay was free of charge (AV, Vítkovice, Vítkovice 1946-1954, inv. No. 1684, reg. No. 218).

Workshop for Disabled People

In 1927, a workshop was set up for employees who became "disabled" as a result of an accident at VI. The workshop gave the opportunity to supplement the accident pension and at the same time, the opportunity to do useful work. The workshop employed 70 disabled workers who worked in a printing shop, bookbinding shop, knitted baskets, tied brooms, sewed work clothes or glued bags. The whole institution did not only pursue economic but also therapeutic purposes. The motto of the workshop was "Better one's own work than other people's compassion" (AV, Vítkovice, VMIC 11, inv. No. 1610, reg. No. 302).

In 1947, the existence of the VI rehabilitation workshops, the so-called invalids' facility, was highlighted as one of the few companies in the country to have set up workshops for employees with reduced working capacity. All printed forms of the company were made at the workshops, bookbinding work was carried out there, jute work clothes and gloves were made in the tailor's workshops, there were a shoemaking workshops, basket-making workshops and brush-making workshops as well. It was planned within the new five-year plan to add further workshops for lung patients, whose number increased significantly after the war (AV, Vítkovice, Vítkovice 1946-1954, inv. No. 1684, reg. No. 218).

The workshops also served for retraining of healthy employees from the previous field of work to a new field more necessary from the national economic point of view (AV, Vítkovice, RTUM 1945-54, inv. No. 53, reg. No. 14).

Hygiene at Work

Hygiene at work became a new activity of the social department after the World War II. Its tasks consisted of ensuring workplaces: were healthy and safe, had dust-free and properly lit work areas, proper changing rooms and washrooms at the workplaces, and general technical sanitary facilities at the plants (AV, Vítkovice, Vítkovice 1946-1954, inv. No. 1070, reg. No. 167).

When a a specific deficiency was reported, an investigation was conducted at the workplace, which was attended by a representative of the directorate, an officer of the Institute for Occupational Medicine and a social-health worker. In the years after 1947, plans were laid to have grass planted along with trees in the factory courtyard, and for proper equipment to be provided in labourers' collective dormitories, factory canteens and other social institutions (AV, Vítkovice, Vítkovice 1946-1954, inv. No. 1070, reg. No. 167).

Recreation

The existence of recreational activities for VI employees is mentioned in archival documents already before World War I. For the purpose of recreation and health, gyms, a sports stadium, a swimming pool, a recreational centre in Stará Bělá, a cycling track, tennis courts, playgrounds, an apprentice home and an ice rink were built, and municipal orchards were extended (Matějček, Vytiska, 1978).

After World War II, VI employees had access to five buildings for recreational purposes: Villa Maryčka in Staré Hamry with a total capacity of 16 places, a wooden cabin in Bílá with a capacity of 48 beds and a shared dormitory with 12 places and 4 buildings in Karlovice with a total capacity of 100 places (AV, Vítkovice, VMIC 11, inv. No. 1636, reg. No. 309).

With a view to maintaining mental and physical freshness, a sports stadium was built, offering 16 types of sports such as football, athletics, tennis, volleyball and others. For swimmers, an open-air swimming pool as well as an indoor swimming pool was available (AV, Vítkovice, Vítkovice 1946-1954, inv. No. 1684, reg. No. 218).

In 1948 the ironworks set up, as a novel idea, a *House of Rest* for those employees who, despite feeling sick, did not report themselves as sick. These employees were monitored by internal recruitment and were sent to this House of Rest in order to protect their health (AV, Vítkovice, Vítkovice 1946-1954, inv. No. 1082, reg. No. 167).

2.2.5   Catering and Clothing

The social facilities of the plant included eating houses, restored in 1880s after the initial failures. The first was a soup kitchen, later several canteens were established. In 1876, a factory grocery shop called Warenhalle was opened, where most workers bought the necessary foodstuffs. Since 1885, a new publicly accessible marketplace was in operation, and since 1899 the marketplace had a new building in which stalls were rented out to merchants. Later, a municipal slaughterhouse was added (Matějček, Vytiska, 1978).

The merchandise sold at the factory market was not evaluated positively only, as evidenced by information from the contemporary newspaper Spirit of Time. "Grocery falsification is happening in Vítkovice on a large scale, there is no market commission for health, so that a labourer is compelled to buy any muck for a lot of money. For example, we find pieces of glass and various other mucks in sausages (the sausage maker is known to us), when a housewife buys some sour cream to season the dish, it smells of vinegar and yeast (one of the merchants in Ocelářská Street), and others more, so that people are poisoned even in this respect" (Vítkovice and Labourers, 1900: 1). The goods sold adversely affected the health of the Vítkovice labourers.

The grocery price list from 1934 shows that basic foodstuff prices were 15 to 47% lower at the marketplace than at the "Future" cooperative stores. More than 3000 buyers visited the factory shop daily. The existence of the marketplace also enabled cheap sale of meals in factory canteens and in the factory hotel. The canteens served an average of 3500 portions a day. The labourers paid 80 hellers for breakfast, 70 hellers – 2,50 CSK for lunch and 1,60 CSK for dinner. According to Matějček and Vytiska (1978), the Vítkovice directorate did not forget to emphasise the charitable nature of the marketplace on various occasions.

In 1937, only the most necessary foodstuffs were sold in the shop, no luxury goods, which, according to Schwenger, was intended to be educational, so as to prevent workers from being tempted towards unnecessary expenses. The goods were sold at 28% cheaper here than at the usual shop, while having the same or often a better quality (AV, Vítkovice, VMIC 17, inv. No. 6099, reg. No. 1405).

In 1889 the first two canteens were established in the ironworks, in 1907 there were twelve of them. They sold beer, wine, soda, lemonade, tea, salami, sausages, cheese, sardines, bread and pastries. Moreover, there were several other factory canteens in different operations. In 1914, a two-member labourer family spent 22,81 CSK a week, a three-member family spent 26,47 CSK, a four-member family spent 30,13 CSK. Food totalled to roughly 50% of the expenses, clothing to 18%, flat to roughly 25% (Matějček, Vytiska, 1978). In 1926, 8 thousand persons a day took their meals in the cafeterias, in 1937 already 9 thousand persons. Breakfast consisted of a soup, coffee and bread for 85 hellers, lunch included a soup, meat, vegetables and potatoes for 2,50 CSK, meat dinner was for 1,50 CSK (AV, Vitkovice, VMIC 11, inv. No. 1610, reg. No. 302). It follows from the documents that the warm meals were of a good quality and healthier than the cold snacks brought from home (AV, Vítkovice, VMIC 17, inv. No. 6099, reg. No. 1405).

Officials could get a lunch with a dessert for 6 CSK and a 25% price discount for all other meals at the factory hotel (AV, Vítkovice, VMIC 11, inv. No. 1610, reg. No. 302).

The company also took care of its employees' clothing, as early as during World War I. After the war, the factory administration entrusted this responsibility to the workers' production cooperative in Prostějov. For this purpose, it was rendered a special sales room (AV, Vítkovice, VMIC 11, inv. No. 1610, reg. No. 302).

After World War II, catering for the VI employees was provided by means of the factory marketplace which had 25 thousand customers, 7 camp kitchens for 4570 boarders, the factory hotel with 760 boarders and thirteen factory canteens (AV, Vítkovice, VMIC 11, inv. No. 1636, reg. No. 309).

Catering events in the canteens followed the effort to satisfy the VI employees on a versatile basis. At the end of 1945, the Mining Corporation paid about 11 CSK extra per person per day (AV, Vítkovice, VMIC n.a., inv. No. 423, reg. No. 29).

In 1947, the economic administration supplied foodstuff to all employees, their families, camp canteens, factory canteens in the factory hotel and the factory marketplace. The boarding fee in camp kitchens amounted to 18 CSK a day (breakfast, lunch, dinner). A lunch or dinner cost 10 CSK in the kitchen of the factory hotel. In addition, there were 13 canteens for immediate refreshment directly at the workplaces. The large farm estates in Vratimov and Rožnov ensured a smooth supply of foodstuff and agricultural products AV, Vítkovice, Vítkovice 1946-1954, inv. No. 1684, reg. No. 218).

Archival materials from 1947 describe the operation of a factory laundry for all employees who could not do the washing at home for whatever reason.; hospital, institutional, canteen and other industrial laundry were washed in the laundry. The fee for washing one kilogram of laundry was 8 CSK. Since the laundry became very popular, building of a new laundry was planned within the next five-year plan (AV, Vítkovice, Vítkovice 1946-1954, inv. No. 1684, reg. No. 218).

In 1949, a dietary eating house was set up for employees with chronic digestive problems (AV, Vítkovice, RTUM 1945-54, inv. No. 53, reg. No. 14).

2.2.6 Wage Policy and Insurance

In 1883, the ironworks founded a savings and credit union association for officials and supervisors, lending money for promissory notes. Similarly, there was a pension institution which paid out an annuity to officials. A second pension office with different contribution rates was set up for supervisors and foremen (Matějček, Vytiska, 1978).

The benefits for the VI labourers were tempting, considering that there were none in smaller enterprises. In addition, the labourers had more advantageous accident, sickness and old-age insurance. Matějček and Vytiska (1978) conclude that the ironworks owners and the company directorate could use these benefits to influence a part of the labourers and to enforce their obedience.

From period press dated 1900 we learn that wages in VI in relation to prices of goods were not high: "And how do the wages of Vítkovice labourers look? The average wage of a dexterous labourer is about 600 to 610 guldens per year. If we compare the costliness of groceries to earnings, then we come to the belief that in Vienna notorious for its costliness, a labourer can live at earnings of 600 guldens yearly cheaper and better than in Vítkovice" (Vítkovice and Labourers, 1900: 1).

In 1928, the jubilee fund was incorporated into the existing charitable funds administered by the General Maintenance Institute, which until July 1926 provided the VI labourers with supplements to their pensions from the Central Social Insurance Company in the amount of up to 3000 CSK per year. In addition to these supplements, there was a 10% children's allowance for each child under 17 years of age. Widows received 50% of the deceased's supplement, a child that lost one parent received 1/5 of the supplement, and a child that lost both parents received 2/5 of the supplement (AV, Vítkovice, VMIC 11, inv. No. 1610, reg. No. 302).

In 1928, the ironworks recapitulated the operation of the VI social facilities in the last ten years. Labourers with at least 20 years of service who were not entitled to a pension supplement received credit notes up to 7200 CSK. Employees who had paid contributions to the Central Social Insurance Company for at least 20 years during their service at the ironworks were entitled to disability and old-age pensions of up to 2000 CSK per year (AV, Vítkovice, VMIC 11, inv. No. 1610, reg. No. 302).

The wage policy was strongly influenced by the situation on the labour market. The wages of foremen, leading labourers and the most important categories of specialised labourers remained traditionally high. Officials' salaries, except for the lowest office categories, exceeded labourers' wages by considerable amounts. According to Matějček and Vytiska (1978), the assertion of "high" wages in Vítkovice was valid only for some groups of labourers. The others only got just enough to stay in Vítkovice.

The wage costs were relatively low especially in the smelter, so VI could afford to pay better than elsewhere. Around 1912, for instance, the production costs for one cent of crude iron amounted to 5-6 CSK, but the wage costs of the blast furnace production were only about 29 hellers. In 1901, the weekly wages of supervisors, foremen and leading labourers at blast furnaces averaged to 58,44 CSK; in the steel mill, rolling mill and open-hearth furnace it was 39,90 CSK. The highest average wage in these categories was found in the steel foundry – 70,13 CSK per week, while the lowest – 27,04 CSK per week in ancillary operations (Matějček, Vytiska, 1978: 92).

Wages were differentiated based on the age and length of employment at the company. For example, in blast furnaces, the highest average wage was in the group of labourers aged 35-40. But within the entire company, the 45-50 age group was the best paid, which however counted only 620 people out of 18,658 labourers, female labourers, foremen and supervisors. In addition to wages, 47,2% of employees (i.e. 5769 persons) received secondary benefits from the company management. The company paid their rents, provided factory flats at reduced rents to them, provided overnight accommodation, cheap or free fuel, provided pieces of land to them and allocated groceries free of charge. These benefits were mainly given to supervisors, foremen and leading labourers (Matějček, Vytiska, 1978).

Matějček and Vytiska (1978) describe that a slight increase in wages did not mean anything to the company financially. On the contrary, it allowed the company to avoid the risk of strikes which were particularly effective in smelters, because stopping the operation by extinguishing furnaces almost meant a financial disaster. Gradually, it became almost common in Vítkovice that the management forestalled any significant wage demands of the labourers by a small "voluntary" wage adjustment.

The social status of labourers was influenced by a number of factors such as wage and housing conditions, working hours, health care, occupational safety, accident rate, occupational diseases, length of holiday, etc. However, the level of real wages and the development of prices of basic life necessities affected the material security of labourers and their families in a decisive way. In the late 1920s, when according to Matějček and Vytiska (1978) the industry was experiencing its prosperity peak, the wages of Vítkovice labourers were amongst the highest in the country.

Table No. 11 – Examples of labourers' wages in 1928

Industrial area	Amount of average wage per shift in 1928
Metalworking industry in Bohemia	28,30 CSK
Metalworking industry in Moravia	26,50 CSK
Labourers in Vítkovice	40,08 CSK
Labourers in Třinec Iron and Steel Works	44,89 CSK

Source: modif. Matějček and Vytiska, 1978: 137

The daily labourers' wages in Třinec Iron and Steel Works were higher, but as for the annual average, Vítkovice labourers (13 157 CSK) earned more than Třinec labourers (12 582 CSK) (Matějček and Vytiska, 1978: 137).

Other factors influencing the social status of labourers in VI included either permanent or temporary termination of employment. A sickness insurance regulation was approved in 1924. Insured persons were divided into ten classes by their wages. Half of the insurance was paid by the employer, the other by the insured person in the form of a wage deduction. In the same year, the Act on Compulsory Accident Insurance came into force (Matějček and Vytiska, 1978).

Creating advantageous wage conditions in VI was one of the forms of management intervention against revolutionary currents developing within the workforce. Wages were based on the age, marital status, education, professional qualification and length of work experience. Furthermore, the wages were adjusted depending on the length of employment in the company and the labourer's physical age. Between World War I. and II., the wage development experienced an upward trend. A very sophisticated wage system forced the labourers to maximise their work performance. Wage tables were disadvantageous for minors under 18 and for women. The result was a wage differentiation by individual plants and professions. Two-thirds of employees were paid task wages and one-third time wages (Matějček and Vytiska, 1978).

In 1947 an average daily wage was 13,88 CSK per hour and the task wage amounted to 19,44 CSK. A year later, an average daily wage stabilised at 14,59 CSK and the task wages at 20,42 CSK. In addition to trainings and incentive wages, social care was given to all who needed it (AV, Vítkovice, Vítkovice 1946-1954, inv. No. 1082, reg. No. 167).

On 1st January 1948, a self-help employee support fund was set up on the initiative of the Works Council Board, aimed at providing for family members of the deceased employee. The measure served as immediate aid to cover the funeral expenses and to ensure the family's livelihood until the widow's pension was assessed. The monthly contribution was 10-25 CSK on average (AV, Vítkovice, Vítkovice 1946-1954, inv. No. 1684, reg. No. 218).

Fraternal Treasury of Vítkovice Ironworks

The first report on the fraternal treasury of Vítkovice in VI dates back to 1843 and it was apparently created using the example of the Frýdlant Ironworks for cases of labourers' illness and injuries (Palát, 1989). The statutes of the Fraternal Treasury of VI were approved in March 1883. It became the successor of the original Fraternal Treasury of Vítkovice. The new Fraternal Treasury of VI consisted of a sickness fund and a maintenance institute. All labourers had to become its members (Machotková, 2000a).

The Maintenance Institute had the function of a savings institute. When leaving the services of the Mining Corporation, accumulated deposits were paid out to the members and, depending on the length of their service years, after 20 years, also a part of the plant's contributions. Both were without interest. Members who became incapable of work due to a work accident received deposits, dividends and a specified insurance capital. The institute provided for widows and orphans with aid based on the amount of the deceased husband's or father's account, or as the case may be, with a lifetime pension based on the liquidated capital sum (Machotková, 2000a).

Starting from May 1891, the Mining Corporation increased its contribution from 2 to 6 kreutzers of one gulden from wages, as 4 kreutzers went to a special reserve fund to ensure minimum pensions for the disabled, widows, orphans and to pay annual accident insurance premiums (Machotková, 2000a).

In 1895 the Fraternal Treasury was abolished in this form. The sickness fund was transformed into the Company Health Insurance Fund and the Maintenance Institute became the General Maintenance Institute (Machotková, 2000a).

Company Health Insurance Fund

This fund was established in October 1895 on the grounds of Austrian Law No. 33 of 1888 prescribing that an entrepreneur employing more than 100 employees could establish a company sickness fund. The insurance fund was a department of the Fraternal Treasury. Membership was mandatory for all VMIC employees. At the beginning of the twentieth century, the insurance business was very fragmented in terms of organisation. When the independence of the Czechoslovak Republic was declared, there was a total of 2,073 sickness funds, of which 832 were company ones. Starting from 1926, insurance companies were gradually merged into larger institutions. In 1946 there were 105 health insurance companies in Bohemia and Moravia, of which 7 were company ones. The insurance coverage provided free medical assistance, medicaments and financial aid in the event of incapacity for work amounting to 60% of wages usual in the given district. The claim period was 20 weeks, in the 1920s it was extended to 1 year (AV, Vítkovice, Závodní nemocenská pokladna, inv. No. 10, reg. No. 1).

The contemporary press reported on the labourers' obligation to pay the fines which went into the account of the company health insurance fund: "If the labourer commits a small offense, he is immediately punished with a financial penalty. Fines collected in 1899 amounting to 11415 guldens and 52 kreutzers allegedly flow into the company health insurance fund, but the labourers have no control over whether it is really the case. And we have mentioned the skilled labourers here. But how does it look like in case of labourers earning an average of 300 to 400 guldens annually, who constitute almost a half? Surely the reader can make their own judgment in this matter" (Vítkovice, 1900).

Over the years, health insurance funds were entrusted with other tasks which were not directly related to health insurance, such as the prescription and collection of unemployment benefits, later renamed "contribution to earmarked assets for work inclusion", making payments of family allowances, issuing employment record books etc. (AV, Vítkovice, Závodní nemocenská pokladna, inv. No. 10, reg. No. 1).

The health insurance rate fluctuated, in 1926 it was 4,3%, in 1948 it was 6%. This was supplemented by a 1% wage contribution to the fund for work inclusion paid half by the employer and employee, and further a 4% contribution to the payment of family allowances, fully paid by the employer. Disability and old-age insurance premiums were set by law at 6% of wages (AV, Vítkovice, Závodní nemocenská pokladna, inv. No. 10, reg. No. 1).

The number of insured persons varied in line with the employment rate at the enterprise. After World War I, it amounted to 10,008 people, in 1944 it was 33,056 people. Until 1931, the management of the insurance fund was exclusively in the hands of Germans, although 90% of the insured persons were of Czech nationality. After 1931, "Czech administration" was introduced (AV, Vítkovice, Závodní nemocenská pokladna, inv. No. 10, reg. No. 1).

Despite all the pressure, it was enforced that all correspondence with insured persons during World War II was conducted exclusively in Czech, while other social insurance institutions of the ironworks, such as the pension institution or the maintenance institute, corresponded only in German (AV, Vítkovice, Závodní nemocenská pokladna, inv. No. 10, reg. No. 1).

Interestingly, archival materials state that the arbitration court (settling disputes between the insured persons and the insurance fund) did not have to be convened for several consecutive years, which proved that the company health insurance fund fulfilled its tasks between 1895-1948 to the full satisfaction of the insured persons (AV, Vítkovice, Závodní nemocenská pokladna, inv. No. 10, reg. No. 1).

General Maintenance Institute

The Institute was founded in October 1895, replacing the former maintenance institution, which was part of the Fraternal Treasury. Its members were supervisors, foremen and labourers. 6% was deducted from their wages and deposited into their personal account. The Mining Corporation contributed the same amount; however, this contribution went to the reserve fund. The maintenance consisted of a one-time payment of the capital or pension (Machotková, 2000c).

After 1,5 years of employment, it provided pensions to people incapacitated due to work and ensured payment of capital in cash to all members in their old age, amounting to even more than 10 thousand CSK depending on the years of service (AV, Vítkovice, VMIC 11, inv. No. 1610, reg. No. 302).

The General Maintenance Institute managed several social funds:

1. Jubilee fund – founded in 1928 on the occasion of the centenary of the ironworks. It provided retirement supplements to former labourers, widows and orphans.
2. Reserve fund – provided periodical monthly regulatory aids to people incapable of work.
3. Fund of care for tuberculosis – founded in 1924. It focused on supporting labourers with tuberculosis and their family members.
4. Supportive fund – it originated in 1939 by a merger of five supportive funds: fund for the support of disabled workers, fund for the support of work of incapacitated labourers' widows, Albert baron of Rothschild's charitable fund, fund for the support of families of labourers summoned to military exercises (AV, Vítkovice, Všeobecný zaopatřovací ústav VI n.p. 35, inv. No. 28, reg. No. 12, Machotková, 2000c).

The General Maintenance Institute ceased to exist in 1954.

Pension Institution

Insurance of Vítkovice officials was introduced in the early 1840s. In the first pension statutes of 1845, a general principle was expressed that an official was entitled to old-age security after a long period of service. In 1878 an Officials' Fund of VMIC was established, functioning on the basis of savings. Officials were deducted 10% of the net annual income from their salary, while the Mining Corporation contributed the same amount for each official. In 1897, a Pension Institution of the VMIC Officials was established instead of the Officials' Fund. It had a total of 161 members. Newly were accepted officials aged 24-40 years, university graduates and employees with school-leaving qualification. The Pension Institution provided its members with a pay-out on leaving employment, as well as a widow's pension and orphan's aid to their wife and children in case of death (Machotková, 2000b).

In 1909, the Pension Institution was transformed into a substitute institution. Contributions remained unchanged at 20% of the pension assessment base. Employees paid a third and the Mining Corporation two thirds. Between 1920 and 1928, a supplementary fund was introduced for all pension institutions (Machotková, 2000b).

Employees who held the positions of supervisors, foremen and clerks at the plant were initially insured with the Fraternal Treasury. A Foremen Fund was created to provide more valuable insurance. Starting from October 1884, the factory contribution was increased from 2 to 4 kreutzers, employees paid 8 kreutzers to the disability fund and 2 kreutzers to the sickness fund. The Foremen Fund was dissolved in 1905 (Machotková, 2000b).

For employees who did not belong to the Pension Institution, a Pension Treasury was established. 212 former members of the Foremen Fund joined it as well (Machotková, 2000b).

2.2.7 Activities of Associations, Financial Aids

An important part of the social activities of VI was association and endowment activities, financial support of charitable organisations and publicity in press.

The Mining Corporation owners established various foundations throughout their history. Some were intended for orphans and an orphanage, there was a foundation for the municipal poor, foundation for war survivors or an almshouse foundation (Machotková, 2000c).

At the time of the deepest depression of the Ostrava industry, the first Labourers' Educational Association[10] was established in Moravská Ostrava, on 19th March 1875. Its main mission was to spread enlightenment and education among miners and ironworkers in the Ostrava region. Augustin Havlíček was appointed its chairman. However, it was not of a long duration, the chairman terminated its activity after a year on the grounds that the association could find neither a secretary or a treasurer, and the association members were not able to invite any labourers to join (Palát, 1989).

In 1893, Petr Cingr founded a mining and metallurgical trade union association "Prokop" in Ostrava. The metallurgical section was based in Vítkovice, in the Fischer's pub (Rohel, 1970). One year later, another metallurgical association was established – "Unity of Labourers" pursuing education objectives, as well as a food association "First Consumer", which provided its members with cheaper and

---

10 Activity of associations was for the first time legislatively regulated by federal law No. 134 on the Right of Association of 15th November 1867. The first association established under this law was the Czech labourers' self-help association Oul (Efmertová, 1998).

better-quality groceries. This was followed by a boom in activities of associations in Vítkovice, which, according to Matějček and Vytiska (1978), was undoubtedly linked to the growth of the miners' movement after the foundation of Prokop.

As for other activities of the VMIC, financial support of the school system is worth mentioning. Specifically, starting from 1901 the ironworks regularly donated a sum of 3-5 thousand CSK to public vocational schools for women's occupations in Vítkovice, which belonged to the Dobromila charitable association. The charitable association asked for sponsorship donations every year. On the first occasion, the gift was donated to the Czech Girl's Continuing School of Housekeeping in Vítkovice, then to the Public Vocational School for Women's Occupations in Průmyslová Street No. 41. In the materials from 1924-1939, the financial donations are generally intended for "schools of the Dobromila association" (AV, Vítkovice, VMIC 11, inv. No. 1383, reg. No. 248).

The Dobromila association organised courses in its schools for the broadest layers of population, which were free of charge for women of unemployed husbands and for daughters of unemployed fathers. Language courses (English, German and Russian) for Vítkovice officials were also organised (AV, Vítkovice, VMIC 11, inv. No. 1636, reg. No. 309).

The Dobromila association substantiated its requests for financial subsidies by the fact that most students at its schools were girls from miners' and labourers' families of VI. The same was true for evening classes. In the case of language courses, the rationale for the financial coverage was that they took place at the school premises. Thus, the finance covered the rental of rooms.

For the local use of the factory, factory broadcasting was in operation as stated in the Social Activity Report of December 1945 (AV, Vítkovice, VMIC n.a., inv. No. 423, reg. No. 29).

VI used the press as one of their means of self-presentation. Starting from 1930, a weekly labourers' newspaper of Vítkovice Ironworks was published under the name "Vítkovák", for the price of 20 hellers (Matějček and Vytiska, 1978). In addition, the "Jiskra" factory magazine was (fortnightly) published, covering the interests and needs of VI employees. In 1946 the magazine published 16,000 copies, and the publisher was the Confidants Body of VI. Starting from November 1946, the publishing company was taken over by the state-owned enterprise VI. Its net profit was dedicated to the benefit of the employees' social needs (AV, Vítkovice, VMIC n.a., inv. No. 423, reg. No. 29).

2.2.8 Cultural Activity

Cultural activity appears only after the year 1945 as a new area belonging to the social group activities. The interests of individual employees of the ironworks were surveyed by means questionnaires. As part of the meeting of cultural confidants, a plan for the cultural section was drawn up. One of the points was the establishment of an enterprise club which would bring together all the components of cultural activity. From the beginning, a theatre group, chess players, musicians, singers, as well as factory physical education and sport joined the club (AV, Vítkovice, VMIC n.a., inv. No. 423, reg. No. 29).

The cultural area included a factory library, too. The report of December 1945 states that the library had 13 thousand volumes of various books, mostly of a technical nature, and that 90% of the books were in German. The effort for the next period was aimed at acquiring Czech books (AV, Vítkovice, VMIC n.a., inv. No. 423, reg. No. 29). The history of the library dates back to the 19th century and is associated with the foundation of a reader's association in 1864. At the time of its founding, which was also financially supported by the ironworks directorate, the reader's association had 63 members, and in 1908 already 286 members. The directorate contributed a larger amount to the activities of the association every year. The association could use three rooms in the hotel and a darkroom (Matěj, Korbelářová, Levá, 1992).

Cultural activities included regular screenings of films in the plants, in the factory hotel, in the new dietary canteen and apprentice canteen, and lectures delivered by doctors and social-health workers. Social workers regularly reported on the screening promotion in the Reports on the Activities of the Enterprise Social Services (AV, Vítkovice, RTUM 1945-54, inv. No. 232, reg. No. 28).

3. SOCIAL POLICY OF THE BAŤA COMPANY

Baťa's Zlín is considered in the conditions of Czechoslovakia as a follower of a new factory town, the North Moravian Vítkovice, the so-called Nové Vítkovice (Matějček, 1977, Ševeček, 2009). Jemelka et al, in their 2015 publication, consider it as an extraordinary example of a corporate town.

Ševeček (2009) argues for the need to enrich the socio-historical discourse of the Baťa company with areas such as personnel and enterprise social policy with regard to the social context by a noticeable lack of modern studies on the history of the enterprise. Czech historiography has a lot to catch up with in this area. There is no significant attempt at an objective, critical evaluation of the phenomenon through the perspective of modern social history. Methodological support and an invaluable source of inspiration is rich foreign literature. The best study on the Baťa business system and its social consequences is considered to be the work of Paul Devinant from 1928 for the International Labour Office in Geneva (Ševeček, 2009; Lehár, 1960). Devinant was one of the first authors to draw attention to the importance of a specific social framework built around the Zlín factory for the development of the Baťa company (Ševeček, 2009). Erdély (2013) considers the Devinant's study the first objective criticism.

Tomáš Baťa gradually transformed his business into an organisation resembling a modern and democratic state. He divided it into hundreds of departments with great opportunities for initiative and a considerable economic autonomy. The organisational structure was reshaped into a pyramid resting on the basis of floors, narrower buildings, even narrower plants, and the top of the building was formed by the close company management and the boss himself (Pochylý, 1990).

Tomáš Baťa is the creator of an original complex ideology, which was called "batism". It is of huge value to humanity. The doctrine can be substantiated by a wealth of evidence on the reported high level of well being of those who were lucky enough to have become his co-workers (Valach, 1990).

The phenomenal success of the Baťa enterprise sparked interest in Baťa topics in the interwar years. This is also evidenced by a well-arranged review of published articles and monographs on the theme of the Baťa enterprise, which can be found in Ševeček (2009). Ševeček compares the attitude of literary production towards "batism" in the period of the communist regime to the most elaborate form of capitalist tyranny. This corresponds to the strongly ideologically burdened text of Lehár from 1960.

Diagram No. 4 – Organizational structure of the Baťa concern

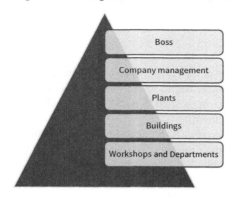

Source: Špiláčková, own construct

The Baťa concern was a system in which no one was forgotten in the division of rights and duties. With its help, a large number of employees got the opportunity to participate in the company management through work which they understood and where they could impact its outcome by their influence (Pochylý, 1990).

3.1 Brief History of the Baťa Company

Tomáš Baťa (1876-1932) together with his older siblings Anna and Antonín invested the inheritance from their mother, an amount of 800 guldens, in a new company – a small shoemaking workshop. An official authorisation was issued on 21st September 1894 with the name of Antonín, because Tomáš was a minor at that time. The workshop was located in one house on the Zlín square (Pokluda, 2004).

Later this small workshop became the largest shoe company in the whole Austro-Hungarian Empire. Already after a year of independent entrepreneurship, the brothers Antonín and Tomáš Baťa employed 50 workers and female workers, 10 in the workshop and 40 home workers (Lehár, 1960).

In 1900 there was a formal change of the company name. The original A. Baťa company became T. & A. Baťa (Pokluda, 2004). In the same year, Zlín was comprised of a total of 2975 inhabitants and 542 houses (Šlachta, 1986).

Immediately afterwards the Baťa enterprise moved closer to the railway station because of the new railway. The Baťa workshop produced coarse wool shoes since its beginnings, but a great commercial success came in 1896 with light canvas shoes with a sole, the so-called "baťovka shoes". They were in high demand mainly in the indigent customer segments. The baťovka shoes spread to all parts of the

Habsburg monarchy. In 1900 new steam-powered machines were installed in the factory. There were already 120 employees working there (Pokluda, 2004).

Tomáš Baťa's participation in public events in Zlín began in 1898 with the co-founding of the Sokol sports organisation (Pokluda, 2004).

In order to maximize profits and to get ahead of other competing shoemakers in Austria-Hungary, Tomáš Baťa made an extraordinary effort to rationalize the production in his factory. To this end, he travelled in December 1904 to the USA, together with three of his employees, to acquaint himself with the methods of business management, technical equipment, manufacturing organisation and labourers' performance in the shoe factories there. In Lynn, Massachusetts, he applied for a job as a factory worker. His three journeymen worked in other factories. Every Sunday, all four Zlín shoemakers gathered in an American "saloon" to exchange their knowledge and experience. They worked in America for a whole year, then nine months in Germany and finally returned to Zlín with a new view of the shoemaker business and shoes. Tomáš Baťa's immediate goal was to bring the labourers' performance in his factory closer to the high performance of labourers in the US factories. (Lehár, 1960, Erdély, 2013).

According to Lehár (1960: 24), the social status of the Baťa factory labourers suddenly deteriorated in 1905 after the American journey. This is illustrated by an article from a magazine of the Association of the Czech Shoemaking Workers entitled "Shoemaker", which read: "Last year Mr. Baťa went on journey abroad to gather experience, where he worked as a labourer and was a member of a labourers' organisation – because he had to. Before he went to America, the work in his factory was more or less tolerable, but since he returned, the labourers' conditions working have been getting worse. Either he has mastered all the bad American qualities, or he wants to quickly draw level with the American billionaires and would prefer to flay the labourers alive".

A strike lasting several months in the autumn of 1906 hit the whole enterprise deeply. After the strikers were dismissed, only a handful of experienced labourers remained in the company. From then on, the company owner and not the trade union held the decisive power (Pokluda, 2004).

According to Pokluda (2004), in the following years the Baťa factory increased production and managed to sell shoes all over the world. After Antonín's death in 1908, Tomáš Baťa became the sole owner of the company. In 1912 he married Marie Menčíková and in 1915, Tomáš Baťa junior was born in the marriage.

At the time of peak production during World War I, Baťa plants were employing 5000 people. Throughout the war period, the Baťa company carried out a feverish investment activity. The company invested a lot of money in the construction of factory buildings in Zlín. Tomáš Baťa invested considerable amounts in land ownership also. In 1917 the company started to build its own shoe shops (Lehár, 1960). The first shops were Zlín, Liberec, Prague, Vienna, České Budějovice, Pardubice,

Moravská Ostrava and others. Their number grew to 18 in 1918. Baťa plants were already well known, in the newspapers they were described as 'America in Zlín', and T. Baťa was considered the embodiment of a dynamic entrepreneur – self-made man (Pokluda, 2004).

In 1919, in an effort to gain new experience, Bata set out on another journey to America. He got himself thoroughly acquainted with the organisation and business policy ("public service") at Henry Ford's car factory. He also got to know the conditions which Endicoll & Johnson, at that America's biggest shoe company, had created for its employees (Pokluda, 2004).

The overall social status of labouring class in the period after World War I was rather inauspicious, as reported by Lehár (1960). But then Baťa won a contract for the Austrian army on favourable terms, which significantly improved his financial situation and helped him to overcome the adverse period of the First Republic. In the years 1922-1923 Baťa masterfully coped with stagnation having reduced the cost of shoes by 50%. Rumours circulated that the company would go bankrupt, but the company survived and Baťa became one of the most famous industrialists. By lowering the prices, he gained the favour of the government, which meant opening up the possibilities of bank loans. His self-assurance grew, he drew on the experience of his youth and began to set bold goals. He invested, planned and surrounded himself with the best experts. After returning from the war, his brother Antonín ceased to take part in the leadership and his sister Anna subsequently got married (Valach, 1990).

In 1923-1925, reorganisation of workshops began in connection with the introduction of continuous production using roller tracks, so-called conveyors, following "the American pattern". With this device the company planned to achieve 20-30% higher efficiency (Šlachta, 1986). According to Lehár (1960), this innovation moved production efficiency a step forward. Manufacturing productivity increased from 8,785,000 to 15,205,000 pairs of shoes (i.e. by three quarters), while the number of employees increased by only 35% over the same period. On the part of employees, work organised in this way could be perceived as stressful. Each stop of the belt was reported by a sound device to superiors who became immediately aware of a failure or an employee fault. Thus, the work was under constant supervision and constant work discipline was required throughout the shift (Ševeček, 2009: 67).

Apart from technical measures, the process of production rationalisation also included social rationalisation. The most important element was the so-called premium system of profit and loss participation introduced in 1924 (Lehár, 1960), inspired by the experience of his stay in America. Profit participation, which grew out of the autonomy of workshops, represented an allowance for many labourers, amounting to about 20-30% of their fixed wages. For leading employees, loss participation was also introduced. The profit participation was paid out weekly. Half was paid in cash, the other half was credited to the participant's account with the company cash office, where it bore interest of ten percent. Although these deposits were a burden for the company, they artificially increased the moral bond between the company and its employees (Erdély, 2013; Pokluda 2014). It is clear from a speech delivered by T. Baťa in 1924 (In Cekota, 1929: 27-29) that the provided profit participation was not intended purely as an act of good will; the aim was to "raise the labouring class both materially and morally". The intention was to make all labourers participants in the company capital and thus to reduce the production costs. The employees should use the increased income for improving the living conditions of their families and for their education. Only then was there a chance that the money spent would return to the enterprise in the increased skills of the labourers, either in the form of work for the enterprise or for the public life of the state. The profit participation could be withdrawn at any time without giving any reason.

The Baťa system also included a whole set of deductions from the labourers' wages or employees' personal accounts. Under the Work Rules of 1923, the company administration could charge employees with wage deductions for faulty work, for loss or damage of tools, instruments and machinery, for the material provided for work. Order fines under the Work Rules were paid to the Baťa Support Fund. Technical and administrative staff were penalised for violating provisions of the employment contract, such as the bribery clause, competition clause, etc. (Lehár, 1960: 101).

In 1924, the Regional Political Administration in Brno imposed a fine on Tomáš Baťa for misdemeanours in connection with a continuous violation of the Act on Eight-Hour Working Time. Tomáš Baťa objected that the labourers were not forced to work overtime, but that they did so voluntarily (Lehár, 1960). Criticism was on the increase, complaints about the situation in the Baťa factory appeared at the inspectorate in Kroměříž, in the parliament and at the Ministry of Social Welfare. Baťa worked much more effectively in this area by developing his own social policy (Pokluda, 2004).

During the post-war economic crisis between 1924 and 1925, industrial production in Czechoslovakia was slowly recovering and the overall economy gradually developed. In 1925 the Baťa company dominated almost a half of the Czechoslovak export of all footwear (Lehár, 1960).

The Zlín factories growing in size attracted new job seekers as a magnet, as Pokluda writes (2004). This is also reflected in the increasing number of employees:

1925 – 5,200 employees
1927 – 8,300 employees
1930 – 17,400 employees

Between the 1920s and 1940s, the Baťa company also expanded abroad with its coexisting businesses[11]. Examples can be found in the then industrial cities: Borovo in Croatia, Chelmek and Otmęt in Poland, Best in Holland, Möhlin in Switzerland, Hellocourt and Vernon in France, Belcamp in the USA, Batanagar in India, Batatuba in Brazil and Batizovce – Svit and Šimonovany – Baťovany, in 1949 renamed Partizánske, in Slovakia. Red brick family houses were a common dominant feature of all these satellite corporate towns. This predominant element reflected Tomáš Baťa's view of "working together, living individually" (Moravčíková, 2004).

The Baťa company used planning as well. The only officially introduced long-term plan was a three-year plan from 1939, which was divided into six groups. The sixth group was social policy. Baťa's planning rested on half-yearly projections (Pochylý, 1990).

In mid-1938, the Baťa concern employed a total of 65,064 persons both domestically and abroad, of which more than a third fell under foreign companies (Lehár, 1960: 231). Between 1931 and 1939, Baťa established 47 plants and companies abroad (Valach, 1990).

Tomáš Baťa died tragically in a plane crash on 12th July 1932 on his way to Switzerland. His half-brother Jan Antonín became the new company boss. However, experienced company directors D. Čipera and H. Vavrečka held key positions (Pokluda, 2004).

In August 1939, Tomáš Baťa junior fled as a student from fascism to Canada, where he, together with his colleagues[12], founded a new factory in the new city of Batawa which employed 170 workers. Their arrival in Montreal caused a tremendous sensation, and not only politically. As a result of the events of the war, the individual parts of the Baťa plants were growing apart. J. A. Baťa settled permanently in Brazil whileTomáš Baťa jr. returned as a Canadian officer to liberated Czechoslovakia in the spring of 1945, however, the family could not influence the Baťa plants in any way. The company Baťa JSC and all the group companies were nationalised on 27th October 1945. This act definitively split the company. Toronto then became the company headquarters and the seat of the Baťa organisation (Valach, 1990; Pokluda, 2004).

In everything he did, Bata thought of the human element; not as a means of conquering political power, but as a co-worker. It was a big mistake that Tomáš Baťa's principles of industrial management were not applied on a larger scale in the country. In the post-war years, the economies of highly developed countries of Japan and Germany were built upon them. In Czechoslovakia, with a few exceptions,

---

11 A detailed list of the Baťa Concern companies abroad between 1921-1943, including the year of incorporation, company name and registered office can be found in appendices of Lehár's publication (1960: 294-297).
12 Tomáš Baťa named all his employees as „coleauges, partners, friends". This is a typical word, fraze for him. This is a reason, why employees liked him and were satisfied.

they were not utilised in large companies, whereas they put their own profits above their customer's interests (Pochylý, 1990).

Tomáš J. Baťa (Tomík) said of his father that, his creation of scientific work management and the use of their results to improve business and social services, put him ahead of his time by more than half a century (Pochylý, 1990).

3.1.1 Foundations Applied in Management of the Baťa Company

"The fundamental and lasting values of Tomáš Baťa's life work must be sought primarily in the social field" (Vavrečka, 2013: 5).

Vavrečka (2013) appreciates Devinant's correct formulation of the fundamental basis of the Baťa system. Baťa wants to achieve a spiritual integration of his co-workers in the sense of "public service", which he seeks not only through legal actions, but above all by enabling direct participation in success. This is where the core of the Baťa's system lies. For Baťa, the aim was not only to enhance performance, as current entrepreneurs are trying to do in a similar vein, but to promote practical economic education in the interest of the enterprise and in the general social interest as well. Baťa criticised, in particular, the large-scale industry for not caring for labourers' education and training, and for keeping the mental and material standards of the labouring class low. Through profit participation, labourers learn new working morale, gain self-confidence, are able to appreciate their own and another person's job in the same way, do not recoil from any work and do not avoid changing jobs, learn to save, do not ask for support if at times they cannot find a job; they simply become more valuable citizens of the state, better humans in the social sense. These thoughts led Baťa when considering the most sensible inclusion of a labourer in the factory work plan.

Baťa understood that an industrial enterprise could not be an educational institution and therefore, he provided social education only through the production process itself. He knew that providing young labourers with vocational training would make him reach his goals faster (Vavrečka, 2013).

These thought processes guided Baťa to socio-economic pedagogics. People can be brought up to social solidarity by various means, such as religion, inoculation of democratic ideas, ideals of socialist parties or by means of power. Baťa created his own method; Vavrečka (2013: 7) calls it positivistic or psychological-realistic. It is based on creating a functional combination of individual benefits with the well-being of society, which is immediately understandable to everyone and what everyone can immediately feel, be it in the company, in the municipality, in the state or worldwide.

The basis of Baťa's wage system was the recognition that in a well-organised enterprise, every individual must achieve a higher profit for their work than when working on their own (Erdély, 2013). Tomáš Baťa (in Cekota: 1929: 54) writes:

"Human desire for higher wages will never stop. It is futile and unwise to stop this desire. It is a promise of better times, a seed of progress."

Cekota (1929) describes Tomáš Baťa's effort to transform people's labourer-wage thinking into business thinking. He materialised his idea in the form of self-governing workshops and a premium system of profit[13] and loss participation. He was seeking such an organisation of work in which an individual, a labourer of a large enterprise, would work with the same diligence and economy of time, energy and responsibility as an independent entrepreneur. A large number of people from workshops and departments were given the opportunity to assert themselves in management and operation (Cekota, 1929; Pokluda, 2004). Erdély (2013) acknowledges this system, stating that the social effects of the Baťa's system deserve attention, particularly the division of a large enterprise into a number of small independent workshops. Baťa tried to create a sense of belonging to a workshop in people receiving their wage and, once being aware of their responsibility, to make them a co-worker with an immediate interest in the company production (Erdély, 2013).

The whole enterprise was a union of many hundred departments. All Baťa plants were organisationally connected into the following main groups: purchasing department, production department, sales department, ancillary plants. Each department had great possibilities of initiative and considerable economic autonomy. The autonomy was manifested by these features:

1. Each department had one manager, responsible for the work, profit and loss of the department.
2. A separate economic profit and loss account with weekly public accounting.
3. Participation of employees – foremen and many workers in the profit of the workshop.
4. Personal responsibility of everyone in the department for their work.
5. Collective effort of the whole workshop to accomplish tasks which are decisive for the profit of the department (Cekota, 1929: 49).

Baťa considered the belief in success and social usefulness of collectivist economic forms to be the most serious economic mistake of modern times. He said that all collectively organised institutions weaken the foundations of any higher economic development as they destroy the working morale. People have a natural tendency towards idleness. It is necessary for people to realise that work is a moral duty, the

---

13 The participation of employees in corporate governance and their share in net profit is known from history as the oldest protective and insurance public care means, as Dr. Josef Gruber, Minister of Social Welfare, states in 1921 (Gruber, 1921). Hence Tomáš Baťa did not apply anything new.

negligence of which is punished by extinction. Work is a duty, it is the law of nature, the law of life (Vavrečka, 2013).

Shortly before his flight to India, Baťa wrote down the socio-moral worldview which he adopted in his last will. It culminates in the proposition that any business which does not knowingly serve the public must necessarily perish.

According to Cekota (in Pochylý, 1990), Baťa constantly created positive and favourable values and distributed them satisfactorily among all business participants, customers, employees and the public. Factories, machines, material values were just a tool in this civilization, a "pile of iron and bricks" in Tomáš Baťa's words. The lasting value does not consist in his material inventions, but in the example of his conceptual thinking, which has created, in addition to material values, a certain type of man and lifestyle.

Many prominent sociologists, psychologists, economists and other specialists have studied in detail the uniqueness of Tomáš Baťa senior's personality. Most agree that although his greatest desire was to produce shoes for the whole humankind, he was above all obsessed with creating conditions for young people so that they could avoid suffering, misery and humiliation which he had experienced. He gave the young people a sense of responsibility and perspective. After all, his junior staff used to walk with their heads up high, caring for their appearance, exemplifying diligence, cleanliness and order. And they were rightly proud of these virtues (Valach, 1990: 32).

Tomáš Baťa's personal philosophy is contained in his last will from the year 1931, which, after his death, got into the hands of his half-brother Jan A. Baťa: "The first condition for the prosperity of our enterprise is that you do not think that the enterprise is only yours, that it is for you … In the development of our plant, we saw the development of the entire region and ensuring its welfare. … with our enterprise we bring a new, previously unknown life to our regions, through its development the general well-being and education of our people are rising. It was the desire to create, to enable increasingly more and more people participation in the benefits which our plant provided to both employees and customers. If you serve this great idea, you will still be in accordance with the laws of nature and humanity. Yet when you are mindful only of yourself, when you stop serving the general with your enterprise, you will become useless and will inevitably fall" (Menčík, 1993: 8-9).

3.1.2 Enterprise Management Styles

As Ševeček (2009: 71) describes, in the first decades of the last century, traditional business management systems underwent a fundamental change attributable to the introduction of industrial innovations. In this context, two American approaches to management are mentioned, which had a significant impact on the current business practice. Both approaches tried to extend the possibilities of managerial control over the workforce in a somewhat different way. The first was (1) the concept of "scientific management" which had an important impact on the technical aspect of the development of a mass production system. The second was a paternalist-oriented (2) concept of "industrial betterment" which sought to extend management from the purely technical sphere to the social and cultural spheres, as well as to the employees' values and ways of behaviour. It was an industrial reform movement seeking to improve the social and moral conditions of work and thus to ease the dissatisfaction of the labouring class with modern ways of production organisation. A specific management system gradually crystallised at the Baťa enterprise, drawing eclectically from both of the above-mentioned significant trends. The socio-psychological dimension of the problem was much more distinctively accentuated in management processes, which was in certain areas developed, for example, by the trend of "human relations".

In 1924, Baťa founded a two pillars business model – profit participation and self-management of workshops. It was aimed at harmony and consensus, i.e. that the labourers did not have to worry about a fair profit distribution. For this purpose, he used the designation of public service. The customer (price) and the labourer (wage), the entrepreneur (growth) should be equally satisfied (Pokluda, 2014).

Baťa's management system originated under the conditions of an industrial organisation which supposed a relatively high level of the human element intervention in the field of production. In these circumstances, the relationships between employees and the company could not be based solely on a mechanical application of the concept of authority and obedience (see Taylorism) but required an inclusion of essential social and psychological aspects of industrial work. The company practice stemmed from an assumption that by organising the conditions at the workplace and in employees' home environment, it is possible to achieve the necessary involvement and loyalty with the goals defined by the organization (Ševeček, 2009).

The new economic philosophy accounted for human biological needs; work is dependent on health. Therefore, work needed to be organised in such a way that the person's strength gets worn out as little as possible. The final output of work was not performance but human happiness. (SDAZ, Zlín, Cutting Service II/8, inv. No. 34, c. No. 194).

Baťa chose the American production model as a pattern, while becoming an enthusiastic promoter of American culture and lifestyle, too. His aim was not only to apply the most advanced form of mass production in the plant, but also to make his native Zlín a "modern town". It was important for the development of the town that his visionary spirit, as Ševeček writes (2009: 335), was able to perceive the development of modern factory production in its essential social context.

3.2 Institution of Enterprise Social Policy

Humans had always been the central focus in the organisational system of Baťa plants. According to Pochylý (1990), everything was done to provide people with the best conditions to work and live. Significant social benefits of Baťa's employees are evidenced by these data:

- The working week had only 40 hours (five working days), Saturdays and Sundays were free, while countrywide the working week had 48 hours (six working days).
- All work was carried out in standardised buildings, located in the greenery of parks and flower beds.
- Workshops in which the employees worked were spacious, with well-designed lighting and ventilation.
- Emphasis was laid on cleanliness at workplace. Some workshops were equipped with air conditioning.
- Employees had such income which enabled them to create savings on condition of cheap housing and provision of basic needs (Pochylý, 1990).

Baťa always cared thoroughly and conscientiously for the means of subsistence of his co-workers[14].

At its beginnings, the enterprise social activity rested upon three pillars:

1. housing
2. nourishment
3. health (SDAZ, Zlín, Social Department II/10, inv. No. 4, c. No. 1332).

For Baťa, it was an organisational problem and at the same time a task to provide his people with a good-quality flat, a sufficient amount of good and nutritious food, health care, upbringing, education and entertainment. It was clear to him that he could win the struggle against difficult social conditions only with a healthy and happy "army" of co-workers. Social care for employees developed as the plant evolved. This is also reflected in social care expenditures. Between 1918-1923 Baťa spent 6,441,000 CSK on social purposes, while between 1923-1928 a further 50,33,5000 CSK (Cekota, 1929).

Baťa literally made contracts with people for life, as his care began from birth in his maternity hospital (Valach, 1990).

---

14 Tomáš Baťa considered the company employees to be his co-workers. Therefore, in the archival sources we can find the notion of employee and co-worker at the synonymous level.

Baťa's social care was not just merciful spending of money which would help people for a while. The line of Baťa's social care was the motto "Help people to help themselves and then to help you as well" (Cekota, 1929: 139).

In archival material of 1930, the socio-health principles of the Baťa company can be found. The main socio-health principle of the enterprise was to "give a job to as many people as possible and to accept all people with disabilities and sick people if they are able to work and if the wok in the plant is suitable for them. That is why crippled people, blind, deaf and dumb, people with physical weakness, anaemia even after a history of TB are hired ..." (SDAZ, Zlín, Social Department II/10, inv. No. 1, c. No. 1331, fol. 1-10).

The second place belonged to granting of gifts and subsidies, both to people employed in the plant and unemployed, their families, and persons and corporations pursuing the same purposes as the Baťa company. Poor children received clothes for Christmas, regardless of whether or not their parents were employed in the plant. Each year between 15th November – 15th March, approximately 160 school children received free meals. Furthermore, 160 school children received 0,25 litres of milk per day as recommended by a doctor. Throughout the year, some children in Zlín were given "case-by-case" reject shoes, the company contributed to various excursions and public baths (SDAZ, Zlín, Social Department II/10, inv. No. 1, c. No. 1331, fol. 1-10).

As for other social-health activities, the following were mentioned:

- Maintaining two kindergartens and two shelters in districts of Letná and Zálešná.
- Donations to schools, institutes and associations also outside of Zlín throughout the year.
- Awarding scholarships and contributing to study excursions.
- Maintaining a holiday sanatorium for 30 children designated by a doctor.
- Providing wedding gifts and sickness allowances.
- Providing aids to widows and orphans.
- Providing care for elderly people in Zlín.
- Care for upbringing of young men at a boarding school and organisation of courses for girls.
- Outpatient department with two waiting rooms.
- Keeping records of people incapacitated for work and injuries.
- Visits of a social nurse to patients.
- Prevention of occupational diseases.
- Care for the health condition of flats and workshops (SDAZ, Zlín, Social Department II/10, inv. No. 1, c. No. 1331, fol. 1-10).

The company also offered free legal and other counselling. Originally, the counselling was conducted by the Legal Department. But in 1937 the function of a social clerk and in 1940 a school clerk was established. In 1943, a legal advice department was created within the wage and labour section. Employees had the opportunity to turn with their issues to these clerks who helped them to the personal problems (SDAZ, Zlín, Social Department II/10, inv. No. 4, c. No. 1332).

3.2.1 Personnel Department

All company employees were recruited by the Personnel Department. In 1923, those who wanted to be admitted to the company had to submit a portrait photograph of 9 cm x 6,5 cm and a home or baptism certificate (SDAZ, Zlín, Cutting Service II/8, inv. No. 34, c. No. 194).

Diagram No. 5 – Compilation of a personal budget of expenses and incomes

Nutrition
Flat, lighting, fuel
Clothing, underwear, footwear
Other basic needs
Entertainment and delights
Total expenses
How much should you earn to get along?
weakly…….annually……..
How much do you want to save?
weakly…….annually……..
How much do you need to earn to be able to save this amount?
weakly…….annually……..
What you intend to do with your savings and what will you use them for?
weakly…….annually……..

Source: Cekota: 1929: 132, modified

It was obligatory to fill out entry forms. The forms also included questions which the jobseekers had never met before. An example is the "compilation of a personal budget of expenses and incomes" (Cekota: 1929: 132).

Every newly admitted person was examined by a doctor and assigned to a training department. At the same time, the new hires received an information leaflet entitled "Doing a new job". It contained a description of all social facilities of the plant which the employee could use.

In November 1937, psychotechnical testing rooms were put into operation as subdivisions of the personnel department. By February 1938, 1,300 people had passed through the test rooms. The task of the testing rooms was to examine newly recruited people and examine the already employed co-workers of the Zlín plant. The tests mainly determined the speed of observation and reaction. In case of newly recruited employees, the tests were deciding whether to hire the person and further determined the skills by which the person was assigned a particular job (SDAZ, Zlín, Cutting Service II/8, inv. No. 34, c. No. 193).

160,000 job applications were received annually. On average, 7,5% of workers were dismissed each year. According to Valach (1990), the reasons were laziness, tardiness, poor quality of work, criminal offenses, unhealthy lifestyle, etc.

A part of the personnel department was the Institute for Human Research. The Institute first drew attention to itself in 1938 through the May exhibition "Human is the Central Problem of Everything". The exhibition showed various devices used for psychotechnical tests and the visitors could test a number for them. The tests formed a basis for the development of new classification standards. During the tests, the Institute observed especially intelligence, performance and accuracy in uniform work, manual skills and agility (SDAZ, Zlín, Cutting Service II/8, inv. No. 34, c. No. 193).

Everyone was primarily interested in earnings. An average weekly wage at Baťa in 1922 was 160 CSK, in 1938 up to 540 CSK. Employees had 113 days off per year including paid holidays (Valach, 1990).

The social activity for 1943 and 1944 shows the wages of the company employees by age and gender.

Table No. 12 – Average wages of the Baťa company employees in years 1943 and 1944

Employee group	1943 (in CSK)	1944 (in CSK)
Adult men over 21	627	655
Other men under 21	438	460
Young men (members of BSL)	271	270
Single women over 18	350	360
Single women under 18	295	300
Married women	324	314
Average wage per employee	**491**	**510**

Source: SDAZ, Zlín, BSF 036, inv. No. 25, c. No. 6; SDAZ, Zlín, Social Department II/10, inv. No. 4, c. No. 1332

In addition to regular wages, employees were paid New Year's bonuses. In 1943 New Year's bonus amounted to a total of 23 373 269 CSK, in 1944 it was 24 045 960 CSK (SDAZ, Zlín, Social Department II/10, inv. No. 4, c. No. 1332).

The employee statistics of the Svit enterprise archives (in Lehár, 1960: 209) indicate the age groups of the Baťa company employees between 1934-1938. An average age of all employees in this period was around 26 years. Workshops admitted young labourers up to the age of 35. In addition to young men, the company employed a large number of women, especially in sewing workshops, accounting for approximately one third of all employees.

Various events were organised for employees. In archive materials (SDAZ, Zlín, Social Department II/10, inv. No. 30, c. No. 1338) we can read e.g. about these events:

Events for the unemployed: in the 52nd week of 1932, a total of 285 unemployed was registered in Zlín and its surroundings. They were weekly delivered 285 pieces of bread weighing 3 kg, piece for 4 CSK, and 285 Christmas plaited buns weighing 1,5 kg, piece for 2,50 CSK.

Table No. 13 – Bread support

Period in years	Number of distributed loaves of bread weighing 3 kg	Number of distributed Christmas plaited buns	Number of supported municipalities	Total financial expenditures
1931-1932	9922	902	84	56 578 CSK
1932-1933	8347	720	85	42 738 CSK

Source: SDAZ, Zlín, Social Department II/10, inv. No. 30, c. No. 1338

Distribution of Christmas presents of the Baťa company: at Christmas of 1933, 50 pairs of shoes for school children (piece for 39 CSK), 50 pairs of "Melton" shoes for old people (piece for 29 CSK), 50 m of fustian (metre for 6 CSK), 40 girls' dresses (25 or 30 CSK each), 30 boys' dresses, sweaters, stockings and underwear totalling to 7560 CSK were distributed in Zlín.

Vánočka (this is a traditional Czech sweet Christmas bread) **for old people:** in December 1933, a total of 700 Vánočka weighing 1,5 kg (4,50 CSK each) were prepared for old people, shoemakers and shoemakers' widows in Zlín and for poor elderly people in the district.

Giving presents to the sick: a budget was created for the sick who spent Christmas Eve and Christmas holidays at the Baťa Hospital. In 1934, 213 persons received a pair of "mikado"[15] shoes, at a cost of 2,511 CSK. In 1933, 180 people received "mikado" shoes costing 2,160 CSK.

3.2.2 Social Department and its Employees

The existence of a social department in Zlín dates back to 1924. It had two sections: (a) a counselling section led by a social clerk and (b) a record keeping section led by a female social clerk (SDAZ, Zlín, Social Department II/10, inv. No. 5, c. No. 1333).

The task of the Social Department was to solve employees' problems of "a social nature". The Social Department was entrusted with implementation of the so-called supportive care for the Baťa company co-workers and their family members. The department dealt with individual applications for aid, proposed the amount of aid and managed their payment (SDAZ, Zlín, BN 035, inv. No. 74. fol. 16).

Baťa employees were granted loans on flat furnishing or on the acquisition of other needs requisite to leading a proper life. They were paid off by weekly wage deductions. In the case of loans granted to employees, the full loan repayment was guaranteed by: (a) a leading foreman in the amount of 10% Supervisor, (b) an administrator 10%, (c) a member of the directorate who signed the loan, (d) 50% of the loss will be charged to the department in which the debtor last worked (SDAZ, Zlín, Social Department II/10, inv. No. 1, c. No. 1331, fol. 1-10).

In 1945, the Social Department carried out 5,992 interventions in wage matters, 2,926 in health insurance, of which 2,622 cases were resolved positively. 3,820 applications were dealt with in respect of sickness allowance. As for housing, the department carried out 780 positive interventions. Furthermore, the Social Department dealt with one-time supports, increases in wages and child allowances (SDAZ, Zlín, Cutting Service II/8, inv. No. 34, c. No. 192).

Tasks of the Social Clerk

The social clerk addressed issues of a social nature, dealt with employees' wishes and complaints, gave advice to all who were dealing with personal problems and asked for advice. Social care for employees included: complaints about dismissal, relocation, superiors, co-workers, wage complaints, complaints related to accommodation, social insurance. Moreover, the social clerk handled applications which could not be handled by the personnel department. These were mainly requests based on social reasons: applications for work, for a job change, for a special remuneration, waiver of punishment, treatment permission, requests for legal advice, requests for aid from the Baťa Support Fund (SDAZ, Zlín, Social Department II/10, inv. No. 5, c. No. 1333).

---

15 There is no explanation of "mikado" in the archival source.

In addition, various suggestions for improving the working environment of employees were managed by the social clerk. The job description of the social clerk included e.g. dealing with discrepancies in marriage, giving advice on divorce proceedings, making housing interventions at the accommodation department, informing sick employees of their claims against the health insurance fund or the Central Social Insurance Agency. If the employee needed legal advice in private disputes against a third person or in family disputes, the social clerk arranged free legal advice from a lawyer for them (SDAZ, Zlín, Social Department II/10, inv. No. 5, c. No. 1333).

The social clerk worked applying methods which were verified by scientists as correct (Zlín, 11. 9. 1940 in SDAZ, Zlín, Cutting Service II/8, inv. No. 34, c. No. 193).

In order to be able to deal with cases objectively, the social clerk needed to know the enterprise organisation perfectly, he carried out some of the work in the plant, he needed to know the employees' life and the way in which the plant managers acted. To check the employees' data, the clerk visited their families, where, as the archival materials state, the cause of employee dissatisfaction could almost always be found in the fastest way (SDAZ, Zlín, Social Department II/10, inv. No. 5, c. No. 1333).

In 1938, a novelty in social protection was introduced in the Baťa company. Based on a report from the Zlín magazine dated 10th December 1938, a social inspectorate was established "to oversee the observance of laws and employees' labour and social rights." The head of the Social Patrol was Karel Huták, a social inspector of the sales department of the Baťa company (Průmyslový úředník, Praha, 1938 in SDAZ, Zlín, Cutting Service II/8, inv. No. 34, c. No. 191).

The purpose of the Social Patrol and Social Inspection was to create an instrument which functioned to serve all people, wherever they were (SDAZ, Zlín, Cutting Service II/8, inv. No. 34, c. No. 193).

The Zlín magazine published specific case reports of solved cases in the "Social Patrol" articles. The cases to be solved by the social inspector included: irregularities in paying wages, unauthorised wage retention, sickness allowance, failure to pay the agreed wage, handling leave, informal labour (i.e. 'under the table'), orphans' clothing and others (SDAZ, Zlín, Cutting Service II/8, inv. No. 34, c. No. 193).

Work of the Social Clerk

The social clerk did his job "to help eliminate worries and bring satisfaction to the employees' families". It follows from the archival documents that he performed everything discreetly to gain the employees' trust, so that the employees would tell him everything which was weighing on them, without fear of arousing hatred or anger of a third person. He needed to use reason, heart and tact in his work. He decided minor cases himself and he dealt with complex matters upon consultation with the head of the personnel department or directly with the plant manager. The plant manager was the last decisive body for handling employee complaints (SDAZ, Zlín, Social Department II/10, inv. No. 5, c. No. 1333).

The social clerk was a confidant and supporter of those in a weaker position, if their applications or complaints were justified (SDAZ, Zlín, Social Department II/10, inv. No. 5, c. No. 1333). At the same time, he was an adviser, friend and supporter for the co-workers (SDAZ, Zlín, Social Department II/10, inv. No. 29, c. No. 1338).

The social clerk's work routine was as follows:

- The social clerk ascertained the visitor's/employee's personal data necessary to fill out the form header.
- Then the social clerk listened to the employee's wish or complaint. He gave advice to the best of his knowledge and conscience. Therefore, only a person with life experience could perform the work of a social clerk, knowledge from the legal field was an added advantage.
- If the visitor/co-worker needed to write something, e.g. to insurance companies or offices, if there was a need for personal intervention, the social clerk did it himself for the employee.
- The social clerk attended to more complex cases even when he had no visits. He noted how the case originated and how it was handled. He had cases on file until they were completely resolved.
- Common cases were sorted into binders by common numbers. The social clerk kept an alphabetical index of social cases on a special form. Therefore, when an employee visited him repeatedly, using the index he could immediately find out and what the social clerk has already arranged for the given person.
- After returning from a family visit, the clerk filled out the designated form and put it in the card file. Once a week, the clerk prepared an overview of the activities of the social department for the past week (SDAZ, Zlín, Social Department II/10, inv. No. 5, c. No. 1333).

As a specific example of social clerks of the Baťa company, we can find in the archive materials the job description of Mr. Otmar Jabůrek, dated 28th March 1938 (SDAZ, Zlín, Baťa, sign. II/2, c. No. 1026, inv. No. 14, p.č. 80). There are two job titles in the entry itself. While at the beginning of the form "social inspector" appears, the text of the content states "social clerk". We can interpret this fact as a variation of synonyms.

The social clerk Otmar Jabůrek had his office in the 11th building (personnel department). He was available throughout the working week as well as on Saturday (SDAZ, Zlín, Cutting Service II/8, inv. No. 34, c. No. 193).

Record Keeping Social Department

The social department included a record keeping section. Extensive records served to capture the social issues of the plant employees. It consisted of several filing cabinets. (SDAZ, Zlín, Social Department II/10, inv. No. 5, c. No. 1333).

Family filing cabinet: a card file on the designated form for each plant employee was created as soon as the employee came into contact with the Social Department. Later, entries were added when a visit was made. Records of various facts which the social clerk learned about the family were also entered in the card file.

New-born filing system: Starting from 1st May 1926, a donation was given to new-born babies. After the birth, an employee reported this to the Social Department and the Social Department, with the personnel clerk, then added the data to the new-born filing system. Where possible, the family visited and a report on family relationships was compiled. On the basis of the new-born filing system, a donation list was made every 14 days and approved by the plant manager. Based on these entries, the cash register issued a passbook to each new-born baby and handed it over to the new-born's father. If the employee was dismissed, the donation was transferred from the passbook to the local financial institution with appropriate restriction of transferability.

Filing system for large families: Starting from 1939, contributions were provided to employees with 4 or more children. If a fourth child was born to the employee, a form for the card file was filled out. A personnel or social clerk made a visit to the family to verify the information provided. The contribution amounted to 40 CSK per month for each child. If there were more children in the family, the company paid the rent, electricity and gas for the family. In September, the social clerk reminded the employee of the large family to bring a document confirmed by the school administration stating how much it is necessary to pay for tuition and school supplies. Depending on the number of children, the parents received 50-100% of the expenses covered from the support fund. A detailed directive on allowances for large family was developed. Once a month, the aid was accounted for. Each personnel clerk had only his large families on his list. Before the monthly accounting, the personnel clerk confirmed that all the employees on his list were still working at the plant, to prevent payment of aid to a dismissed person. The aid was paid monthly either by postal orders or by a collective cheque of the postal savings bank.

Aid filing cabinet: Aid was paid out through the Baťa Support Fund. The aim of aid was to secure the employee's family when the breadwinner was unable to provide for the family from his or her earnings for whatever reason. During the annual Christmas event, various gifts funded by the Support Fund were given to families of those employees who needed help. In case of a one-time assistance, the aid was entered in the personal or family card file. Otherwise, a registration form for aid card files was filled out.

Illness records: If an employee became ill, he was obliged to report this fact to the personnel department. Every day a list of all those who have become ill was drawn up and handed over to the Social Department. After when fit for work again, the employee contacted the personnel department again for a checklist. The illness card file was used to record how long and how many times each employee was ill. If someone was ill for more than a year, disability proceedings were carried out under the Health Insurance Act. In this case, the Social Department ensured that the employee was not left without funds. Occasionally, a random visit was made throughout the period of illness, for which the Social Department had specially trained employees.

Death records: If an employee died, a relative was asked to come to the Social Department and complete the card file of the deceased. The card files were aimed at providing for the deceased's family until the appropriate annuity or pension was assessed, depending on deceased's insurance years. Widows were given special consideration so as to provide them with suitable employment in line with the given possibilities and their skills.

3.2.3 Department for Public Benefit Institutions

Administration of childcare, housing, provision of groceries and other basic needs, socio-hygienic measures and entertainment facilities was entrusted to the Baťa Department for Public Benefit Institutions. Generally speaking, it cared for the standard of living of the labourers, which was incomparably higher than the standard of living of the social strata from which most of Baťa's labourers came. The department had its own budget (3 million in 1928 and already 50 million in 1932) and was subjected to the same discipline in performance and duty to work as profitably as the factory shoe workshops. The department was located near the factory entrance (Erdély, 2013).

The department organised various festivals several times a year. Celebrations of 1st May belonged to the most important ones. In 1931, Baťa's celebrations of May Day were attended by 80,000 people (Erdély, 2013).

The department's tasks also included administration of boarding houses and flats, checks of the cinema business management, testing the quality of meals served in factory canteens, organisation of sports meetings, etc. Apart from these activities, the department was in charge of managing the treasury, which Baťa founded on the day of his 50th birthday in 1926 (Erdély, 2013).

3.2.4 Economic Department

It can be traced from an overview of the activities of the Economic Department for 1944 how many vouchers were processed at the department, who received the employee supplementary allowances, how much coffee was provided free of charge, how much milk was distributed to chemical workers free of charge and others. Vouchers were issued for work clothes, work shoes, bicycle tyres and bicycle identification marks. Supplement vouchers were given to workers in the categories of "hard working", "very hard working", "long working", "working with poisons". Employees working with poisons received milk supplement vouchers (0,25 litres per day per person). Milk was delivered directly to individual workshops in the morning break. Milk and all expenses were paid by the given department to the Department Store by transfer orders (SDAZ, Zlín, BPF 036, inv. No. 25, c. No. 6).

Examples of the activities of the Economic Department can be found below:

- Free black coffee was provided in departments where co-workers worked in the heat, such as in the tyre workshop, foundry, power plant, during the hot weather in summer and after air strikes. In 1943, 93,600 servings were distributed, in 1944 it was 410,573 servings.
- As a special Christmas ration for the whole enterprise in 1943, 919,750 individual cigarettes were distributed at a cost of more than 400,000 CSK.
- Also vouchers for a special ration of soap and soap powders were distributed to co-workers who became particularly dirty at work.
- In 1944, 700 dry batteries were distributed to women who went to and from work in the dark from the surroundings of Zlín.
- In the period from 10th October 1944 to 31st December 1944, 308 pieces of various linen were repaired in the clothes repair shop for married women. The purpose was to keep the married women working all day long, without having to devote evenings and Sundays to darning, mending linen and clothes (SDAZ, Zlín, BPF 036, inv. No. 25, c. No. 6).

3.2.5 Baťa Support Fund

Employees who were temporarily or permanently eliminated from work due to circumstances of no fault of their own, unable to earn their living needs by earnings, or who were affected by a disaster or an accident, were assisted by the company's financial Support Fund (SDAZ, Zlín, Social Department II/10, inv. No. 4, c. No. 1332).

In September 1928, the "Baťa Support Fund" was established instead of the existing "Support Fund for Employees of the T. & A. Baťa Company". It obtained financial means through employees' fines and from contributions of the Baťa company which were not subject to taxation. The fund provided contributions to employees, such as social support in the form of money, needed items, advice etc.. For the greater part, the fund financed the construction of single-family houses, boarding schools, schools, hospitals, land purchases, etc. It addressed all the consequences in connection with health and social care for employees. The fund was managed by the Head of the Baťa Hospital, Dr. Albert (Cekota, 1929).

As per the Statutes of 11th December 1935 the fund activities included:

- Providing aid to company employees at the birth of a child.
- Providing aid to company employees in case of a long-term illness.
- Providing aid to company employees at death in the family.
- Betterment of widow's pensions in cases deserving special consideration.
- Betterment of disability pensions in cases deserving special consideration.
- Establishment of sanatoriums, hospitals, medical, humanitarian and other auxiliary institutions and companies.
- Supporting housing events.
- Granting aids to elderly employees and their family members.
- Social care for employees' children.
- Supporting all educational, cultural and sports as well as other events for employees (SDAZ, Zlín, BN 035, inv. No. 74. fol. 16).

In addition to the aforementioned activities, the fund set itself a task of providing support to dismissed employees if they do not get a new job (Cekota, 1929).

Starting from 1942, the event of wedding gifts to newlyweds was introduced in the enterprise, funded by the Support Fund. If both newlyweds had been in the company for at least three years, they received a wedding gift of 500-1000 CSK depending on length of their employment (SDAZ, Zlín, Social Department II/10, inv. No. 31, c. No. 1339).

Any employee of the Baťa company, as well as associated companies, could become a member of the Baťa Support Fund. The admission conditions were a minimum age of 20, at least one year worked at the company, and a submitted application. The member's fund contribution was set at 50 CSK per year. In addition to regular membership, the Statutes also allowed honorary membership and a so-called contributing membership. A "contributing" member paid at least 100 CSK per year. However, the membership is not more specifically described in the Statutes (SDAZ, Zlín, BN 035, inv. No. 74. fol. 16).

In 1939, the company began to pay out regular monthly allowances to its employees who had 4 or more children of compulsory school age. Until the end of 1943, they these families obtained 40 CSK per month for each child. In addition, the fund also covered tuition and school supplies and, in some cases, the flat rent as well as consumed electricity and gas. Starting from 1944 the allowance[16] was increased to 50 CSK per month (SDAZ, Zlín, Social Department II/10, inv. No. 4, c. No. 1332).

The Baťa Support Fund disbursed aids during the war, too. In 1943, the fund disbursed more than 22 million crowns, of which the sum for social care for children and employees' families totalled to almost 10 million CSK (SDAZ, Zlín, BPF 036, inv. No. 19, c. No. 5).

In 1947 the fund was renamed the "Baťa State-Owned Enterprise Support Fund". The defined activities of 1935 remained the same in the Statutes of 1947 (SDAZ, Zlín, BN 035, inv. No. 74. fol. 16).

On 1st September 1947, together with the new Fund Statutes, an informative summary of the rights and obligations of the co-workers of the Baťa State-Owned Enterprise was published. In particular, the supportive care was reorganised. As per the overview, all wishes and difficulties of any kind were handled outside working hours, primarily through confidants. Until then, this activity was carried out by the Social Department. Confidants were a trade union body. By means of confidants, the trade union influenced and regulated activities of the works council (SDAZ, Zlín, BN 035, inv. No. 74. fol. 16).

3.3   Areas of Social Services Provided to Employees

Regular employment and decent income of employees, spent reasonably on means raising the standard of living, have profoundly changed the life and character of not only the city of Zlín but also its wide surroundings. As evidenced by published statistics, industrial prosperity also had an impact on human destinies in terms family. In October 1928 the National Statistical Office issued statistics on marriages in the Czechoslovak Republic. While there was an average of 10 marriages per 1000 inhabitants a year countrywide in this period, this average was exceeded in Zlín, with almost 15 marriages per year per 1000 inhabitants (Cekota, 1929).

Baťa also employed people with physical handicaps in his company. As noted by Cekota (1929), in 1929, there were 208 people with various physical disabilities working at the enterprise. They worked mainly in organised workshops under the same conditions as their co-workers. They were selected for such work, in which their performance, quality of work and, naturally, their earnings almost equalled their healthy colleagues.

All measures raising the standard of living of people working in the company, from good wages, orderly workshops, good nutrition, housing, etc., reduced the

---

16 The company paid these allowances voluntarily, they were not required by law (SOkA, Zlín, Social Department II/10, inv. No. 4, c. No. 1332).

risk of accident and loss due to illness, thus making the enterprise more capable of serving the public well (Cekota, 1929).

The Baťa enterprise cooperated with major entities to which it donated financial contributions. Examples of the entities and the amounts of the financial contribution in 1942 can be found below.

Table No. 14 – Financial contributions of the Baťa company to important entities in 1942

Entity	Financial contribution
Red Cross	637,600 CSK
National Fund	1,922,500 CSK
National Assistance	1,100,516 CSK

Source: SDAZ, Zlín, Social Department II/10, inv. No. 4, c. No. 1332

In 1932, Tomáš Baťa founded "Svedrup", a self-help cooperative for the improvement of the shoemaking craft following Baťa's principles. Its purpose was, among others, to take care of members and their children socially, in particular by counselling, unemployment benefits, distributing repairs from cooperative collection points and supporting elderly and sick members. In 1942, 310,000 CSK were disbursed for these activities (SDAZ, Zlín, Social Department II/10, inv. No. 4, c. No. 1332).

3.3.1 Housing

Accommodation of employees was the responsibility of the accommodation department. The right to use a flat was an inseparable part of the service employee-to-plant relationship (SDAZ, Zlín, Ubytovací oddělení II/9, inv. No. 8, c. No. 1331, fol. 0-68).

The Social Department participated in the decision-making on flat allocation (SDAZ, Zlín, Social Department II/10, inv. No. 5, c. No. 1333).

According to Baťa, a good-quality flat has the same effect on a person's health and working ability as proper nutrition. His ideal was for all people working in the enterprise to live near their work so that they could spend their free time recovering and not wasting their energy on a long journey by foot or commuting by train. The principle of good housing was to combine the advantages of a country stay with the comfort of living in a city. Based on experience, they found that single-family houses and semi-detached houses freely located in a garden best suited family housing. The streets were planted with ornamental shrubs and trees. Three living rooms (a family's daily living room, children's bedroom and parents' bedroom) and a kitchen with fixtures were set as the minimum living space. Water supply, sewerage system, dust-free roads, electricity and gas networks were built everywhere to ensure all sanitary and health measures (SDAZ, Zlín, Ubytovací oddělení II/9, inv. No. 8, c. No. 1331, fol. 0-68).

Baťa built the first series of family houses designed by architect Kotěra before the war. In the years 1912-1913, these were the first six houses for employees (Pokluda, 2004). In 1924 he proceeded to a thorough solution of the employees' housing problem in line with his own opinions. He had family houses built based on these principles:

1. The house shall be free from all sides and surrounded by greenery of a garden and trees.
2. Each family living in the house should have its own entrance. It needs to be independent from all its neighbours in all directions.
3. The family flat should have a water supply, electric lighting and bathroom.
4. The weekly rent must be so low that a person can earn it in two hours of work (Cekota, 1929).

In accordance with these principles, 800 single-family houses were built in 1926 on a woody slope behind the factory. Each house had four flats. One flat had an area of 56 m² of living space and contained a bathroom, pantry, kitchen and bedroom upstairs. A cellar and woodshed belonged to the flat, too. Weekly rent was 15 CSK. Cekota (1929) states that the 800 flats eliminated the imminent housing crisis in Zlín. In 1927, 167 houses were built, in 1928 another 300 houses. Special homes with shared accommodation were built for single employees. The girls' home, with a capacity of 2,500 persons, was opened in 1925, a boarding school for young men for 1000 people in 1927. Housing care was supplemented by 23 smaller boarding houses for about 800 people, scattered in the garden districts of Letná and Díly (SDAZ, Zlín, Social Department II/10, inv. No. 4, c. No. 1332).

The standard for a workshop employee was a flat with three rooms, with a kitchen, bathroom, cellar and small garden. Electricity, water supply and gas were commonplace in the accommodation also (SDAZ, Zlín, Social Department II/10, inv. No. 4, c. No. 1332).

In 1929, 1,364 families, comprising of 6,069 persons and 3,222 single persons, were accommodated (Cekota, 1929: 158).

In each house of the Baťa company a house order was posted, in which the users' obligations were regulated, including the monthly contribution for the flat maintenance. Rent in a single-family house ranged between 49-61 CSK/week depending on the house type, rent of one family in a semi-detached house amounted to 35 CSK/week (SDAZ, Zlín, Ubytovací oddělení II/9, inv. No. 8, c. No. 1331, fol. 0-68).

Procedure for the Allocation of a Family Flat

The applicant picked up an application at the accommodation department, filled it out and had it signed by his leader. Subsequently, a record on family relations was drawn up with the applicant. The application was then signed by a personal clerk, the head of the Social Department and the head of the Personnel Department. Before the family could move in, the staff of the accommodation department gathered information about the new families in various ways. They either contacted the owner of the existing flat of the family, asked other company employees who were from the same municipality as the family in question, or they directly visited families from Zlín before they moved in (SDAZ, Zlín, Ubytovací oddělení II/9, inv. No. 8, c. No. 1331, fol. 0-68).

When assigning the flat, the applicant filled out a supplement to the work contract, a list of family members and a card file. The new tenant inspected the flat and wrote down any defects. The card file was made out in duplicate; a copy was for the Record Office which confirmed on the original that the tenant has been duly registered in the municipality. The original was then handed over to the payroll department, so the rent was deducted directly from the employee's wage every week. The tenants had to report subtenants and "incidental" visits to the Record Office and the accommodation department. It follows from archival documents of the accommodation department that the tenants were frequently visited. Families were usually visited twice a year, households which were not in good condition were kept on file and visited more often. The accommodation department had its craftsmen and minor repairs not caused by the tenants were repaired at its own expense. Major repairs were ensured by the construction department. If the employee was dismissed, he received a letter from the accommodation department stating that he was obliged to move out of the rented flat within a month, as per the tenancy agreement (SDAZ, Zlín, Ubytovací oddělení II/9, inv. No. 8, c. No. 1331, fol. 0-68).

3.3.2   Health Care

In Zlín, an entire system of health care facilities was built to provide health care for people from birth to old age. The main emphasis was laid on prevention. The major medical facility was the Baťa Hospital (Pochylý, 1990).

The Baťa Hospital started to be built in March 1927 according to the plans of Dr. Albert. Already in November of the same year, the first ward was in operation. The construction of the hospital was financed solely by the company T. & A. Baťa without assistance from public funds. In addition to the medical treatment itself, health care also focused on prevention: "It should go on the offensive against illnesses, it should be a wall, protecting people from illnesses at all, as much as possible" (SDAZ, Zlín, BN 035, inv. No. 74. fol. 16; Cekota, 1929: 172).

Baťa's dedication to the hospital construction reflects how much importance he attached to health care: "It is not possible to remain permanently healthy among the sick, just as it is not possible to be happy among the unhappy" (SDAZ, Zlín, Social Department II/10, inv. No. 4, c. No. 1332).

In its original intention, the hospital was described as an Institute with a Clear Health and Social Mission, which also appeared in the Statutes. From the very beginning, the Institute was planned as a socio-health and medical centre for the future large Zlín and Podřevnicko region. Following tradition, the institute was known as a "Hospital" (SDAZ, Zlín, BN 035, inv. No. 74. fol. 16).

The hospital provided care both to employees of the Baťa company and the general public of the town. The following table indicates the occupational status of people given inpatient treatment in the Baťa Hospital between 1928-1935.

Table No. 15 – Occupational status of people given inpatient treatment in the Baťa Hospital between 1928-1935

Year	Number of admitted patients	Employees of Baťa enterprise and their family members		Employees of other enterprises and trades, self-employed people	
		Number	%	Number	%
1928	1 511	806	53	705	47
1929	2 575	1 215	47	1 360	53
1930	3 568	2 127	58	1 441	42
1931	4 565	2 813	61	1 752	39
1932	5 148	2 963	57	2 185	43
1933	5 455	3 394	62	2 061	38
1934	5 906	3 932	66	1 974	34
1935 (31.10.)	6 016	4 099	69	1 917	31

Source: SDAZ, Zlín, BN 035, inv. No. 74. fol. 16

The hospital was situated outside the city, in a quiet environment and protected from northern winds. It consisted of a main building and hospital wards. One ward was intended for 27 patients. The rooms were occupied by 1-7 patients. There were also operating theatres and a delivery room in the hospital, all equipped with up-to-date diagnostic devices. An electric lift was used for transport to the operating theatre, where even a patient on a bed could be transported. The operating theatres were furnished in compliance with the latest professional experience of surgeons – prof. Sauerbruch from Germany and a Czech surgeon doc. Rychlík (Cekota, 1929).

In 1938 the hospital had 340 beds. The hospital included two surgical departments, a department for internal diseases, infectious diseases and tuberculosis, an orthopaedic, dental, gynaecologic department, maternity hospital, a department for children's and infants' diseases and for diseases of the ear, nose and throat (Pochylý, 1990).

There was a general health advisory centre at the hospital where the patient received medical advice as needed. Well-off people had to pay a fee for this service, but it was free for poor people. Over time, the advisory centre was expanded by special advisory centres for treatment of, alcoholism, venereal diseases, cancer, dental and orthopaedic issues. Within the infectious department, a theoretical department was built with a dissecting room (pathology) and laboratories. The orthopaedic department was meant to work as a scientific institute for the study of feet and footwear. As a result, the individual departments of the hospital also significantly affected production in the plants (Cekota, 1929).

Special attention was paid to the dental care of Baťa employees. There was a dental clinic was not only in Zlín, but also in Třebíč, Zruč nad Sázavou and Ratíškovice. In addition to adult care, the Baťa Hospital also carried out special dental care for school children at all Zlín schools (SDAZ, Zlín, Social Department II/10, inv. No. 4, c. No. 1332).

In spite of the initial failures, the Socio-Health Institute of the Baťa Hospital was finally established in 1932. In its building, an office of the District Health Insurance Company and its central outpatient clinic for the Concilium and Revision Service were located. Furthermore, the Institute housed institutions of voluntary social-health care such as the Cs. Red Cross, District Youth Care and Masaryk League against TB (SDAZ, Zlín, BN 035, inv. No. 74. fol. 16).

Part of the work of the Institute was to keep a medical registry of all company employees. Health records of the enterprise employees were given great importance. The medical registry worked in close cooperation with the Zlín Industrial Health Care Department (SDAZ, Zlín, Social Department II/10, inv. No. 4, c. No. 1332).

According to Pochylý (1990), 52,400 records of citizens' health status were collected in the medical registry in 1939. Every citizen of Zlín received their card immediately after birth. The existence of the registry enabled conduction of various studies on the general health of the population and the impacts on it.

The files of individual employees contained records from the anthropological and clinical field. There was also a medical and social history, results of detailed general and special examinations, e.g. chest X-ray radiology and serological blood tests for tuberculosis and syphilis. The main branches of work were complemented by other events of publicly beneficial and socio-health institutions, such as the event of school medicine, courses for voluntary nurses, advisory centre of the

Masaryk League against TB or advisory centre for Mother and Child Protection etc. (SDAZ, Zlín, BN 035, inv. No. 74. fol. 16).

The aforementioned activities have become arguments for an extension of the Institute and the need to build new combined socio-health and medical institute in Zlín. (SDAZ, Zlín, BN 035, inv. No. 74. fol. 16) The new institute was architecturally designed by F. L. Gahura in collaboration with Dr. Albert and Dr. Tolar (SDAZ, Zlín, BN 035, inv. No. 131. fol. 16).

Industrial health and factory hygiene as health care sectors were a subject matter of a special department of the Baťa Hospital with four doctors and a head physician. The tasks of the physicians included regular monthly inspections of workplaces in terms of hygiene. They focused on the overall adjustment of workplaces such as lighting, ventilation, heating, cooling, drinking water distribution, sewerage system, waste disposal and workshop cleaning (SDAZ, Zlín, Social Department II/10, inv. No. 4, c. No. 1332).

According to Erdely (2013), Baťa achieved massive success in the fight against tuberculosis. In his hospital, he appointed two specialists for lung diseases. At the same time, he arranged for thorough treatment and nursing of tuberculosis diseases, so that in 1928 the number of tuberculosis diseases was reduced to 1,53%, in 1929 to 1%.

Due to poor water supply in Zlín, cases of typhoid fever occurred once in a while. Therefore, Baťa had a factory water supply built and elaborated plans to reform the Moravian water management (Erdély, 2013).

Every year the Baťa enterprise regularly provided its employees with opportunities for recreation, spa treatment at spas and convalescent homes. In 1942, a total of 588 workers from various plant departments were sent to Luhačovice, Slatinice and to the resort at the Bystřička dam. Until 1942 the Baťa Support Fund owned a chateau in Březolupy. Every year, the fund lent the chateau to the District Youth Care which organised a children's sanatorium there in the summer months (SDAZ, Zlín, Social Department II/10, inv. No. 4, c. No. 1332).

In 1936 the Scientific Institute for Industrial Health was established. Its main task was to study working conditions, health condition of employees, prevention of injuries and health damage caused by work (Pochylý, 1990).

Care for Children

The social and health department of the plants carefully organised care for children from infancy. Maternity ward of the Baťa Hospital provided the best treatment to both mother and child. The price for medical and nursing assistance was set at 19 CSK per day, which was supposed to ensure cheaper treatment at the hospital than treatment at home even for poor women (Cekota, 1929).

On the occasion of his fiftieth birthday on 1st May 1926, Tomáš Baťa donated 1,000 CSK to all new-born babies with 10% interest, as a proof of friendship.

From Tomáš Baťa's speech:

> "Let us remember that the future of our work lies in our children. Therefore, I greet first of all the new-born babies of our faithful co-workers. I welcome you as a member of our working family, the youngest heirs of our work" (SDAZ, Zlín, Social Department II/10, inv. No. 1, c. No. 1331, fol. 1-10).

The donation was deposited for each child on a passbook in the corporate savings bank for 24 years. At that time the amount reached 9,846.90 CSK. In the case of girls, it was possible to collect the donation earlier if they got married before reaching the age of 24 (Cekota, 1929).

There was also a company kindergarten in which nurses took care of the employees' children for free. However, the families used its benefits only temporarily, especially when traveling, shopping, on a visit, etc. Tomáš Baťa did not favour the idea of married mothers working at the plant. He held the opinion that a woman should take care of her children and husband so that the husband could carry out a great deal of work. As he saw it, a woman should not waste her own capital (Cekota, 1929). In addition to the company kindergarten, there was another kindergarten of the Baťa company, intended for children from the whole of Zlín. There was a nursery for younger children, too. In 1932 there were about 150 children (Erdély, 2013). In 1927, an experienced social worker Heřma Fridrichová was working in the nursery (SDAZ, Zlín, Cutting Service II/8, inv. No. 34, c. No. 193).

Between 1926 and 1933, 3,200 children were born in total, which meant that these children had altogether 4 million CSK including interest (SDAZ, Zlín, Cutting Service II/8, inv. No. 34, c. No. 192).

Care for Elderly People

Care for old co-workers was thought out in detail in the social system of Baťa enterprise. Care for old people was concentrated in Baťa's homes which were set up within the Baťa Hospital as a self-governing unit. The homes were founded in 1935 at the expense of the Baťa Support Fund and with the assistance of the Baťa Company. In 1940, a second building intended for elderly men was built. In 1942, 50 men and women were accommodated here (SDAZ, Zlín, Social Department II/10, inv. No. 4, c. No. 1332).

The Baťa Hospital took over all care, including accommodation, meals and medical supervision. The home residents could grow flowers or vegetables on garden beds depending on to their preferences (SDAZ, Zlín, Social Department II/10, inv. No. 4, c. No. 1332).

The homes provided refuge not only to the elderly, but also to those who, due to a mental or physical defect, were unable to assure their own existence (SDAZ, Zlín, Social Department II/10, inv. No. 4, c. No. 1332).

In 1938, an article on social services for Zlín workers was published in the Zlín magazine. It gave a summary of the measures the Baťa company took to look after the elderly amongst the Zlín industrial workers:

- Extensive possibilities for personal improvement and education at an early age.
- The nature of Zlín industrial work, forcing as such to think for the future by developing a living, personal and economic precondition.
- Wages for work so high that they allow savings to be made, while meeting the subsistence needs of a family.
- Profit participations constituting a capital over the years of working activity.
- 10% interest on personal participation deposits.
- Continual need for older people in educational and leadership positions at industrial workshops where their composure, wisdom and rich life experience can be utilised (SDAZ, Zlín, Cutting Service II/8, inv. No. 34, c. No. 193).

3.3.3 Catering

In the Baťa company, catering was developed in a sophisticated way. Baťa was an enemy of coffee pots and bread rolls as a labourers' lunch (SDAZ, Zlín, Social Department II/10, inv. No. 4, c. No. 1332). The food had to be valuable and in sufficient quantity, which was regularly checked (Valach, 1990).

The nourishment issue was divided into two parts:

a) Nourishment of single employees took place in common canteens, where they could get a lunch containing meat with soup and side-dish for 2,50 – 3 CSK, i.e. an average wage earned for 20 minutes of work.
b) Family nourishment was ensured by a delivery service resting on the same principles. Thanks to it, workers in the Zlín region were not exposed to rising food prices. Nobody had a monopoly on catering, so people could choose. Quality and price were decisive (Pochylý, 1990).

Meals were served in several large halls of factory canteens (with area of 80 x 20 m each) in the building of the Department Store and the Market Hall, but also in other canteens directly in the plants. In 1942, over 10,000 lunches and 8,000 dinners were served daily. Menus contained 6 types of meals daily except Monday and Thursday, when a single meal was prescribed (SDAZ, Zlín, Social Department II/10, inv. No. 4, c. No. 1332).

Cekota (1929) describes in detail the condition of catering and the prices of individual meals in 1929. Factory canteens provided hot and nutritious meals three times a day. Breakfast consisted of coffee or milk (0,33 l for 50 hellers), together with white bread rolls (5 pieces for 1 CSK) or bread (10 dkg for 25 hellers). It was served between 6-7 a.m. Lunch was served between 12 a.m.-1 p.m. in triplicate: meatless for 1 CSK, with meat (15 dkg) for 2 CSK, with roast meat for 4 CSK. In addition, desserts were offered, 1 piece for 50 hellers and white coffee for 50 hellers. Coffee or milk for 50 hellers were available as snack. At the time between 5-6 p.m., dinner was served. The price of dinner ranged from 1-1,50 CSK (a meat dish). 6000-7000 employees were catered daily in the self-service canteens of the Department Store. A pair of scales was also found in the canteens to check the set weight of the portion.

The quality of food was checked daily by personnel clerks, educators or sometimes also social clerks (SDAZ, Zlín, Social Department II/10, inv. No. 5, c. No. 1333).

In 1942 the price of lunch ranged from 3,50 to 5 CSK (SDAZ, Zlín, Social Department II/10, inv. No. 4, c. No. 1332).

Distribution of groceries and other products for families of the enterprise employees was carried out by the Baťa Department Store with its branches (Pochylý, 1990).

3.3.4 Upbringing and Education

The Baťa enterprise took great pains to build up a school system in Zlín from kindergartens through general and main schools up to numerous and remarkable institutions of secondary and vocational education (SDAZ, Zlín, Social Department II/10, inv. No. 4, c. No. 1332).

It was necessary to build schools for the growing number of children. In 1924 it was the Zlín Paseky School, in 1928 the Masaryk Schools, in 1932 Letná, in 1933 and 1938 Zálešná, in 1937 Díly. An auditorium and gymnasium were added to the Masaryk Schools (1932-1934), a whole school district with a Trade School (1931), other buildings and a summer swimming pool were built in the adjacent area. In large, airy and bright school buildings, teachers sought to apply modern, experimental teaching methods (e.g. the Masaryk Experimental Differentiated Secondary Modern School). Foreign teachers were appointed to teach the main world languages, e.g. at the Foreign-language Secondary Modern School. The experimental school system of Zlín became a well-known notion of its day (Pokluda, 2004).

The school system of Zlín included:

- **A Study Institute** with rich technological and natural history collections, and a pedagogical department to organize professional courses.
- **An Export School** to prepare for the field of foreign trade.
- **A Higher People's School** focusing mainly on language education.
- **A Zlín School of Art** with an exhibition department which regularly held large art exhibitions in Zlín several times a year (SDAZ, Zlín, Social Department II/10, inv. No. 4, c. No. 1332).

Apart from basic (called obecné) and secondary modern (called měšťanské) schools, establishment of industrial education is worth mentioning. In 1925, the so-called Baťa School of Labour (hereinafter 'BSL') was founded in Zlín, which answered the purpose of training all young men and women who were admitted to the services of the Baťa Company after a secondary modern school or a lower secondary school. At that time, an advertisement appeared in the newspaper saying that: "Baťa is looking for 200 young men to turn them into independent and enterprising people". About 80 pupils were admitted in the first cycle. The school programme cycle lasted three years. Each pupil worked a regular number of hours per week at a workshop as an adult labourer and, in addition, spent three hours a day at school (Pochylý, 1990).

BSL was divided into several branches: shoemaking, mechanical engineering, electrical, chemical, tannery, knitting and construction. Young people could attend a lower or higher technical school in all these fields (SDAZ, Zlín, Social Department II/10, inv. No. 4, c. No. 1332).

BSL school leavers received a school-leaving certificate or a certificate of passed examinations valid outside of Zlín as well. For each pupil, a special card file was created which recorded the following data: evaluation at the workshop, at school and boarding school, wages, savings and possibly scoring in the factory. The school never had a lack of applicants. Those who applied had to pass entrance exams, consisting of several parts, such as psychotechnical examinations, intelligence tests, readiness, speed of judgment, etc. Less attention was paid to the knowledge acquired at previous schools (Pochylý, 1990).

BSL were established not only for boys but also for girls. Boys were called 'young men', girls 'young ladies'. A BSL for girls was founded in 1929. In 1932, the first 420 female school leavers completed their education there. The upbringing of young girls was different from that of young men, as it was envisaged that young men would form the factory workforce, while women would only earn money for a dowry and cease working after getting married (Pochylý, 1990). In the three years of the Baťa School for Young Women programme, subjects of housework, home accounting, physical education, singing, health science, foreign languages, sewing of clothes and linen, cooking, typing, shorthand, etc. were taught. (Kolektiv autorů, 2013).

Valach (1990), too, described the Young Man and Young Woman movement as the most remarkable in the field of education. With this school, Baťa interconnected exemplary work with education. The Young Men's homes were beautiful single-storey buildings of their day, equipped with all sanitary, cultural and sports comforts. They wore uniform formal clothes, white trousers, blue double-breasted jackets, and white caps, girls wore white skirts and blue jackets. The school courses lasted three years. After getting acquainted with the entire production process, the pupils also got to know office work. They received a very decent salary-480 CSK per month, whereas the cost of living did not exceed 280 CSK. Especially for children from poor families it was a "veritable miracle". According to Valach (1990), a three-year stay at school was a marvellous start to life for young people.

Compulsory subjects for young men included accounting, business correspondence, drawing and languages. Everyone had to learn German and English. After three years of study, young men and young women became BSL school leavers, and could wear a badge with golden letters "ABŠ" (Pochylý, 1990).

Table No. 16 – Total number of BSL school leavers

Year	Number	Year	Number
1928	44	1935	2180
1929	256	1936	2567
1930	417	1937	3190
1931	663	1938	3591
1932	871	1939	3840
1933	1182	1940	4280
1934	1957		

Source: Pochylý, 1990: 89

The first class of school leavers consisted of 44 pupils, from a first year class of 80. Thus, almost half did not finish the programme. Even in the following years, according to Pochylý (1990), the school was successfully completed by only 50% pupils, which testified to its difficulty. Most of the school leavers continued to work in the Baťa enterprise. Almost a third of employees underwent a systematic training in one of the factory schools.

In 1933 and 1935, meetings of BSL school leavers were convened, where the idea of founding the ABŠ Club emerged. The elite among the ABŠ were the so-called Tomášovci. The name was derived from the boarding school, established in 1937 and named in honour of Tomáš Baťa – Tomášov. Tomášovci were obliged to go to the factory in jackets, white vests, with top hats and gloves. A lot of them carried an elegant walking stick, but in the factory, they changed clothes just like other workers. After returning from work, they learned to ride horses, play rugby, golf, debate, dance, etc. They were educated to become prominent industrial entrepreneurs (Pochylý, 1990).

In addition to the above-mentioned types of schools, the Baťa Business Academy, the Grammar School with Emphasis on Science, the School for Women's Occupations and the Music School functioned in Zlín with the support of the Baťa company (SDAZ, Zlín, Social Department II/10, inv. No. 4, c. No. 1332).

Tomáš Baťa believed in developing a good basis for young people. He knew from his own experience that the environment could shape their character, their soul. Therefore, he tried to create optimal conditions for young workers, but at the same time, he required appropriate work performance (Valach, 1990).

With the support or on the direct initiative of the plant management, a number of associations and groups was established, offering the employees self-education and entertainment. Language courses, specialised courses, cooking courses, sewing and household management courses were organized (Cekota, 1929).

To obtain further education, employees had the opportunity to attend the Study Institute. The Study Institute had two parts: (1) technological and (2) pedagogical (Pochylý, 1990). Various aids of natural science, zoological, botanical and geological collections were available in the Institute. Furthermore, there were graphical overviews of various production processes, industrial plant models, as well as a blast furnace model, a waterpower electricity generation model, an artificial silk production process model, a sugar mill model, a coal mine model, and various other models. The Higher People's School and the School of Arts had their seats in the Study Institute, too. Furthermore, courses of the Export School and various professional courses for enterprise employees took place there (SDAZ, Zlín, Social Department II/10, inv. No. 5, c. No. 1333).

All employees were offered further education in all fields through evening courses. In 1939 they had two study institutes, an equipped library and teaching staff from all fields available. Great attention was paid to language learning (SDAZ, Zlín, Social Department II/10, inv. No. 29, c. No. 1338).

Exhibitions of works of art, painting and sculpture, as well as exhibitions of pupils' works by pupils of the School of Art and pupils of Technical Schools were held at least twice a year. (SDAZ, Zlín, Social Department II/10, inv. No. 5, c. No. 1333).

There was a library with ample choice of books and a reading room at the Study Institute. There were also specialised libraries in individual departments, such as the library of designers, chemists, etc. (SDAZ, Zlín, Social Department II/10, inv. No. 5, c. No. 1333).

Training workshops were set up for adults coming from other factories. Foremen and workshop leaders deepened their knowledge in Saturday follow-up courses. On Saturday mornings, the plant manager summoned educational conferences in the administrative building which Pochylý (1990: 91) called the "University of Zlín Science".

The area of upbringing and education also includes publishing of magazines, weekly and monthly magazines. Archive materials emphasised the magazines Zlín, Svět, Náš kraj, Výběr, Průkopník and Technický rádce (SDAZ, Zlín, Social Department II/10, inv. No. 4, c. No. 1332).

One of the important educational methods was concentration of thoughts into short and witty slogans. It was based on the experience that a slogan which is constantly visible has a tremendous impact and penetrates the thinking of the subject. Slogans were found in workshops, on buildings, factory walls (Pochylý, 1990).

3.3.5 Free Time Activities and Recreation

For the social activity to be complete, it had to contain, in Baťa's opinion, a number of opportunities built upon a careful plan, which would uplift people both physically and spiritually during the time outside work (SDAZ, Zlín, Social Department II/10, inv. No. 4, c. No. 1332).

The centre of entertainment was a local ten-storey hotel – Společenský dům (Community House), located on Náměstí práce. There were dining rooms and playrooms on the ground floor, cafés with dance floors on the first floor, association rooms on the second floor and 300 guest rooms on the upper floors (SDAZ, Zlín, Social Department II/10, inv. No. 5, c. No. 1333).

The employees had inexhaustible possibilities to fill up their free time. There was a factory library with 15,000 volumes of both entertaining and professional publications (Pochylý, 1990). The S. K. Baťa Sports Club performed various sports on its own playground, tennis courts, volleyball courts, at the swimming pool and in gyms. Cycling, ski, chess, gamekeeper and other groups were organised. The fees were regulated so as to allow everyone to become a member. Baťa also operated a factory cinema with a total of 2000 seats. Two screening apparatuses played twice a night daily. There was a new programme every day with a 1CSK entrance fee. In addition to the cinema, there was also a permanent theatre in Zlín. The company used to give free tickets to its employees (Cekota, 1929).

As for musical life, there was a Music School in Zlín which in 1938 was attended by 350 pupils and included several musical ensembles. The most famous were the Dvořák Choir and the Zlín Trio. Fine art was represented by the famous Salon exhibitions (Pochylý, 1990).

The outdoor swimming pool was equipped with showers, slides and bridges to practice jumping into water. The changing rooms of the swimming pool were heated in the winter and served the non-resident employees as a place to rest during lunch breaks, so that they would not have to stay outside in cold weather. There were plenty of forests around the plant and the town. The forest paths were adapted and provided with benches which the employees could use to relax and refresh in the summer (SDAZ, Zlín, Social Department II/10, inv. No. 5, c. No. 1333). In 1937, 110 showers placed on grassy areas between individual buildings were put into operation. They were mainly intended for refreshment in the summer heat and their use was free (SDAZ, Zlín, Cutting Service II/8, inv. No. 34, c. No. 193).

For employees' refreshment and recovery, the company rented several boarding houses in Luhačovice Spa. Later, the resorts were expanded by Bystřička, boarding house Foltýn in spa Slatinice and boarding house Domov in Frenštát pod Radhoštěm. Long-term employees, whose health condition was described by doctors as so "appalling", that a stay in convalescent home was absolutely necessary, were chosen for recreational stays. These stay would regularly be one – two weeks and in extraordinary cases three-four weeks. During the patient's stay at the spa (the costs of which were fully covered), the employee's family received support in the amount of the average wage (SDAZ, Zlín, Social Department II/10, inv. No. 4, c. No. 1332). The recreational vacation was not deducted from employees' regular holidays, but it was allocated, extraordinarily, in an additional length of 14 days (SDAZ, Zlín, Social Department II/10, inv. No. 31, c. No. 1339).

3.4 Presentation of the Enterprise Social Policy in Baťa's Press

In most cases, the cutting service was provided for the Baťa enterprise by the "Central European Cutting Office ARGUS" with its seat in Prague – Smíchov. Individual reports from printed materials from the time illustrate the content of social care of the Baťa enterprise. The contributions exemplify the information preserved in the archive documents of the Baťa company. The analysis was based on a selection of documents by theoretical categories and subcategories, these can be found in the methodology of this publication.

3.4.1 Care for Employees

In the field of care for employees we find topics of psychotechnics, social inspection and care for large families of co-workers.

Psychotechnics

Modern care for working people is demonstrated by the use of lunch breaks as relaxation time. The Zlín workers could use the lunch breaks in line with their needs. Short films were shown for them, they could relax on the lawn around the fountain or spend time on sun loungers on the lawns (České slovo, 13. 9. 1944 in SDAZ, Zlín, Cutting Service II/8, inv. No. 34, c. No. 191).

An event was organised at the Baťa enterprise, aimed at strengthening the relationships with former workers living outside the Protectorate. The main organiser was the plant manager Josef Hlavnička in cooperation with the club of Baťa School of Labour school leavers. A large number of Czech books were sent to the former company co-workers during this event (Lidové noviny Brno, 25. 1. 1943 in SDAZ, Zlín, Cutting Service II/8, inv. No. 34, c. No. 191).

Supervision of 1,700 children from schools in Zlín and in Baťov was taken over by a school officer of the Baťa enterprise. This was due to the fact that the vast majority of children came from families employed in Baťa's factories. The school officer was in constant contact with children's schools and their families. He provided guidance and support wherever the child was failing for some reason. He also south to ensure children were prepared for the everyday practicalities of life. According to the period press, the function of the school officer was a great reinforcement to the Zlín school system (České slovo, 22. 11. 1942 in SDAZ, Zlín, Cutting Service II/8, inv. No. 34, c. No. 191).

To facilitate shopping for the working women of the Baťa enterprise, specific times, namely between 12 a.m.-1 p.m. and 5-6 p.m., were reserved for them at the department store and in other Zlín shops. Other co-workers and the Zlín public were advised to do their shopping outside the reserved times (Venkov Praha, 18. 8. 1942 in SDAZ, Zlín, Cutting Service II/8, inv. No. 34, c. No. 191).

Employees who had proven that they know more than one world language received a bonus of 50 CSK to their weekly wage (Spolupráce Praha, č. 12, 1936 in SDAZ, Zlín, Cutting Service II/8, inv. No. 34, c. No. 191).

Every year, the Baťa House of Service organised a Christmas Eve dinner for its employees who did not have their own home in "U Vašatů" rooms. The attendees at the dinner were given a Christmas gift of food. The best workers received a free week-long recreational stay in the Giant Mountains (Nedělní list Praha, 25. 12. 1936 in SDAZ, Zlín, Cutting Service II/8, inv. No. 34, c. No. 191).

Baťa, described as a sensible entrepreneur, introduced serving nutritious snacks after two hours of work. His young men were given the so-called English breakfast in the morning. All of this contributed to a good working mood, health and, of course, to increasing the factory performance (Hlasatel Přerov, 16. 12. 1932 in SDAZ, Zlín, Cutting Service II/8, inv. No. 34, c. No. 191).

Tomáš Baťa promoted a healthy way of life with reference to his experience from America. He constantly called for abstinence. It was forbidden to smoke in the premises of his enterprise. In this spirit, various events were implemented which the contemporary press wrote about. In 1925, an abstinence group (Abstinent Club) was founded in Zlín with 100 members in the beginning. Baťova Beseda, where alcohol and smoking were totally prohibited, was referred to as the pub of future. Smoking was forbidden in all company offices and workshops. New Year's Eve was also celebrated without alcohol and cigarettes. Celebrations of May Day in Zlín, attended by 50 thousand people in 1932, were presented as the largest alcohol-free festival countrywide (SDAZ, Zlín, Cutting Service II/8, inv. No. 34, c. No. 191).

In Baťa's workshops, the following inscription was placed: "Whoever puts garbage at home on the floor, whoever throws papers and food remnants on the floor, whoever spits on the floor, do it also here in the factory so that you can feel at home. This will make it easier for me to know what it looks like in your household and who you are… The way you keep yourself and your surroundings clean, that way it is in your household, and I can appreciate you accordingly"(SDAZ, Zlín, Cutting Service II/8, inv. No. 34, c. No. 191).

The company purchased a larger number of cars for its employees in 1931. It was interested in supplying its employees with cheap vehicles, thus allowing everyone to use a car (SDAZ, Zlín, Cutting Service II/8, inv. No. 34, c. No. 191).

Social Care – Social Inspection

In 1945, a conference of social workers of the Baťa company took place in Napajedla at the Fatra plants. The all-day programme focused on issues of convalescence, treatment and social care. The aim of the conference was to exchange experience and unify working procedures (Stráž lidu, Olomouc, říjen 1945 in SDAZ, Zlín, Cutting Service II/8, inv. No. 34, c. No. 191).

Social workers represented an element of support for employed women and mothers. Care for these women was entrusted to an institution of specially trained female social workers. Their mission was to take care of proper functioning of the household when women were employed or ill and where it was necessary to take care of children, cooking and cleaning (Večerní české slovo, 3. 10. 1944 in SDAZ, Zlín, Cutting Service II/8, inv. No. 34, c. No. 191). In 1944, Mrs. M. Mikuláštíková was a social clerk. She attended to both work and the private problems of married women. More and more women were turning to her, reflecting that she played an enormously useful role, as the newspaper České slovo states (České slovo, 30. 1. 1944 in SDAZ, Zlín, Cutting Service II/8, inv. No. 34, c. No. 191).

Baťa's labourers went on a regular two-week holiday stays to Slatinice near Olomouc. By 1943, 1300 employees participated in these stays. Every 14 days, 65 labourer holidaymakers arrived to enjoy their holiday (Večerní české slovo, Praha, 6. 11. 1943 in SDAZ, Zlín, Cutting Service II/8, inv. No. 34, c. No. 191). The sales department provided winter holidays for its sales assistants in Frenštát pod Radhoštěm. During the stay, which was free of charge for the employees, married couples were paid a family allowance. In exceptional cases, family members were also allowed to come and stay (Práce, Ostrava, 28. 10. 1943 in SDAZ, Zlín, Cutting Service II/8, inv. No. 34, c. No. 191).

The cutting service captured an article from the Venkov Praha newspaper dated 26th October 1941, in which a broadcast lecture on the activity of a worker in an industrial enterprise, called a social clerk or social inspector, was presented. The lecture focused on social care in the Baťa enterprise which was performed on a particularly large scale. The social clerk watched over the employees' health, cooperated with other departments to ensure that the working environment complied with safety and health regulations, and used factory broadcasting to give educational and informative lectures. The social clerk was also the employees' confidant and representative in various meetings with the plant management. Furthermore, he attended to young employees' morale and took care of a happy family life of the employees. He often acted as a magistrate in families or helped with both advice and debt in cases of financial indebtedness. The work outside the factory included care for accommodation, establishment and maintenance of sanatoriums, establishment of holiday convalescent homes, establishment and administration of various support funds, mediation of contacts with social institutions such as pension institutions and health insurance funds (SDAZ, Zlín, Cutting Service II/8, inv. No. 34, c. No. 191).

Factory radio was considered an interesting component contributing to employees' awareness and education. It broadcasted daily from 9 a.m. to 9.10 a.m. It was also used by the social clerk. The social clerk also introduced a special service at the Baťa company, placing a small box on the main gate into which co-workers could throw slips of paper with their problems. For instance, a husband whose wife fell ill had no time to seek a doctor because he had to go to work. That is why he threw a slip of paper into the box and, on the basis of it, the social clerk called a doctor for the employee's wife. The social clerk handled about forty cases weekly (SDAZ, Zlín, Cutting Service II/8, inv. No. 34, c. No. 191).

The social clerk Mr. Huták was presented in the press at the time as "Uncle Huták" (Zlín, 9. 5. 1941 in SDAZ, Zlín, Cutting Service II/8, inv. No. 34, c. No. 193).

An article on the establishment of several social advisory centres in the Baťa industrial enterprise was published in the Lidové noviny newspaper in June 1941. These were legal, health, tax, economic, nerve and social insurance advisory centres (SDAZ, Zlín, Cutting Service II/8, inv. No. 34, c. No. 191). There were also advisory centres of social nature. As an example, the Zlín press mentions an advisory centre for social topics. This group included an advisory centre for adolescent girls and young women, and an advisory centre for pregnant women (SDAZ, Zlín, Cutting Service II/8, inv. No. 34, c. No. 193). A career advisory centre played an important role, too (SDAZ, Zlín, Cutting Service II/8, inv. No. 34, c. No. 194).

In 1923, all employees were granted 50% discount vouchers for shoe repairs. Each labourer was given as many vouchers as there were members in his family (SDAZ, Zlín, Cutting Service II/8, inv. No. 34, c. No. 193).

In 1940, the personnel department advised on how to use the lift correctly through the Zlín paper: "The lift is a means of transport, not a conference room." In this article, we find the slogan "Who shortens his journey, extends his life" (SDAZ, Zlín, Cutting Service II/8, inv. No. 34, c. No. 194).

Care for Employees with Large Families

Baťa helped many families financially. A cash allowance, discount on rent, electricity, gas, tuition and school supplies was determined for families with four or more children. The implementation was entrusted to the Baťa Support Fund. In 1939, 256 families ,with a total of 1000 children, were included in the measure. The father of a family with the highest number of members was a baker at the Baťa Department Store, Mr. Sebastián Skála, who had eleven children (Týden, Plzeň, 2. 6. 1939 in SDAZ, Zlín, Cutting Service II/8, inv. No. 34, c. No. 191).

An overview of the individual discounts for large families can be found in an article of the Legionářská stráž Brno paper dated 2nd March 1939. Discounts on rent of a family flat, on electricity and gas amounted to 10% for each child. The discount on tuition was 50% for 4-6 children and 75% for 7 children. Parents with more than 4 children received free tickets to one cinema show each week. Families with 4-7 children were paid 50% of the costs of school books, with more than 7 children the entire costs of school books (SDAZ, Zlín, Cutting Service II/8, inv. No. 34, c. No. 191).

3.4.2   Saving and Employees' Savings Balance

In December 1938, a Monday issue of the Zlín daily paper wrote about an announced competition in domestic economy on the initiative of the company head Mr. J. A. Baťa. In particular, it was aimed at creating an exchange of experience among Zlín women on how to manage their husbands' income while still saving. Based on the tests carried out, an improvement in economy by 20 percent was expected, which would mean saving every fifth crown from the husband's income. Zlín women were also presented as an example to other women in the country (SDAZ, Zlín, Cutting Service II/8, inv. No. 35, c. No. 195).

In 1931, the savings of 25 thousand employees of the Baťa company in Zlín amounted to 101 million CSK. These savings not only insured the employees as individuals at critical times, but also secured jobs for the employees as a whole (SDAZ, Zlín, Cutting Service II/8, inv. No. 35, c. No. 195).

In 1930, the Národní Listy newspaper released an article entitled "Flight through the Baťa's World", which compared the conditions of Baťa's employees and state employees. Baťa did not only wish, but even forced his people to become capitalists. For instance, Baťa gave his co-workers a profit participation. In addition to the minimum and, in many ways, also a maximum wage, a diligent worker could earn an extra crown. At the same time, Baťa allowed his employees to lodge savings in the Enterprise Savings Bank, where the interest rate on deposits was 10%. In his School of Young Men, Baťa raised capitalists. A young man who, at the age of fourteen, entered the school and at the same time the factory, had to save up a minimum capital of 100 thousand CSK until the age of 21. The result of the article was a wish for the state administration to get inspired by Baťa (SDAZ, Zlín, Cutting Service II/8, inv. No. 35, c. No. 195).

3.4.3   School System and Education

35 municipalities in the Zlín region were involved in the Board of Trustees for youth education in Zlín. The youth were led by 311 instructors. As an example of protectorate events, the 1944 event entitled "We Sew for the Little Children" can be mentioned. The aim was to make 1,000 pairs of slippers for children aged 2-10 years, which were handed over at Christmas (České slovo, 21. 9. 1944, In SDAZ, Zlín, Cutting Service II/8, inv. No. 37, c. No. 206).

The evaluation of the Czech Social Assistance in Zlín for the first three months of 1946 proved that this institution had done a lot of work in the field of social assistance. Individual events required more than 400,000 CSK. One-time aids constituted the largest item (SDAZ, Zlín, Cutting Service II/8, inv. No. 37, c. No. 206).

The České slovo paper from January 1945 (In SDAZ, Zlín, Cutting Service II/8, inv. No. 37, c. No. 206) published a statement of activities of some departments in Zlín. In 1944, the Legal Department made 222 interventions in total, the Social Department handled 1,068 wage matters, more than 1,500 supply issues and 500 labour protection interventions. The School of Labour organised 250 courses attended by more than 5,000 people. The Department of Women organised 61 courses, mostly for housewives focusing on household work.

3.4.4   Housing

Mila Vegrová published an article entitled 'Where to Go for a Good Housing in our Country?' The content is a presentation of the high housing standard in Zlín. The author asks why it is possible to build well, in a modern way, comfortably and at a low price only in Zlín and not elsewhere (Ženská rada č. 6, 1937 In SDAZ, Zlín, Cutting Service II/8, inv. No. 38, c. No. 212).

Jaroslav Zapletal made the public acquainted with the housing question of teachers. In an article from 1939, the author points to the quality of labourers' housing in Zlín. He writes that it should be the employer's duty to take care of the teacher's flat. The Baťa company is given as an example. Zapletal writes that even the lowest Baťa's labourer lives in a better house better than a rural teacher (SDAZ, Zlín, Cutting Service II/8, inv. No. 38, c. No. 212).

In the press in 1941, the housing culture in Zlín was presented as extremely high and worthy of following. Care for good housing never ceased. The construction department was very busy in 1940. For example, it announced a competition of using the cellar space. In the field of housing care, employees considered the Baťa enterprise as one of the most advanced companies in the world (SDAZ, Zlín, Cutting Service II/8, inv. No. 38, c. No. 212).

In 1945, the Housing Board of the National Committee in Zlín received a total of 5,000 applications for flat allocation or relocation. 500 most needy applicants were selected from the total number, among them those affected by bombardment. A solution seemed to be to acquire more flats when some of Baťa plants were transferred to the border regions (SDAZ, Zlín, Cutting Service II/8, inv. No. 38, c. No. 212).

3.4.5 Social Care, Donations

The Baťa enterprise was involved in the organisation of care in the Zlín region. In 1938, the Zlín paper published an evaluation of social work in the Zlín region for the last two years (1936 and 1937). Social work was concentrated in the District Youth Care which cooperated with a number of local humanitarian corporations. The leading effort of social and health workers was to raise the living standard of population in the Zlín district. The Baťa company supported the mission of the District Youth Care most effectively. The chairwoman of the District Youth Care in Zlín was Mrs. M. Baťová (SDAZ, Zlín, Cutting Service II/8, inv. No. 45, c. No. 244).

Baťa Support Fund

After 15 years, the existence of the Baťa Support Fund (hereinafter 'BSF') was highlighted in articles of the period press as an expression of the true social feeling of the enterprise founder. Its scope of activities exceeded the usual framework of similar facilities České slovo, 18. 2. 1943 in SDAZ, Zlín, Cutting Service II/8, inv. No. 45, c. No. 239).

In 1945, BSF paid out more than 17 million CSK for purposes of social nature (childbirth allowance, long-term sickness allowance, allowance in case of death in family, betterment of widow's and disability annuities, sanatoria and medical care, housing events, support for the elderly, care for children and family members, cultural and social events, wedding gifts, social-health events, contribution to an increased operation of the dental department, support for soldiers and their families, support for university students). In the first ten months of 1946, it was already 12 million CSK. The Fund contributed heavily to the alleviation of social burdens and sought a higher living standard for its employees (Národní obroda, 28. 11. 1946 in SDAZ, Zlín, Cutting Service II/8, inv. No. 45, c. No. 239).

BSF contributed financially to the establishment of homes for the elderly in Zlín instituted by the town administration at the Baťa Hospital. The first was built in 1935, the second five years later due to a capacity shortage. All those who were unable to take care of themselves because of their old age or other ailments found shelter, maintenance, social and health security in these homes (České slovo, 2.7.1946 in SDAZ, Zlín, Cutting Service II/8, inv. No. 45, c. No. 239).

Employment of Blind and Crippled People

In April 1926 the Czechoslovak Central Care for the Blind asked the Baťa plants in Zlín, whether they would be willing to employ a few blind people in their factories as a test. The head of the company's health and social department, Dr. Gerbec, and the head of the plants very willingly agreed. The willingness of the company to employ the blind was reported to the Ministry of Social Welfare. The Minister subsequently thanked T. Baťa for his understanding of this issue. Average salaries of the blind ranged between 61-75 CSK per week. 13 activities, mostly in the area of packaging of items, were selected for the blind. In 1932, 12 blind women and 7 men were working in the company (SDAZ, Zlín, Cutting Service II/8, inv. No. 45, c. No. 239).

In 1926, the company was employing 10 blind people and prepared to accept 30 deaf-mute apprentices (SDAZ, Zlín, Cutting Service II/8, inv. No. 45, c. No. 239).

In 1935, the Social Department of the Baťa Enterprise published statistics on the number of employed people with physical disabilities:

deaf-mute	11 people
fully blind	5 people
one-eyed and with eye defects	34 people
with amputations and defects of lower limbs	76 people
without an arm	13 people
with defects of upper limbs	322 people
with deformed spine	23 people
total	484 people

Employees with physical disabilities performed their work in the same way as employees without defects and their wages were not different (SDAZ, Zlín, Cutting Service II/8, inv. No. 45, c. No. 239).

The blind proved themselves to be reliable workers in the Baťa plants. In 1942, the company was employing 20 blind people. The Baťa company was described as a pioneer in employing this group of people in Czechoslovakia (SDAZ, Zlín, Cutting Service II/8, inv. No. 45, c. No. 239).

A number of deaf-mute children from the Pilsen Institute were employed at the Baťa enterprise. Here they proved to be 100% workers. Two of the Pilsen wards earned so much in Zlín that their wage was equal to that of the Institute director. By becoming involved in the operation process, the deaf-mute became rightful members of society (Práce, 30. 7. 1946 in SDAZ, Zlín, Cutting Service II/8, inv. No. 45, c. No. 239).

Donations for the Unemployed

In 1932, the press reported on a one-million donation by the head of the Baťa enterprise, Jan Baťa, to fight unemployment. The money was donated to the Moravian-Silesian country, destined for use to enable regulatory work on the Morava River Moravě (SDAZ, Zlín, Cutting Service II/8, inv. No. 45, c. No. 241).

In 1932, Enterprise Employee Committees of the Baťa company complied with a request by the Town Council and decided to pay a heller from wages regularly on a weekly basis over to the Municipal Authority for the care of the unemployed. A special fund was created from the financial means. The money was used primarily for productive care of the unemployed. Support was granted mainly in kind (SDAZ, Zlín, Cutting Service II/8, inv. No. 45, c. No. 244).

As in other years, in 1936 the Social Department of the Baťa enterprise launched a winter relief action for families of unemployed people in the Zlín district. Almost 700 families in need in poor villages of Moravian Wallachia received, a sufficient ration of bread every week. On Christmas Eve, the company delivered large Vánočka to all poor families through the Municipal Authorities (SDAZ, Zlín, Cutting Service II/8, inv. No. 45, c. No. 241).

In 1939, an issue of the need to increase the marriage rate and fertility in order to prevent "the nation from dying off" was discussed in the Moravské slovo newspaper. Tomáš Baťa, as the first employer, understood the importance of this event with his measures for families with four or more children (SDAZ, Zlín, Cutting Service II/8, inv. No. 45, c. No. 241).

Donations to Cultural Purposes and for Schools

In 1930, the press reported about the placement of benches in the orchards of Zlín. It was a gift from the factory owner Baťa to the town (SDAZ, Zlín, Cutting Service II/8, inv. No. 45, c. No. 241).

In 1943, employees of the sales group of the Baťa enterprise abandoned Christmas and New Year's greeting cards and donated the saved amount to the Social Department of their group to purchase children's books. A book was given to every child born in the years 1929-1936. The books were distributed to a total of 3,000 children (SDAZ, Zlín, Cutting Service II/8, inv. No. 45, c. No. 241).

The Baťa enterprise distributed free tickets to theatres and cinemas. By doing so, a theatre visit was possible also for young people who otherwise could not visit theatres due to the too high interest (SDAZ, Zlín, Cutting Service II/8, inv. No. 45, c. No. 241).

3.4.6 Reflection of Press Releases

First of all, it is necessary to appreciate the rich archive of the cutting service in relation to the Baťa company, which can be studied in the State District Archives of Zlín. The press releases in most cases contributed to the positive image of the Baťa company and the social policy of its representatives. Individual partial activities and events were presented in the press, giving specific examples of their implementation. In the articles, it is possible to trace details which have not been preserved in official documents. Despite the fact that the explanatory power of the press information is reduced by the significant influence of the Baťa company owners on the content of printed materials, the preserved cuttings complement the rich archive of the Baťa company.

4. SOCIAL WORK AS AN ELEMENT OF ENTERPRISE SOCIAL POLICY METHODOLOGICALLY LED BY FMLSA OF CSSR

The basis of the socialist economy was central planning. Practical attempts to implement social planning were dominated by projects of social development plans in enterprises, so-called enterprise social plans, or comprehensive programmes of care for workers. This focus stems from the conception of social policy of that time, which emphasised particularly the employment field, and specifically the working population. According to Kutta, comprehensive programmes of care for workers were used to test the possibilities of "programming social life in individual enterprises and organizations with the aim of creating the most favourable conditions, not only for effective work but also for further all-round development of workers" (Kutta, 1980a: 14). Long-term programmes of care for employees were deemed the first stage of a social plan and a social policy instrument.

Preparation of social care plans was not generic only in our country. Materials for the 20th session of the United Nations Commission on Social Development (hereinafter 'UN'), held in New York in 1969, indicate a clear emphasis on the preventive and developmental role of social care programmes. "Social care programmes can no longer be seen as marginal activities linked mainly to charitable ways of solving social problems". According to the Commission, the programmes should be seen as: "an essential means to ensure equal opportunities and decent living conditions for all citizens and to accelerate the development of society by facilitating the desired institutional and social change, with an active participation of people in order to improve their own lives and the society as a whole" Commission, 1969: 14). During the talks, a five-year programme of social development for the years 1969-1973 was created, containing 38 sub-projects in total. As per project No. 12 (Commission, 1969: 63), the area of social planning has been shifted to enterprise social plans.

With hindsight, Tomeš (2013) described the enterprise, "development of care for workers", as a transfer of public social tasks to enterprises and municipalities. Typical for the welfare state was delimitation of social activities to employers, i.e. development of the communist concept of delimitation, leading to significant corporatisation of the welfare state. In parallel to this process, social planning of municipalities and regions took place, which basically transferred the responsibility for social care to National Committees.

Organisational care for workers should be connected with the state system of society-wide care for population. However, enterprises were supposed to build the necessary sanitary, cultural, catering, accommodation, recreational and children's facilities and to operate them using their own resources (Tomeš, 2013).

A higher social activity was required from enterprises for the following reasons: (1) enterprises were the basic social units of the state and their interest targets could not conflict with the interests of society, (2) efforts and resources expended in the system of state social services nullified the passivity of employee organisations when tackling problems (3) enterprises had enough material and personnel possibilities to create suitable conditions both for work performance of employees and for the non-working life of employees and their families, (4) comprehensive care for people increased the satisfaction of workers, motivated their work attitudes and influenced the overall results of the organisation and society as well (Šálková, 1970).

The main principles and tasks in organisational care for workers were set by the Resolution of the Government of the Czechoslovak Socialist Republic No. 66 of 1973, which laid a foundation for the system of care for working people. Comprehensive plans fell within the competence of the Federal Ministry of Labour and Social Affairs of the Czechoslovak Socialist Republic. Some larger enterprises, such as Třinec Iron and Steel Works, prepared their first enterprise social plans as early as 1971-1973. Between 1972-1974, the Czechoslovak Research Institute of Labour elaborated a methodology for planning social development of enterprise collectives, to be a framework for the years 1976 to 1980 (Kutta, 1980a).

In connection with the preparation of comprehensive programmes of social care, all ministers were assigned tasks. One of them was to specify the need for school leavers from social schools and university-educated professionals for social work for the years 1976-1980 (Kohout, 1976).

A starting point for elaborating comprehensive programmes of care for workers in enterprises was an extensive social analysis of the enterprise work collectives. Attention was focused especially on the social structure of collectives, working conditions and social climate (Kohout, Kolář, 1978). Comprehensive programmes of care for workers were considered as a partial pre-stage of social development plans for collectives in organizations. The main difference between a social development plan, as a higher type of care, and a comprehensive programme of care for workers was the presence of a target social prognosis or prediction of the future situation (Kohout, 1976).

The importance of introducing social work in enterprises rested on the assumption that if a worker experiences an unfavourable personal situation, this in turn affects their work performance and consequently causes issues in interpersonal relationships at the workplace, in their family environment, or in the worker's immediate vicinity. Preventing these situations and solving workers' problems was the task of a qualified social worker who was a desirable professional support, and at the same time, a contact person if a professional consultation with a doctor, psychologist, lawyer etc. was needed. The worker's social milieu, i.e. the family, work collective or the work performance itself were seen as the basic source of the worker's problems (Špiláčková, 2015).

One methodological aid for experimental verification of the principles of enterprise care for workers was material by Růžička and Šálková from 1971, with the title "Social Worker in Individual and Group Care for Workers in Enterprise". It was created for internal use by workers. "The authors tried to clarify the mission, status and importance of the function of enterprise social worker" (Růžička, Šálková, 1971: 53).

4.1   Characteristics of Enterprise Social Work and its Methods

Care for workers in enterprises/organisations was defined as follows: (1) In a broader sense, it was a set of measures laid down by the Labour Code and other legal regulations. This care consisted in the placement of workers, their recruitment, personal screening records, monitoring of development and their evaluation, adjustment of relations pertaining to labour law, care for professional growth, protection of life and health at work, increasing the culture of work, carrying out health insurance, drawing up applications for retirement and factory recreation. It was a whole system of personnel management. Its organisational basis was the personnel/ staff department. (2) In a narrow sense, care for workers included the work content of departments of care for workers, the so-called social departments. The main task was to provide comprehensive care for workers, to monitor and implement measures laid down by legal regulations and collective agreements, and to be an advisory unit for dealing with workers' personal matters (Polášek, Keller, Šálková, 1969).

Enterprise care for workers paid attention to social activities for workers' benefit. Those facts which adversely affected the worker's subjective profile were prioritised, that is, those which the worker perceived as inconvenience, hardship, worries and difficulties. In all cases of personal problems, the worker became the subject of social activities. The content of social activities was understood in terms of "efforts to remedy, to improve conditions for satisfying the legitimate needs of workers, or as the case may be, to prevent processes which could undermine the workers' interests". One of the main tasks of social workers was screening and actively searching for workers who needed help (Růžička, Šálková, 1971: 11).

Organisations created conditions of varied nature for the work of social workers:

- Formal conditions – by defining the work content, authority and obligations.
- Organisational and material conditions by supporting their activities within its socio-economic objectives and making workers acquainted with their mission and work tasks.
- Necessary working environment near the given workplace.
- Conditions for contacts with managers and employees of non-enterprise institutions.
- Conditions for access to necessary information, i.e. documents and records necessary for fulfilment of tasks and enabling participation in educational events on the content of social work.
- Conditions for operational discussions on their proposals to address social problems and incorporation of the approved measures to be implemented (Šálková, 1989)

The social worker's position at the enterprise was influenced mainly by the tradition and peculiarities of each enterprise. According to Šálková (1980, 1981), the basic forms of care were:

- General care for workers, so-called enterprise social service, or organised care for workers
- Individual and group care for workers

General care had an institutionalised base in the form of facilities offering to meet certain needs of all workers. For example, for health care, catering, recreation, culture, hygiene, childcare, housing and accommodation care, care for workers' qualifications. In the area of individual and group care these were e.g. departments of care for workers, in which social workers applied methods of social work, provided social-legal counselling, psychologists carried out research surveys and counselling. Archival materials indicate that, pregnant women and lone mothers, adolescents, pensioners, alcoholics, citizens of Roma origin, persons with reduced work capacity or released from serving a prison sentence, were categorised into care for groups of workers. (Šálková, 1968; Polášek, Keller, Šálková, 1969).

The relationship of general care, individual and group care, including the extent of general and special needs of workers was schematically expressed by Šálková, Tomeš (1983). General care for workers, i.e. enterprise social work services, met general needs, while individual and group social work attended to the needs of individuals and groups. Both components intertwined and complemented each other.

Diagram No. 6 – Relationship of enterprise social services and individual and group social work

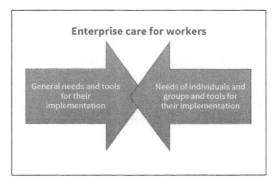

Source: Šálková, Tomeš, 1983: 76, modified

The following diagram expresses the proportion of implementation of the workers' needs within the system of care for workers, whereas the extent of care was determined by the given need.

Diagram No. 7 – Model expression of the share of implementation of the workers' needs within the system of care for workers

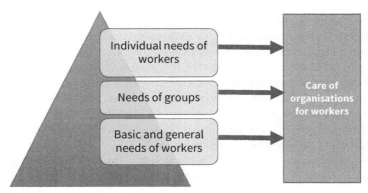

Source: Šálková, Tomeš, 1983: 77, modified

In materials from the time, enterprise social services and individual and group care for workers were collectively referred to as differentiated care for workers.

Various components of the organisation were involved in the development of differentiated care for workers. According to Šálková (1981; Polášek, Keller, Šálková, 1969) they were, for instance, managers, personal screening and personnel units (as for conceptions and coordination of social development), KPC, RTUM and SUY officials, specialists in social science (especially sociologists and psychologists, social workers conducting social analyses, formulating draft measures, in social-legal counselling and applying methods of social work), lawyers (in providing legal counselling), doctors and medical staff, work collectives and individual workers.

Social work contributed significantly to accomplishing the goals of differentiated care for workers. Literature from the period on social policy in organisations understood social work as a scientifically based professional discipline and a working method of human care, resting upon a wide system of theoretical and scientific knowledge. Social work was defined as ways, procedures and techniques of identifying and addressing social needs or a social situation or an issue of an individual, group or social unit, with the active participation of the subject to whom social work was directed (Šálková, 1981; Šálková, Tomeš, 1983). Its aim was to provide both groups and individuals with professional assistance in preventing adverse life situations and eliminating their causes and consequences. Social work included preventive measures and face to face work with people, mostly in extraordinary situations (Šálková, Tomeš, 1983).

Social work in organisations focused primarily on (a) certain groups of workers, a collective in which individuals were in a particular relationship, or groups whose members were mutually unrelated, and on (b) individual members of a collective (Šálková, 1981).

As a rule, social work was ensured by a social department or a department for staff care included in the personnel and personal screening division (Růžička, Šálková, 1971). For enterprises with up to 10 thousand workers, it was recommended to create a department of social work (Šálková, 1981). Ideally, there was a maximum of 1000-1500 workers per social worker (Šálková, 1989).

To support the need for social work in enterprises, Šálková (1980: 56) quotes the results of sociological research indicating that only 37% of men and women were not disturbed by personal and family problems at work. From this we can conclude that 63% of workers in enterprises felt problems which limited them at work, and thus could become a focus for social work.

Formation of social work in organisations was based on the social structure of working collectives consisting of people of different age, sex, education, professional orientation, health status, life experience, personal qualities, value orientation, interests, attitudes and goals (Šálková, 1980).

As stated by Šálková (1981), there were few theoretical publications on social work in the 1970s, and there were none on social work in enterprise practice. Both the theory and practice of social work in enterprises were enriched by the results of implemented research. Period literature considered the research conducted by the Technical and Economic Research Institute of Metallurgical Industry as research of the widest scope. Their research results on social work were put into practice of metallurgical enterprises and other organisations through instructions of the Director General of Iron Metallurgy, which had the nature of instructive methodological directives.

In annexes of the book by Šálková (1981) 'Social Policy of Organizations and Socio-Legal Activities' published in the series "Helping Enterprise Practice in the Management of Personnel and Social Development", we can find numerous methodological instructions of the Directorate General of Iron Metallurgy, published with the consent of the Personnel Director Dr. Zdeněk Jadrný. This confirms the great importance of the research results of the Research Institute of Metallurgical Industry, which served as a basis for methodologies precisely in this branch of industry.

Enterprise social work particularly included:

- Care for the needs of workers or their families included care for the social and health needs of workers and their families, care for housing, nutrition, transport, cultural and recreational needs, socio-legal protection and counselling, and others.
- Care for individuals and groups of workers requiring special and increased assistance in organisations included care for women, single men with a small child in care, adolescents or new workers, workers with disabilities, group care for children, care for elderly workers or workers just before retirement, in extraordinary life situations, care for conditionally convicted persons, for workers of Roma origin or care for persons released from serving a prison sentence and others.
- Care for former workers of the organisation and their families included care for pensioners, workers with disabilities due to a work accident, surviving family members, and care for workers dismissed from the organization due to structural changes (Šálková, 1971).

There were three types of enterprise educational facilities in the field of employee qualification care: factory schools of work, enterprise technical schools and enterprise institutions (Polášek, Keller, Šálková, 1969).

All the above activities (care for the needs of workers, care for individuals and groups requiring special and increased assistance and care for former workers) were complementary, intertwined and formed part of social activities. Social services/activities were carried out by means of social work. It was teamwork. The scope of services for workers was determined by the size of the enterprise, the nature of work, the regional location and the enterprise prestige as well (Polášek, Keller, Šálková, 1969).

4.2   Methods of Social Work in Enterprise Practice

Applied methods of social work were derived from the forms of social care. The methods of individual and group social work are most often mentioned (Šálková, 1981, Šálková, Tomeš, 1983).

Polášek, Keller, Šálková (1969) state that social work was methodically applied in three forms: (a) individual work which prevailed, (b) group social work, (c) social field research, e.g. in a factory or workshop.

In 1971 Růžička and Šálková included among the basic methods of social work: (1) collective or general work, (2) work with groups and (3) individual or case work.

According to Šálková (1971), socio-legal protection and counselling were implemented in the 1970s as part of individual social work. They included provision and mediation of expert information, support towards self-help, handling social affairs, written submissions to institutions on socio-legal issues, negotiating in the employee's interest with state administration bodies, institutions and individuals on issues such as social security and social welfare, issues pertaining to labour law, family, childcare, etc. In the 1980s, socio-legal activities/services or enterprise social services are already mentioned, forming an important part of social work in enterprises. The content of the services was to provide socio-legal assistance to workers in social adaptation to work at the organisation. Organisations helped workers using the service especially if they were not able to solve their social problem on their own (Šálková, 1981). The system of social work with groups of workers and individuals was a subsystem of care for workers (Šálková, Tomeš, 1983).

Social workers provided socio-legal counselling to workers who found themselves in difficult life situations or in need of advice, especially in case of family irregularities, divorce proceedings, paternity suits and maintenance adjustment proceedings, preparation of written submissions in socio-legal matters and in conflicting social situations arising between parents and children (Šálková, 1981).

An advantage of individual and group social work was a relatively low need for material and technical equipment, because its institutional arrangement was mostly of organisational and personnel nature (Šálková, Tomeš, 1983).

The applied methods of individual or group social work had these phases:

1. Social-diagnostic:
    a. Screening – searching for individuals or groups in need of social help.
    b. Establishing, creating and consolidating an optimum relationship between the individual or group and the social worker.

c. Identifying and analysing the social problem (threat in form of an undesirable phenomenon), identifying the causes, relationships and the individual's or group possibilities to solve.

d. Synthetic all-embracing view of the social problem in terms of possible solutions.

2. Social-therapeutic:

a. Projection of best practices and measures for individuals and social interventions.

b. Mobilisation of activity and all material and psychosocial resources of the individual of the group, and promoting the application of social assistance or intervention of an organisation or other social system, ascertaining the effect of measures and evaluating the results (Šálková, Tomeš, 1983: 95)

According to Šálková (1981), a basis of the individual method of social work was examination of the social situation and acquisition of available sources of material and psychological assistance, required to solve the case. It was intended to bring individuals to understand their own situation and not to impose opinions as to a solution for which they had not yet been prepared. Group social work focused on identifying and addressing the needs and interests of groups. For this purpose, various forms of group activities (working, cultural, artistic, by organising group talks, discussions, interviews on determined topics of interest or concern to the group) were used to solve the group problems.

Enterprises ensured organised programmes through factory clubs and pensioners' clubs (Šálková, 1981).

Group and individual social work helped to clarify the nature of the social issue and enabled ways in which to solve it, through either individual or group efforts to apply the necessary measures. At the same time, it was necessary to create the right conditions for the group members or the worker to participate successfully in solving the situation themselves, which usually was of the highest effectuality in respect of solving the problem permanently (Šálková, 1981).

The objective of working in groups was to act through a collective towards changing individuals' attitudes and behaviour. Its benefit was that it also developed the desired solidarity among the collective members, i.e. that workers themselves gradually implemented social work within a certain range of their activities (Šálková, 1981).

Continuous evaluation of the results achieved so far was of great importance for the course of social work. The main tool of social workers was an interview. Another necessary source of information for social workers consisted in regular visits to individual workplaces of the enterprise and the related direct contact with employees. The presence of a social worker at the workplace often speeded up the decision of a more hesitant employee to request help. Getting to know the employees' non-working environment was also part of social workers' work. Knowledge of family and personal background of members of work collectives was vital (Růžička, Šálková, 1971). Work dissatisfaction or workplace conflicts were seen as a disruptive factor transmitted to family life as well. Therefore, the effort of the social workers was to promote harmonious family relationships which became causally a prerequisite for balanced relationships at the workplace.

Another important feature of social work was a described change in its orientation from the so-called classical "social cases" to the area of care for the so-called "socially non-defective" population, such as: children and youth, working women especially with small children, workers who worked in high risk/dangerous roles and retired people. (Šálková, Tomeš, 1983). Social work thus had a significantly preventive nature.

4.3   Social Worker as an Agent of Enterprise Social Work

Social workers were entrusted with performance of social work at the enterprise. They were regarded as specialist in the field. They could be classified in four function grades:

1. Socio-legal clerk
    a. Ensures social activities
    b. Required qualifications: completed secondary specialised education, socio-legal field, 3 years of professional experience

2. Independent social clerk
    a. Manages smaller working groups and sections of care for employees
    b. Required qualifications: completed secondary specialised education, socio-legal field, 6 years of professional experience

3. Leading social clerk
    a. Manages a group of clerks and sections of care for employees
    b. Required qualifications: completed secondary specialised education, socio-legal field, 9 years of professional experience, university education in the field of humanities, 3 of experience

4. Head of the department/division of social affairs
    a. Manages care for workers in organisation
    b. Required qualifications: completed secondary specialised education, socio-legal field, 12 years of professional experience or university education in the field of humanities, 6 of experience (Šálková, 1981).

In addition to general character traits such as honesty, responsibility and others, specific personal prerequisites were required of a social worker: social initiative, independence, acceptance, sociability, intellectual prowess, civic maturity and a "basic set of fundamental moral qualities" (Šálková, 1980: 75-76). In some situations, social workers could not do without the ability to improvise (Šálková, 1968).

According to Šálková (1980), when performing social work, social workers abided by the following principles: respecting the worker's personality, maintaining confidentiality, building on the worker's individuality, building on the experiential consequences of the worker's traumatic events, communicating with people at the workplace in usual contact.

The research, "Position and Role of a Social Worker in an Enterprise", conducted by the Czechoslovak Research Institute for Labour and Social Affairs, in cooperation with the Pardubice House of Technology, was carried out within the process of developing a state economic plan (called "Working Conditions of an Intangible Nature"), and was concerned with defining the role of social workers in enterprises. Šálková (1980: 78) also reported on the research results.

Šálková's text (1980) reveals that the content of work of social workers consisted primarily of preventive measures and individual work with people, mostly in extraordinary situations, with the aim of providing help quickly. The basic and fundamental tenet of social workers' work was the principle of a comprehensive view of humans. Early detection of a signal about workers' problems was considered to be a success of social work.

Methodological manuals for performance of enterprise social work focused on the following points: (1) mission of a social worker in the organisation, (2) concept of the function of a socio-legal clerk, (3) labour relations of a socio-legal clerk, (4) personal prerequisites of a socio-legal clerk for the function performance, (5) ways of work of socio-legal clerk, (6) prerequisites and conditions for work of a socio-legal clerk, (7) initial experience of school leavers from social schools, (8) further professional development of socio-legal clerks.

An indispensable presupposition for the work of social workers in enterprises was to gain the trust of the company employees. Social workers paid a great deal of attention to the course of interpersonal contact with the company employee. Tolerance and factual self-evaluation on the part of the social worker were important for its success. Furthermore, it was essential not to impose own opinions in an authoritative way, to express the willingness to listen and to emphasise a focused interest, to try to empathise with the employee's situation. Social workers searched for enterprise workers in need of help, investigated the worker's social situation, i.e. performed diagnostics and finally proposed a solution. They maintained an individual approach to clients.

Social card files provided methodological assistance in the work of a social worker. It was used to record the activities of a social worker. Social workers made statements as to employees' requests in social matters addressed to the company management or trade union. Furthermore, they elaborated analyses of employees' social needs and reported to the company management on the work results (Růžička, Šálková, 1971). Social cards contained basic personal data such as: name, surname, date of birth, residence, status, number of children, profession, workplace. The worker's personal social history was compiled, too. Successively, the cards were supplemented by records of how the given social matter was handled, the development of the worker's social situation or their adaptation in the work collective. It seemed expedient to enter records of individual meetings into the social cards and to record crucial information important for further procedures (Šálková, 1980).

Social workers in enterprises were members of a team which professionally and systematically dealt with employees of the enterprise collective. Růžička and Šálková (1971: 23) describe the position of social workers as follows: "They examine legitimate social needs of workers, apply social work methods in enterprise practice, suggest, promote and ensure measures to improve the employees' living and working situation, thus to improve the programmed business results as well as the social and political goals of the state". The team also included sociologists or psychologists who participated in deeper analyses of social processes in organizations.

Social workers performed professionally qualified activity in enterprises. Preparation for this activity was a specialised course of study at school in social law. Future social workers encountered the area of care for workers within the school subject "Personal screening and personnel work", this was taught at both secondary and secondary technical schools of social law (Keller, Charvátová, 1977). As the number of social workers in enterprises was very low in the 1970s, it was not possible to organise effective in-service training through factory courses, meetings, seminars and training (Růžička, Šálková, 1971).

The activity of social workers in enterprise was a specific form of social care for humans. In its implementation, it respected the following principles:

- Social workers were employees of the given company, so they had to respect the political and economic concepts of the enterprise, the business goals and the decisions of its management.
- Social workers participated in the preparation and development of the personnel and social policy of the enterprise.
- Social workers maintained constant working contact with managers.
- Social workers did not accept tasks falling within the state welfare system unless there was a serious reason for doing so. On the contrary, they passed suggestions and information in regard of solving social problems on specialised

enterprise units or non-enterprise institutions and cooperated with them in implementing the proposed measures (Růžička, Šálková, 1971).

Principally, social workers were expert advisors to the enterprise management or personnel department on issues of collective, group and individual care of workers, they cooperated with specialised company departments such as the factory health centre, department of health and safety at work, the personnel department, and also with non-enterprise institutions e.g. National Committees, facilities of state health administration or courts. Furthermore, they made analyses and prepared situational reports with a view to solving the company employees' social issues comprehensively. Based on the analyses, they proposed, enforced and implemented measures to solve the worker's social problems (Šálková, 1968).

The status of social workers at the enterprise was conditioned by (a) inclusion of social activities in the system of personnel work at the enterprise, (b) relationship of the social worker and the company collective, (c) relationship of the social worker and managers, (d) relationship of the social worker to other employees, (e) relationship of the social worker to social organizations at the enterprise, (f) relationship of the social worker to non-enterprise organizations, and (g) relationship to professional institutions dealing with people at work (Růžička, Šálková, 1971).

Social workers' activities were also focused on the living conditions of workers outside the workplace. Therefore, they also entered into relations with state administration authorities and with a number of non-enterprise institutions, such as National Committees, courts, housing cooperative administrations, etc. Enterprise care was conceived in connection with the state system of social and health care. Enterprise social worker was one of the agents helping to harmonise the interconnection of the state and enterprise systems of care for people. Mutual awareness of workers' problems was a prerequisite for meeting the goals of both the enterprise and non-enterprise institutions (Šálková, 1980). Considering the continuity of services and activities of social workers, Šálková (1980) recommended modifying the methods of social work of non-enterprise social institutions to the conditions of enterprise social practice.

4.3.1 Main Tasks of Social Workers in Organisations

With their activities, social workers helped to achieve the social and economic goals of the organisation. Their activities were part of the personal screening and personnel work.

Social workers in organisations (Šálková, 1980, 1981):

- conducted analyses aimed at identifying the workers' social needs, the causes of undesirable social influences, processes and their interrelations.
- helped to resolve social problems of individuals and groups, and when fulfilling their legitimate needs and interests, they acted to ensure that the workers' conduct was not contrary to legal and moral standards or to the interests of the collective, and also helped to foster positive interpersonal relationships.
- preferentially addressed problems of those individuals and groups whose work and social adaptation was of a particular interest for the organisation, and problems of workers in difficult life situations or threatened by socially undesirable influences and processes.
- provided socio-legal consultations especially in the field of civil, labour, social and administrative legislation.
- provide employees with information on enterprise social services and activities and encouraged workers to use them.
- passed suggestions and information on social problems to other departments of the organisation, RTUM as well as non-enterprise institutions, while winning them over for solutions.
- worked with experts in the organisation and non-enterprise institutions, especially doctors, lawyers, psychologists, sociologists, educators, and other workers of social organizations, elaborated the necessary solution proposals for them, including written submissions for workers, and acted in the sense of a coordinated procedure in the social field.
- to fulfil the educational tasks, they created a network of volunteer collaborators from the ranks of collective members, and methodically directed them towards the set goals.
- acquired information and deepened their knowledge of theory and practice, particularly in social policy and social work, attended meetings, seminars, educational events focused on their activities.
- participated in the elaboration of social analyses for preparation and deepening of forecasts, concepts, programmes and plans of social development within their sphere of competence, and in their implementation.
- kept records of workers' social conditions and the ways to solve them (social card file), prepared comprehensive analytical and control reports for their area of activity with proposals for further steps to remedy the identified problems.

4.4   Employee as a Subject of Enterprise Social Work

Enterprise workers and their family members were perceived as a subject of social workers' care (Polášek, Keller, Šálková, 1969; Hodek, 1978; Šálková, 1981). The term "socially needy worker" was also used (Šálková, 1981).

For the purposes of social analyses, formulation of objectives and tasks of long-term programmes and social development plans, organisations identified groups or individual workers requiring increased attention in accordance with determined criteria. The definition of groups was not accepted as permanent and unchangeable in enterprise social work. It was based on the results of continuously conducted social analyses (Šálková, 1989). An example of such criteria is found for instance in a text by Šálková from 1981. The order of the criteria is completely random.

– Psychophysiological peculiarities of the organism and specific functions and position in the reproductive process of society (women, women with children, pregnant women)
– Age (minors, pre-retirement workers and working pensioners)
– Adverse health condition
– Unsuitable working conditions or nature of work (hazardous operations, workers separated from their families for a long time, workers performing unattractive or repulsive work)
– Economic and social priorities of workplaces or professions
– The need to accelerate the adaptation process and strengthen the desired stabilisation in the organisation (new staff)
– Temporary interruption of a closer contact with the organisation (the long-term ill, women after maternity leave, people doing military service)
– Special features of national cultures (workers and apprentices of foreign nationalities)
– Threatening by socio-pathological influences or behaviour, with reduced ability of work and social behaviour
– Cultural, especially hygienic backwardness
– The need to fulfil the moral functions of the organisation in relation to certain former employees or their family members (former employees of the organisation, retired persons)

Due to the many criteria by which employees were assigned to groups requiring increased attention, it was necessary for individual and group care to be performed by a sufficient number of "social department specialists", as stated by Šálková (1981: 27). The organisational concept and rules of the organisation functioning – the system – were tailored to this requirement.

Clients of an enterprise social worker can be divided into three groups:

– Those who sought the social worker out themselves in the event of a problem.
– Those who came to the social worker at the recommendation of their co-workers after a period of hesitation or if their problem escalated.
– Those who were indifferent to resolving their problems with the assistance of a social worker and refused interference in their personal matters (Růžička, Šálková, 1971).

Differentiated care for workers required increased attention and assistance to be paid to some workers and groups of workers, allowing for their psychological peculiarities, difficult and extraordinary situations which they were experiencing or threatened by. Within the text by Šálková (1981), as well as in other publications (Šálková, 1980; Šálková, Tomeš, 1983), we can find a definition of specific groups of workers at whom differentiated care was pointed:

1. women, particularly:
   a. expectant single mothers, lone mothers with minor children, mothers with more children, mothers taking care of a disabled child,
   b. performing work in which they are subject to increased physical and mental strain,
   c. before returning from maternity leave,
   d. women in menopause and older lone women.

2. minors, particularly:
   a. entering the work process, apprentices and school leavers,
   b. orphans and half-orphans,
   c. minors living in dormitories,
   d. young spouses,
   e. coming from children's homes, disrupted families, offenders and juveniles considered to have insufficient moral principles, including issues of alcoholism, prostitution or other anti-social influences.

3. workers:
   a. who had recently joined the company,
   b. soldiers doing their basic military service,
   c. who had applied for a flat or accommodation,

4. physically disabled workers, particularly:
   a. with reduced working capacity,
   b. at workplaces with a health risk and frequent work accidents,
   c. after a work accident or long-term ill,

5. workers whose abilities of working or social adaptation are lower than usual, particularly:
   a. workers of Gypsy origin,
   b. returnees from institutions of remedial education,
   c. violators of work discipline and absentees,
   d. recidivists and alcoholics,
   e. workers with antisocial elements of conduct,

6. family members:
   a. workers severely affected by a work accident,
   b. survivors of workers who died in work accidenta,
   c. old-age and invalided pensioners who worked in the enterprise before their retirement.

Tackling the social issue of a socially needy worker was carried out with regard to the possibilities of the given enterprise, but also in cooperation with authorities, organisations and institutions outside the enterprise.

4.5 Strengths and Weaknesses of Comprehensive Programmes of Care for Workers

Based on a methodological recommendation, between 1974 and 1975, 24 organisations were experimentally testing complex programmes of care for workers with the intention to use the acquired knowledge in the next period. During the trial period, organisations faced various obstacles to ensuring the fulfilment of these programmes. Experience of the organisations' employees was a very valuable tool for generalising the experiment results and for their application in all fields and sectors (Sborník referátů, 1976; Kutta et al., 1980a).

The experimenting organisations passed information to other enterprises at seminars, conferences, meetings, trainings, etc. At a nationwide meeting on comprehensive programmes of care held on 2nd September 1976 in Prague, contributions were presented in which both the positive and negative aspects of the programmes were outlined.

The economic results of the experiment were described as interesting. The nationwide staff fluctuation amounted to a maximum of 0,5%. However, most of the experimenting organisations achieved a deeper decline.

Table No. 17 – Decline in staff fluctuation between 1972-1975

Organisation	Fluctuation between 1972-73 in %	Fluctuation in1975 in %
Lidové spotřební družstvo Jednota Nitra	27	12,4
Východoslovenské lesy Košice	12	7
Důl 9. Květen Stonava	6,54	3,96

Source: Sborník referátů, 1976: 37

In the area of enterprise catering, three organisations showed a decline or stagnation. In other organisations, the number of those using the canteens increased by 3-10%, and in some cases even doubled. Yet the year-on-year increase of those using the services of the enterprise catering in CSSR reached only 0,6% in the period from 1973-1975.

Table No. 18 – Increase in the number of diners in enterprise catering between 1973-1975

Organisation	Number of boarders in 1973 in %	Number of boareders in 1975 in %
Státní statek Česká Skalice	7,8	16,8
Tlačiarne Martin	10,2	23
Technické služby Bratislava	23,7	34,2
Pragoexport	29,6	42,4

Source: Sborník referátů, 1976: 37

Experimenting enterprises Ostravsko-Karvinské doly and Stavební závody Praha, where the implementation of programmes in practice met with a really good methodological and consulting background, were very positively evaluated.

A record of the discussion at the nationwide meeting illustrates the above-stated positives and negatives of the comprehensive programmes (Sborník referátů, 1976).

– In Třinec Iron and Steel Works, the findings of the programme verification were positive. Many analyses were routinely carried out in the company before a programme was put into practice. In contrast to other enterprises and branches, long-term analyses of enterprises in iron metallurgy, resulting in "metallurgical" standards, were positively evaluated. Another positive experience was the introduction of a unified information system. The number of workers in individual sections was described as a negative. Implementation of care for workers required a reduction in the number of workers in the production section in favour of the personnel and social sections.

– The company Chemko, Slovchemie Strážské reported good results in the following areas: reduction of strenuous night work and material handling, decreasing accident rate, improvement of working environment, reduction of sickness rate, increased number of medical examinations, creating of conditions for recreation, improved material conditions for activities of the factory club, improved advisory care for employees going on pension, granting of loans and allocation of flats. Shortcomings occurred in the area of factory catering due to an insufficient number of workers in the kitchen and the kitchen equipment. Another problem appeared to be non-existing evaluation of the investments used in the social section. A theoretical assumption spoke of 5% of investment in the social section, but in practice this amount was not taken into account.

– In the company Konstruktiva Praha, inadequate staffing of social care was countered.

– At Důl 9. května Stonava, they scored negatively against the experimental verification that the programme had made a financial forecast which did not have the necessary coverage in the company's financial resources. They evaluated positively the extension and variability of factory recreation.

– At the District Institute of National Health in Trnava, the introduction of a programme containing social care for employees as such was considered as positive. A representative of the Institute, Mr. Vyšinský (in Sborník referátů, 1976: 85) said: "We health care workers who are actually bearers of ideas of healthy living and work, who have always helped others to solve their problems in social care, we, in fact, somehow forgot our own enterprise workers in the past".

– Klement Gottwald Steelworks (hereinafter 'KGS') in Ostrava faced shortcomings in mutual interconnectedness of the various areas of social programme activities and in interconnection of social programming to other business activities through an economic plan. As a solution, there was a proposal that all intentions and activities in the social programme should be fully supported by economic instruments and capacities. A programme of care for workers was deemed necessary, but the enterprise was not sufficiently financially prepared to implement it in practice.

– In the enterprise Perla Ústí nad Orlicí, there were negative comments as to insufficient training of personnel clerks and other workers in care for workers. To implement social policy, appropriate theoretical knowledge base was considered essential. Their suggestions included not forgetting the training centres of all levels and follow-up trainings. A positive aspect was the operation of a pre-school facility thanks to which the return rate of mothers after maternity was increased by 15%

- A representative of the District Construction Company of Český Krumlov appreciated the methodological support from the Ministry of Construction. He identified the need for issuing an instructive guide for managers, summarising all available materials of all aspects altogether. It would certainly facilitate the practical problem-solving.
- In the state-owned enterprise ČSAD Ostrava, a social programme was implemented, containing the following point:
  - Improvement of the workers' social structure
  - Improvement of working and living conditions
  - Establishment of sanity facilities, dormitories and their betterment
  - Increasing the workers' qualification and education
  - Addressing the housing issue
  - Education of youth apprentices
  - Provision of medical examinations
  - Decreasing the accident and injury rate
  - Care for pensioners, women and youth
  - In implementation of the social programme, they encountered problems in employing workers with reduced working capacity, a lack of work tools and a lack of dormitories for long-distance and foreign drivers (Konečný in Sborník referátů, 1976: 116).

Reports of representatives from companies and organisations testing the comprehensive programmes of care in practice particularly pointed to problems with unclear financing of enterprise social policy (meaning comprehensive programmes of care for workers). Another mentioned shortcoming was the width of the programmes. It covered increasingly more areas, such as increasing qualification, improving the social structure of working collectives, issues of work activity and political-educational activities. There was no sufficient bond among the comprehensive programme, the economic plan and the collective agreement. There was a lack of professionally trained workers who could put the care programmes into practice. A reduced staff fluctuation after the introduction of comprehensive care was seen as a positive aspect, which was also confirmed by sociological surveys. The experiment results showed that the comprehensive programmes increase the level of care for workers. On this basis, the Government of the CSSR decided by Resolution No. 139 of May 1975 that comprehensive programmes would be applied in all organisations (Kutta et al., 1980a). The experiment results were a basis for the government's decision to implement comprehensive plans in all socialist organisations in the period 1976-1980. Related to this was the need to conduct deeper analyses of social processes in organisations and to make sociologists, psychologists and social workers more involved in enterprise practice (Šálková, Svobodová, 1988).

4.6   Importance of Enterprise Social Work

Social work in enterprises was of a significant preventive nature. It prevented processes which could adversely affect the worker and thus secondarily, also disrupt the interests of the enterprise and society. The informal development of social work in enterprises showed positive results, as overcoming the worker's personal difficulties had the effect of stabilising the enterprise collective. Although the main importance of social work consisted in prevention, social workers were functioning mostly curatively, which meant attending to life situations and problems (Růžička, Šálková, 1971). This is also reflected in a discussion of the Section of Enterprise Social Workers at the Social Workers' Society, recorded in minutes of the meeting of 10th October 1969, stating that even the most sophisticated system of state services cannot achieve optimum results unless it involves enterprises, i.e. employers and workplaces, in certain efforts and objectives of the state social policy, and provides professional social services within their own units, whose importance in prevention and re-socialisation of individuals is clear (Šálková, 2016).

Social planning in enterprises represented complex planning which enabled programme changes in the social structure in line with the economic possibilities of the manufacturing companies. Plans of enterprise social growth included, for example, construction of factory canteens, flats, factory outpatient departments, libraries, vocational schools, factory clubs, recreational facilities, but also professional and cultural growth of the enterprise collective. The planning rested upon analyses of the company condition, often carried out on the basis of sociological surveys. These surveys were intended to particularly include research on the social climate of workshops, operations, organisational units and workplaces, research regarding work discipline, morale and conditions for the development of work activities and initiatives, research on leisure-time activities, the housing standard, transport to work, and research on issues of special groups of enterprise employees, especially women, youth, and elderly workers (Bauerová, Kolář, Růžička et al., 1972).

Social work in enterprises was of great importance for the development of professional social work, which is also evidenced by the establishment of a section at the Social Workers' Society in 1969. On 19th June 1969, a separate section of enterprise social workers was created at the Social Workers' Society. The section chairwoman was Helena Šálková from the Federal Ministry of Labour and Social Affairs, and the vice-chairwoman Ing. Anežka Červenáková from the Higher Socio-Legal School. The aim was to bring together social workers engaged in care for workers in enterprise practice. The notion of enterprise practice included agricultural and industrial plants, as well as other manufacturing and non-manufacturing organisations regardless of the size and structure of their basic unit (Šálková, 1969).

Results of social work in enterprises were achieved in the area of solving housing issues, factory catering, accident rate, sickness rate and recreation of workers. Some larger companies, such as Třinec Iron and Steel Works, prepared their first enterprise social plans in 1971-1973. Enterprises built their own flats, health care, educational, cultural, sports, recreational, catering facilities, but also factory nurseries and kindergartens. They cooperated with National Committees on the operation of certain facilities, pooling of resources, granting of contributions and in-kind assistance. In the years 1972-1974, the Czechoslovak Research Institute of Labour elaborated a methodology for planning social development of enterprise collectives, to be a framework for the years 1976 to 1980 (Kutta, 1980a).

From the above, the importance of care for workers can be deduced. Polášek, Keller and Šálková (1969) state that the progressively organised and performed care for workers was of far-reaching social importance. From an economic point of view, it contributed to the growth of both individual and enterprise labour productivity. The motivational effect on workers, associated with the care of workers, was often mentioned as well. Workers did not expect only material reward from work. From the cultural and educational point of view, care led to an improvement in objective working conditions, a higher level of relationships at the workplace, and an overall humanisation of work. From the social and health care point of view, care was deemed as a practical implementation of the principle of "everything for humans and their well-being".

Comprehensive programmes of care for workers were to be gradually improved and expanded into comprehensive social programmes of territorial units (Kutta et al., 1980b).

The social development of working collectives was legislatively regulated for the last time before 1989 by the Act on State-Owned Enterprise No. 88/1988 Coll. The main instrument consisted in economic and social development plans. The mandatory minimum for organisations was to ensure health and safety at work, occupational hygiene, health care and factory catering. Organisations covered these activities from their own resources. Beyond the scope of the mandatory minimum, enterprises could organise other services. After 1989, when democratic changes took place in the then Czechoslovak Federative Republic, a discussion began on the continuation of social work in enterprises. In connection with the economic changes, the extent of social measures implemented by enterprises from their own resources was significantly narrowed. Many companies underwent reorganisation and division into smaller units, whereas their production programme and product sales were not clarified. This naturally led to declining profits and curbs of funds for social purposes. Therefore, also a reduction in performance social work occurred.

Despite the given situation, the role of social work in enterprises was considered difficult to substitute. With the appropriate competencies and in collaboration with other experts and managers at the enterprise, enterprise social workers had greater possibilities to influence the solution for a number of workers' social problems than social workers of regional state administration bodies (Šálková, 1991). Based on the available materials, we can claim that in 1989 enterprise social work gradually began to disappear. Its tasks were taken over by a system social of services which was coming into existence in the 1990s. Nevertheless, with its content and extent of social activities, social work in enterprises significantly contributed to the development of professional social work in Czechoslovakia and in the subsequently established Czech Republic. Helena Šálková (1991) saw the future of maintaining the level of enterprise social policy in organisations of state, private or joint-stock companies only on condition of their prosperity. Berka, Šálková, Tomeš (1987) considered the main features of further development in enterprise social policy to be its internal differentiation, caused by natural differences among companies, objectively given differences among the needs of workers and the created resources to attain the targets beyond the mandatory minimum scope.

4.7   The Role of the Social Workers' Society in Application and Development of Enterprise Social Work

At the beginning of this subchapter, I would like to give factual information about the establishment, existence and re-establishment of the Social Workers' Society (hereinafter 'SWS'), especially in connection with foundation of the Section for Enterprise Social Workers. I obtained most of the data through an interview with Ing. Helena Šálková in May 2016. Hers are authentic memories of a direct participant in the establishment of the Social Worker's Society in 1968, along with supporting documents from a personal archive, listed in the references as 'Šálková, 2016'.

The profession of social worker has been in existence in Czechoslovakia since 1920, when the first school leavers of the Higher School of Social Welfare in Prague entered the profession . Establishment of the association "Organization of School Leavers from the Higher School of Social Welfare" in Prague in 1921 is directly related to the first official education in social work. Its foundation is associated with the first establishment of the Social Workers' Society. Completed education at a social school was a condition for membership in the SWS. As a result of World War II, the SWS was forced to terminate its activity. This was also due to the cessation of activities of all associations in 1948.

In January 1968, a preparatory committee met to set up a new, second SWS. The constituent meeting of SWS took place on 28th February 1969 at the Ministry of Labour and Social Affairs of CSSR in the presence of Minister František Toman. Ing. Ludmila Vávrová became the chairwoman. Honorary membership was granted to the former chairwomen of SWS Věra Vostřebalová, JUDr. Marie Machačová, Dr. Marie Machačová, Dr. Marie Krakešová and Dr. Josef Krakeš. On 28th December 1969, a preparatory committee was held to create a Section of Enterprise Social Workers (hereinafter 'the Section') within the SWS. In June 1969, the Section was established with a membership base of 70. Ing. Helena Šálková became the chairwoman. Starting from 1969, SWS was the only one to transmit and develop information on social work in all areas of social work. Membership was still subject to completion of any school of social focus, but a new option to become a member was added for those who occupied the position of social worker. Apart from the set tasks, the Section defended the social workers' interests, strengthened their authority, social status and financial evaluation as well. In the second half of 1970, Ing. L. Vávrová emigrated, meaning that SWS was threatened by dissolution. JUDr. M. Machačová took over the chairmanship and Ing. Šálková became the secretary. The duo Machačová and Šálková began negotiating to save the society which had 600 members in 1970. They managed to transfer the society into the Czech Medical Society of J. E. Purkyně under the Nurses' Society, as a Social Workers' Section. The "subsection" of social workers in enterprises functioned within its framework. As of 1ˢᵗ March 1986, the number of SWS members was 573. On 18ᵗʰ January 1990, social workers Jana Torová, Helena Šálková, Markéta Skalická, Zdenka Pflegrová, Alena Poubová and Věra Novotná met together to form a preparatory committee for the establishment of an independent SWS for the territory of the Czech Republic, a third one. On 9ᵗʰ February 1990, candidates for membership were summoned to the Assembly Hall of the Motol Hospital. 253 social workers participated. A plenary constituent meeting was held on 2ⁿᵈ June 1990, as the third organisation of the SWS in the twentieth century. The society was registered as a civic association. In 2007, it had 280 members from all over the Czech Republic.

The SWS regularly organised conferences with a thematic focus in cooperation with FMLSA. Anthologies of these meetings were published, containing the full text of the presented papers. On their basis, it was possible to trace the development of enterprise social work, to identify the methods used and define the activities of social workers. Already during the first year of the Section of Enterprise Social Workers, five professional seminars were organised, three in Prague, one in Ostrava and one in Brno. The participation confirmed the interest of social workers in obtaining information for their own work, as the annual recapitulation of the Section indicates (Šálková, 2016). The members became acquainted with findings of the issues of enterprise social work at that time, with the position of social workers, as well as with the prospects for the development of social work in factories. Thematically, the seminars focused on the fields of problems of employed women, citizens with reduced working capacity, combatting of alcoholism, and care for young people in and outside the work process.

In 1969, the Section identified the following problematic areas, to which it wanted to pay increased attention in the future:

- Clarification of the notions of social activity and care for workers
- Clarification of the task of social workers in enterprises
- Clarification of the relationship among psychologists, lawyers, sociologists, physicians etc.
- Absence of a model of social activities in the models of personnel activities
- Pay undervaluation of social workers in enterprises
- Unequipped research workplaces focusing on social work
- A lack of study materials and methodological management
- A lack of university-educated social workers as a counterweight to university-educated technicians and economists (Šálková, 2016).

At a constituent meeting of the Section in June 1969, Šálková identified one of the serious problems. In her presentation, she said: "The social worker ceased to be a social worker because the content of social work was misinterpreted as an activity ensuring the operation of the enterprise social and sanitary facilities. Thus, today's social worker manages the factory canteen, manages housing, calculates rents, ensures maintenance of social facilities, allocates vouchers for recreation, ensures medicaments for wall-mounted first-aid kits, or even ensures replacements of dirty towels with clean ones" (Šálková, 2016).

Enterprise social work was not only a matter for the Czechoslovak territory, it was also discussed at an international level. In the autumn of 1971, an international seminar of the United Nations Commission for Social Development (hereinafter 'UN') was held in Moscow to discuss issues of social work in industry. Ing. Helena Šálková, as an expert executive of the Ministry of Labour and Social Affairs of CSSR, participated in the seminar to represent the Czechoslovak Republic. The main target of the seminar was to discuss and evaluate results following from the report on industrial social care prepared by the United Nations Commission for Social Development as part of the five-year plan drawn up for the years 1969-1973. In her introductory paper, Mrs. Aida Gindy (director of the seminar on behalf of UN) highlighted the importance of social care in industry for the social development of the population and the provision of its basic needs. She informed the participants about the project "Social Aspects of Industrialisation", in which the part on social care in industry is elaborated in a balanced way. The project was prepared by the UN Secretariat in cooperation with specialists from international organisations, especially the International Labour Organisation (Šálková, 2016).

5. MEMORIES OF CONTEMPORARY WITNESSES

An important stage of historical research is the triangulation of acquired findings. Choice of the triangulation type depends on many factors, such as the existence of a living witness of the monitored period, the availability of a sufficient amount of relevant literature on the topic, or the possibility to utilise collaboration with another researcher. With regard to the topic of the treatise, I had a great opportunity and honour to contact the direct participants of social policy of Vítkovice Ironworks, the Baťa Enterprise, as well as care for workers in enterprises after 1969. I consider verifying and supplementing the findings from written sources and literature with the knowledge of living participants of the past social work practice as exceptional and unrealisable in all other scientific fields. Social work has a fully exceptional position in this respect. After all, its professional path started only at the beginning of the 20th century.

Based on the possibilities offered by Hendl (2005), methodological triangulation was used. The data were collected using the technique of a semi-standardised interview with witnesses[17] of the given period and topic.

5.1 Memories by Spouses Heczko of Vítkovice Ironworks

Arnošt Heczko (born in 1925 in Ostrava Vítkovice, Sirotčí Street), attended basic and secondary modern school in Ostrava Kunčičky. In 1941 he started his apprenticeship at the Factory Trade School of VMIC in Kotkova Street, where he passed his journeyman examinations in 1944. Subsequently, he got a job at VMIC as a moulder. He worked in the foundry until 1972, then moved to the quality management department at plant 5. He stayed there until his retirement in 1986.

Stanislava Heczková, née Šubrtová (*1930 in Hartmanice in district of Prostějov). She completed secondary modern school in Bučovice, and then began working as a maidservant in household of the headmaster of the secondary modern school Mr. Fráňa in Bučovice. She moved to Ostrava after her marriage to Arnošt in 1950. After her maternity leave in 1960, she joined the Vítkovice Ironworks, the quality department, where she remained until her retirement in 1986.

---

17 The next text is based on naration of each witnesses, so it will be told in the first person.

In April 1951, after the birth of their first daughter Marie, the newlyweds moved to the Jubilee Settlement in Ostrava Hrabůvka. The spouses died in 2018 in the stretch of fourteen days.

Mr. Heczko's Childhood in Ostrava-Vítkovice and in Ostrava-Kunčice

We lived on Sirotčí Street, but it was not a Vítkovice Ironworks flat, it was a private flat. Flats and houses were given mainly only to officials. Ordinary workers didn't receive anything. I'm from five kids. Three were older than me, two sisters and a brother. I had a younger brother, too. But he moved somewhere to Hranice. I have never seen him again. All I can remember from my childhood is that I was sitting on a window in a house at the junction of Zengrova and Sirotčí Street, and tramways were going there. There was a cop standing at the junction. He watched over me so that I didn't fall down from the window. I still remember that in 1929 it was so cold that my feet became frostbitten in my shoes. So, I didn't go to kindergarten. I don't know much about my dad. Actually, nothing. He was a Vítkovice Mining and Iron Corporation clerk. They called it "Bergbeamter". He died when I was two, I don't remember him at all. When my father died, we didn't have any benefits from Vítkovice. My mum was only receiving an orphan's pension for me. But I don't know exactly how it was then. We often went shopping to the Vítkovice shopping centre, we called it 'marketplace' or "Warenhalle". All people from the neighbourhood did their shopping there, it wasn't just for employees. Mainly there were groceries, and everything was quite cheaper there.

I was once at the Vítkovice Hospital, when our dog had bitten me. But my mother said at the doctor's that I fell down on a glass. But they recognized that it was from a dog. It was our domestic Alsatian dog. I was about a year and a half at that time. Later they told me that I had had a fight with my older brother. My brother was ten years older. And the dog thought that I was beating my brother, so he jumped at me, once on my head and then he bit my face. It is said that my dad killed him then. And there was no other hospital, so we couldn't choose where to go.

In Vítkovice, I also remember a gym next to the 'Czech House'. I think it was called Hasal. My brother and sister used to go there to do exercise.

My mum moved from Vítkovice to her home in Kunčičky. Her mum and dad were still living there, so we lived with them. And in Kunčičky I started attending the first grade. First, I went to basic school, and then to secondary modern school, which was a little further at the church. I attended two classes of the secondary modern school and then my mother died in 1938.

In Kunčičky we had bakers, the Future (cooperative store) and the Benkovský shop. I liked going there because every time we made a bigger purchase, I got a candy. But, of course, my mum bought things on credit. And once a month, when she got money, she went there to pay. That's how we lived. But I don't remember anything more from Vítkovice.

When my mother died, my sister took me with her and when she went to South Bohemia for her husband. He worked repairing roads. So, I visited the third grade of the secondary modern school in Janové u Železné rudy. Then I wanted to go to the fourth grade of the secondary modern school, but it was only in Klatovy. So, I had to go back to Kunčičky to my other sister. There I completed the fourth year of the secondary modern school, and then started my apprenticeship. But you know what it was like ... I was going from one sister to another. Each of them wanted to get rid of me after a year. I was a nuisance everywhere.

Factory School which Mr. Heczko Visited

The choice of school was not random. Vítkovice was a tradition in our family. My father, my brother, worked in Vítkovice, so I went there and today my son works there, too. When I came to the foundry, there were foremen who knew my dad. My dad died in 1927, I was two years old. And the foremen told me, yeah, it's you... and your brother is working here too, right? Yes, he was in the foundry, too. Then he changed from the foundry to the pipe mill.

I entered the factory school in Vítkovice based on an admission procedure. They wanted to see a school report from the secondary modern school. Then they determined for everybody what they were going to learn. They said, you're going there, you there. The greatest interest was in learning to become an electrician and turner. But it is clear that everyone couldn't do it. The apprenticeship lasted three years. It wasn't depending on your interest, if you'd like to do this or that, but it depended on the current needs of Vítkovice, whom they wanted to have. I know that a founder or moulder was considered as a less attractive profession.

They mostly accepted everyone for apprenticeship. For example, to become a founders and patternmaker, where I was, they accepted everyone. We had apprentice workshops at school. Then I went directly from the workshops to the foundry. There I did various things as a moulder.

The school was almost every day. For example, school was one day and then practical training in the foundry. And whether I particularly enjoyed school? I was glad to be doing an apprenticeship.

At school we got free school supplies and lunches from the ironworks. They gave us soup and a piece of bread. But in fact, it wasn't soup, just water with something and a slice of bread.

We brought our snacks to the workshops. At the workshop, there were apprentices of all three grades and four journeymen. One was in charge of two apprentices, the other of four apprentices, it was different. The foreman's name was Musial, he was German. I still remember him. But we spoke Czech everywhere, we didn't have to speak German. But Germans were employed there. They were about three or four in our class. One was from Hlučín. He told me that he didn't want to do the military service, that he was afraid.

There were about 25 of us in the patternmaker's class. As many of us started, that many of us also completed the apprenticeship. No one broke off the apprenticeship earlier. For example, in the apprentice workshop there was Polda Ronovský from Stará Bělá with me. He eventually became the foundry director; he got an engineering degree. It is also interesting that Polda accepted our son Jenda to Vítkovice into the pattern-shop. So Jenda is actually the third generation employed in Vítkovice.

As apprentices we also received some financial reward, 80 pfennigs in the first year, 90 pfennigs in the second year and one mark in the third year per month. In addition, our journeyman added 50 pfennigs to us. When I completed my apprenticeship, they automatically employed us all at Vítkovice.

Life in the Ironworks through Arnošt Heczko's Eyes

In 1944 I finished my apprenticeship, I joined Vítkovice and in 1947 I went to do my military service. I lived alternately with one or the other sister. I kept shuttling somewhere.

There were eight-hour shifts at work, but when they started bombing, we went only in the afternoon. When the air raids began in 1944, everyone was ready, so whoever had bikes or something, we all had to get out of Vítkovice quickly. I always went to hide at the slag heap, together with Polda Ronovský. And when it finished, we all returned to work. They bombed around the gas tank, blast furnaces. It was a bit destroyed there, but the factory wasn't hit. Most of the bombs fell on the iron ore storage place. This is today's Rudná street in Kunčičky. There used to be a mill where ore was ground. A wagon went up the hill and the ore fell into the mill. 92 bombs were dropped there. We counted the holes that were created. They released the bombs early. If they had let them drop a little later, the blast furnaces would have been hit directly. When I was working in the foundry after school, we used to run to Kunčičky during air raids.

Surely there was a difference between working as an apprentice and as an employee. We were working for ourselves. We were evaluated as a "squad". And then we split the earned money among ourselves. Of course, the youngest got the least and the older got more. At the foundry, there were for example 5 to 6 such squads. The headman divided the earned money among his people. Always in the same way. The headman always had 105%, and the others 100, 90, 80% and so on. I worked with a headman Řehák from Janovice. And when he was ill, I was the headman.

While I was living in Kunčičky with my older sister, her husband worked as a foreman in Vítkovice at the disability department. Those who couldn't use their hands or feet worked there. But I don't know if they were the ones who got injured directly in Vítkovice. They printed papers, made gloves. My brother-in-law even wanted to accept my wife there to drive the fork lift. But the doctor didn't recommend it. Then she went to the quality management department and was a head at the smithy.

The work in Vítkovice was good for us. When I wanted a bigger wage, for example for Christmas, we did overtime. Until 6 or 10 o'clock in the evening. Or we went on night shifts. In this way, we helped us to have better money and to be able to buy something. I know now people grumble that there were no bananas available then. So what. Now we can buy bananas here and what should we do with them. We didn't go abroad at that time and we don't go now, either. We don't need it. What matters for us is just Kloboučky near Brno, where we have a cottage that belonged to our grandpa. I can't complain about Vítkovice. Of course, one earned more and the other less. Then they argued. Or there were strikers who earned more. So it caused mischief among people. Otherwise there was no resentment among people.

If Vítkovice had prestige? At that time, the 'Donbas in Kunčice' – KGS – had been built. And the director told us: If you go there, you'll work in white smocks. But no way. It's not like that, even nowadays. Some of us left for the new steelworks, but only because it was closer to their homes. It wasn't for other reasons. The work was the same everywhere.

Life in the Ironworks through Stanislava Heczková's Eyes

I liked working there. I checked, stamped and released the forgings. It used to be a good time. I was in charge of the whole workshop. Next to us, there was a cylinder making plant, where they made propane-butane gas cylinders. I could do the job immediately even without the necessary education. I just had to pass some exams at school. I attended the course during the working hours. After all, I like to remember my work. I had my name there. What I had checked, they knew it was all right. It was good in Vítkovice. For example, we had sewing classes there after work.

Working morale in Vítkovice

My wife used to say that people began to work only after she arrived, that's from eight o'clock. Until then, they were just sitting. Such a relaxed morale was everywhere in Vítkovice. Many times, I got home as early as ten minutes to two o'clock. There was a time stamp clock, but the last one who was going home punched everyone out. And it was the same in the morning, for example, when I went to work at 5, I punched in everyone who came later. No one checked that someone was punching more people.

My wife had a lot of good acquaintances there. One had a tipper truck available, the other could do something else. So, when we were building a garage, one brought stone, sand or gravel for us – just what we needed. As matter of course, he brought it during the shift, he also took my wife with him in the truck, and then she didn't go back to work. Someone punched her out. The driver got 100 CSK for transport.

They were telling us that the working hours must be observed. We worked until 2 p.m., 15 minutes were intended for taking a shower. We had a snack break until half past nine or a quarter to ten. But it always stretched to ten because we used to have discussions on politics. Then the foreman came, and we all had to start working fast. So, the working hours were basically kept, but who could, they escaped earlier. For example, there were holes in the fence, so people also ran through it. And when it was a working Saturday, we were at work until about half past eight. Nobody was checking it. Everybody went home. The execs knew that were doing it, but nobody did anything about it. They let it be. It was important for us to have our work close.

Social Department

We didn't have anything with them. I don't remember that at all. It was rather the communists' realm. I had to be with them, too. In 1947, I joined the party and was lucky to have left 2 months before the Russians arrived in 1968.

Living in Jubilee Settlement

I had applied for a flat as soon as I started working. I didn't want to shuttle between my sisters anymore. And as I married my wife, we got the flat right away. The wedding speeded it up. We moved in spring of 1951, our Maruška was 2 months old. The rent was 60 CSK per month, and I had got my wage of 1100 to 1200 CSK and the deposit was 500 CSK. And my wife and I always got along with the money. But how it was with the flats, I don't know anymore. There were enough flats in 'proudovky' houses (houses constructed in such a way that the builders moved continually from one house to another). But for example, the RTUM chairman had a cottage built, I think somewhere in Vratimov.

Social Benefits

We got a flat, our kids went to kindergarten. As a family, we could go on a holiday to Bílá. Not everyone could get there. It was a matter of choice. We also went on a holiday to Morávka and Staré Hamry. There was only a small villa in Hamry. But today it's flooded, it's not there anymore. We were there, I think, three or four families. I don't know how they chose who would go. They said: you're lucky, you haven't been anywhere for a long time, so you're going on a holiday. But some "sly boots" went there every year, or even more often. The holiday stays were outside the compulsory factory holidays. And there were summer camps for children, too, but our children didn't go there.

Or I remember that we were getting extra meat vouchers for the hard working. Then there were vouchers for rum. We went to get it at the "Warenhale". That was fine.

And my wife got work relief, so she could start at 8 a.m. and work until 2 p.m. because she was bringing Jenda to kindergarten. Kindergartens were automatically for all children. We didn't have to wait for a place in kindergarten. It belonged to Vítkovice.

When someone was celebrating a jubilee, or when we retired, we were given gifts. People also used to drink at the workshop on such occasions. Or we got some money for the years of work, for 25, 30, 35 years. And a small badge was added to it. It was about 1000-1500 CSK extra to the wage.

Joint Memories of Work in Vítkovice

It was good, we like to remember that time, except for the communists. Some managers were terrible. As for our manager, I didn't like him. His name was Arnošt, too. There was a draught in our workshop, we had been telling him, but he didn't do anything. Or those taskmasters. They kept cutting our money. First, we did something for 500, then they gave us only 450 CSK. Out of five percent, they gave us three or only two percent. From the beginning, we had been in RTUM. The meetings were the worst thing. They were mandatory, but we tried to escape after fifteen minutes. We were still paying contributions while retired, maybe it's still valid even today. When we went to another plant, we had to have a passing permit. Or for example, I went to JZD Stará Bělá for a check, I wrote out the passing permit, I set off to be there 8 o'clock and at 9 I was already at home. I have always been accustomed to saving. I've been saving since I was a kid, and with my wife, too. Every time when I got my wage, I tried to put an extra crown aside. My youth was worth nothing. I don't like to remember that. That's why I got married for the first time in 1945 to have a home. But it didn't work well much. At that time, I first applied for a flat, but I got it only with my wife. I cannot complain about working under the communists. We didn't mind standing in queue for bananas and oranges. We were what we were, we had what we had.

Text authorised by the Heczko spouses on 30.6.2016 in Ostrava.

5.2   Memories by Mrs. Štěpánka Vitásková of the Baťa Company

Štěpánka Vitásková, née Marková (* 1927 in Píšť) was born in the family of Štěpánka Marková, née Schaffartziková and Bohuslav Mark, a chief police officer, as the oldest of four siblings. The family lived in Píšť, later in Třebovice in Silesia. After the German occupation, her father was transferred to Vracov in South Moravia and his family moved to him. After the war, they all returned to Třebovice as repatriates. She attended basic school in Třebovice between 1933 and 1938, then three years of secondary modern school in Vracov and the fourth year in Bzenec. Between 1942-1945, she was staying in Zlín where she attended the Baťa School of Labour in 1942/1943 and in 1943/1944 the Experimental Evening Vocational School for Women's Occupations. During her schooling in Zlín, she was working in the shoe workshops of the Baťa company. She was one of Baťa's Young Women. After the end of the World War II, she returned to Ostrava, where she completed her education at the Vocational School for Women's Occupations in 1945/1946. Then she joined the Mannesmann pipe mill – later renamed Klement Gottwald Vítkovice Ironworks – as an administrative worker. In 1950 she married a technical clerk František Vitásek and they brought up four children together. She is currently living with daughter's family in Ostrava – Třebovice.

Working at the Baťa Company – Completed Schools

I was at the Baťa company between 1942-1945. I just finished school; I was 15 years old. We were repatriated from Ostrava to Vracov and from there I went to Zlín. I was staying at the third boarding school and working in shoe workshops. In the first year, I attended the Baťa School of Labour, where the subjects were only for professions in the company, for example sewing on a machine, the so-called "double needle". Everyone who started with the company had to go to the Baťa School of Labour first.

And then we could decide where to go next. There were various kinds of schools. I remember, for example, an economic school or a technical school of mechanical or construction engineering. And I chose a vocational school. It was called the Experimental Evening Vocational School for Women's Professions. I completed one year, then both universities and secondary schools in Zlín were closed. Work at the workshop was also adapted to the school. We were in the workshop from Monday to Saturday from 7 a.m. to 2 p.m., then there was lunch at the Department Store, and then at 4 p.m. the school started, going on until 8 p.m. But I think there was no school on Saturday, I can't remember exactly. We had basic subjects like Czech, German, maths and accounting, and then specialised subjects like sewing, embroidery, cooking, pedagogy. It's all in the school report/certificate. Basically, it was a preparation for housework. The next year I attended again back in Vítkovice, that was already after the war. We had Russian instead of German. When completing the education, a vocational certificate such as for seamstresses, designers was issued. But I did the general preparation. Then I found work as an administrative clerk.

Admission procedure and Joining the Company

We had a dictation, a mathematical example, and then we had psychotechnical tests. We got papers, and there were squares and circles, and they told us: Check only the squares with the right corner filled. A specific time was set for that. Then there was another interesting test. We got an envelope, a wire and a template. A square spiral was drawn on the template. And we had to bend the wire following the template in a certain time. I bent it, but wrongly, and when I straightened the wire, there was a ripple. I had been trying it for a long time, everyone had already gone, my dad was peeping in the classroom to see where I was. Then the one who was monitoring us said, please just put it in the envelope. There was also an interview, they asked me if I could sew. And I immediately said yes, I had sewed this blouse myself. So, when I was accepted, I didn't have to sew at school anymore and they assigned me directly to a workshop. It wasn't easy to get to Zlín, they didn't accept everyone. When I joined, it was in July, and just after a week the company holiday began. So, I also got a leave and went home. After the holiday, the usual regime began.

Young Women

I belonged to Young Women. Young women wore uniforms like young men, namely blue ladies' suits, white blouses, skirts. Personally, I didn't have a uniform, I didn't buy it. It wasn't mandatory. Here, for example, this is the young woman's yearbook. Various things were recorded in it. For example, a week's wages at the workshop. We had to account it for regularly. Or when I wanted to go home, I had to ask for a leave paper and my dad had to sign it at home to confirm that he saw it and checked the yearbook. Because I was a minor, I needed confirmation from both our female educator and my parents. And when I saved my money and wanted to withdraw it, I had to have my parents' confirmation.

Life at the Boarding School

I lived in room number 49, where we were about 15 or 16 girls. We slept on the bunk beds. I was a captain of the room. Points were awarded for room cleaning. After a certain period, it was also evaluated, and rewards were distributed. There was a duty system for cleaning of corridors and toilets. But when someone committed an offence, she had to help there, too. The floors in the rooms were red and we had to wax them. We put sanitary pads on our feet and polished the floor with that.

Or there was a girl with lice. She came from such a tiny village and was even more naive than I was. She was so lice-ridden. It was the first time that I had seen lice crawling on our blankets. Then they disinfected it everywhere.

Working at the Workshop

The management of buildings, workshops was interesting there. For example, we were making baby shoes and I stuck small heels on them. And, for example, someone fell ill, and I had to switch to another job. And immediately, a henchman hurried to me and brought me a voucher for milk, for soap. Every job, every position had its advantages. When I started another job, I immediately had the benefits. So, it was all really going smoothly.

The old workers rather criticised it. They said the foremen were very strict. For example, there was a foreman, Mr. Nesrsta. One worker messed something up, so Nesrsta got angry and threw that bad shoe out the window. And he told that guy he had to pay for it now. Well, the labourer got angry, too, that if he was to pay for it, then both shoes at once, and he also threw the other shoe out the window. I personally didn't experience it. They weren't so strict. It was assembly belt production. At the end of the belt, there was a headman as final check, looking at the products. Well, and if something was wrong, he called out through the intercom, for example: Miss Marková, come to the back. And I knew there was something wrong. When I did something wrong, I stayed longer after work and repaired it. But once, during the lunch break, two friends came to help me so that I didn't have to stay after work. We were three inseparable friends.

And at the porter's lodge, there were very strict checks. Once I forgot to take yarns, a spool from my home to school. So, I took one from Baťa's workshop and went to school. But in front of the porter's lodge I instead turned around and returned to the workshop with the spool. I was really frightened. They made a lot of checks of everything, bags and stuff. When I had something of mine, I had to have a special ticket for it, too.

After work, when the machines were turned off, everyone had to tidy up their workplace and sweep it into the middle aisle. Finally, a cleaner passed through the middle with a wide broom and swept it away. Those who didn't clean their own place, they had to put it away themselves. The cleaner was interested only in cleaning the middle of the workshop. He just went back and forth like a statue. A machinist came every day to check the sewing machines. And when he finished checking them, the electricity was turned on and we could start to work.

Financial and Other Benefits

I don't know anything about the profit participation, it may have been reflected in the wages somehow, but I don't know. Maybe it was different for us as apprentices.

As far as I know, we had 10% interest on deposits. But the wages there were nice, as they said. Mainly the foremen's ones. We had a weekly salary and statement. It's all listed in the yearbook. The benefits were, for example, for different groups, as was the case with the vouchers. There were vouchers for pregnant women, for children under 2 years, under 6, under 14 years, for hard working people. So, if they also granted other allowances on the same basis, I don't know. I personally got extra vouchers from Baťa just for soap and milk. And once I got an extra voucher for shoes, I believe. When we went to the vocational school, we received vouchers for the class so that we could learn to cook, sew, for ingredients, for material.

Life at the Baťa Company

They took care of us in Zlín. For example, there's an invitation to a medical check. Everything was written half in Czech and half in German. We only went to eat to the dining hall. And because there were food stamps at that time, they always cut the stamp for the meal. We couldn't even go anywhere else to eat.

Also, the female educator once sent a letter to my parents where she praised me. And I didn't even know that they had sent it.

Or there was a research institute where they lent shoes for free. Once I bought small shoes, so I went to the institute and they lent me shoes in which I had to walk in any weather for some time. Then I came to show them how they were damaged, and they either they took them back or I had to continue wearing them.

We also had dance classes in the gym. But we had only one advanced class, because the dancing was always on Sundays and on Monday, bombardment took place, the Community House was hit, and the dance classes ended. We used to go to the cinema, but we always had to have a confirmation where it was written when we were about to return. The doorman always checked it. Old Czech films were screened at the cinema, for example My Country (Má vlast), Musician Liduš-ka (Muzikantská Liduška), Madla sing for Europe (Madla zpívá Evropě).

Then there was a Board of Trustees for the Education of Youth, something like a youth union today. But I wasn't a member of any organisation. Or there were Sunday trips, games at the stadium, football was played. Otherwise, Saturday was still a working day, time off was only on Sunday. I went home once a month because it wasn't that far away for me. A friend from Nymburk used to go with me. I also went to a Catholic circle. It was led by Dr. Hlouch who then became bishop. At least, we didn't get into mischief.

Those who knew a foreign language, it was appreciated at work. But mainly boys had great opportunities. They could travel abroad. There was also a large library.

I took my dirty clothes home. Maybe there was a possibility to wash it, but I didn't use it, so I don't know about it.

Something has now come into my mind regarding disciplinary offenses. It was there, too, and I remember that some pupils were even expelled. For example, a girl named Máňa Patriková, after the lights-out, after the female educator checked us, she jumped out the window and went to the merry-go-rounds. And she told us to leave the window open so that she could come back. But she mistook the window and she crawled into room the of our female educator who was sleeping next to our room. And she got into a scrape.

Everything was for vouchers, like fabrics, so-called "dress vouchers". When I missed something, my parents had to bring it for me. Ahh, now I realize that maybe it was the reason why I didn't have the uniform because it was for the dress vouchers. There were also food vouchers, shoe vouchers, I think we were entitled to one winter and one summer pair. And at work we wore our normal clothes, we didn't have any work clothes.

At times, there were also things that we didn't like. For example, once we weren't allowed to go home because one of the 'big cheeses' was supposed to come, and we had to go to the cinema to welcome him. You can image that we all rebelled against it.

Catering

It was during the war, so that's probably why it different. In the morning we came for breakfast and we had bread with jam. But they had to prepare it in advance, so the marmalade soaked in it and the result was red bread. There was no butter at that time. And it was almost every day like that. With that we had black coffee, milk was just for vouchers. For a snack to work, we got bread with something spread on it, or my mother always gave me, for example, lard. We went to the Department Store for lunch. What I liked most, it was something called "tennis balls". These were potato dumplings and cabbage. It cost 2,50 CSK, so we didn't even have to spend a lot of vouchers. I was satisfied, and I enjoyed it. My friends, when they saw what was on the menu today, called to me: Štěpánka, tennis balls! They were joking. But otherwise the lunches were quite good. Once we had soup, a dill soup, and it seemed to me that there were algae. I found it so disgusting that I brought it back. There was a conveyor belt where dirty dishes were put. It was a self-service system. And immediately, a female educator stood next to me and asked me: How come that you're bringing your lunch back, didn't you enjoy your lunch? I didn't know what to answer, so I said it was sour. And the female educator went straightaway to the kitchen to report that the soup was sour. So, my lie didn't pay off. It seemed to me that there were algae and I told her that it was sour.

For dinner, we only went downstairs, there was a snack bar, it was called 'bifé'. We could buy there what we wanted, to get something extra, or we had something from home. But there were no kitchenettes.

Social Department

I know that there was a Social Department. But I practically didn't make any experience with it. For us apprentices, everything was handled and negotiated by the female educator. Only when I was ill, I went to a social-health institution, from where I was sent to the hospital.

There was also a small box at the porter's lodge, into which slips of paper could be inserted. For example, improvement proposals could be thrown there.

Alarms and Bombardments

Alarms were frequent at that time. I wasn't used to it from home. It meant finding our shoes quickly in the dark, put something over the pyjamas, and we couldn't even take a blanket. Then we went to a nearby forest where the shelter was. There we waited, maybe two hours, and because it was cold, I caught a cold. I had angina and I had to go to the hospital in Vizovice where I spent two months. Due to it, I developed joint rheumatism, all my joints, my hands hurt, I limped. When I told this to the headwoman at the workshop, she sent me to a doctor, it was called "at the gate". And because of joint rheumatism, I was the only one at the boarding school to have a duvet cover for sleeping.

When it was the main bombing, it mainly targeted the Department Store, kitchen, power plant, gasworks. That way, everything was defunct because it functioned with electricity, gas. So, they brought to our boarding school some sea creatures, fish to be eaten. And after that we were so thirsty! We had water at the boarding school on each floor in a kind of trough. Some girls washed their teeth, and some did the washing there. Well, it was terrible after the bombardment.

The bombing was regularly after the snack time. Before we started the break, all machines were turned off, when we returned, the machines weren't turned on anymore. So, in fact, we worked only about 4 hours. We ran into the forest during the alarms. We used to do voluntary work and helped to build the shelters. But they were just surface shelters. Once, on 20th November 1944, we came to work, and old co-workers from Moravian Wallachia said: Today, Zlín will be bombed. And they knew it because they listened to foreign radio programmes and were in contact with partisans.

Well, when the alarm started again, but it wasn't the big one of the 20th, we ran into the forest as always. But we didn't go into the shelter, we stayed outside. And then we saw a bunch of planes flying, from below we could see such small silver crosses. Something looking like a small blood sausage was falling down from one of the planes, and the older ones who already knew what it was called: that's a bomb! We all started to jump into the shelter head-first. Panic started. But the entrance was slanted, so people jumped one on the other. There were so many injuries, and it wasn't even related to the bombing. When someone died there, they just filled the cover with lime.

But on the 20th, it was the big bombardment, we went to the large shelter. It was underground because it was made by miners. Carbide lamps on the walls were emitting light. It was terrible, we felt the earth trembling. Some people cried, some prayed, some cursed. Then we got an order to go out of the shelter, there was a kind of detector at the entrance. It was November, there was so much mud everywhere, everything was muddy. We went out. Smoke was coming from Zlín. We still heard the bombing, so we thought, how come we should go out? And one person who knew, said: A timed bomb was dropped directly on the cover, but it hasn't exploded yet. So, we had to run away. We went into the woods, the other way around. When we were coming back, it was dark. We saw the boarding school buildings, especially the boys' ones. There was a piece of bed hanging here, the rest of a wardrobe there, windows completely smashed. We spent the first night still at the boarding school. There was a terrible draught because there were no windows. The next day we were given mailing-cards with the words "I'm alive and well", we added our signature and our parents' address and had to send it home. We were dirty, black. We went by train to Moravský Písek and from there on foot, because the trains didn't go any further. From that day on we didn't have to work, we went home, but we had to report after some time. I think it was every two weeks. And to make it official, we got leave from Zlín for agricultural work.

Travelling

And something more as to the travelling. The trains were so crowded, you can't imagine at all. There were people standing even in the toilets. That was horrible travelling. We agreed with the girls that we wouldn't say that we were coming from Zlín, because the Zlín girls had a reputation for being rather nasty. So that men weren't impudent with us. The female educator didn't check those who were already 18. But how could someone tell if I was 15 or 17 and a half?

I went home once a month. Those who didn't go to school worked until 5 p.m., and I only until 2 p.m. So, when I was going home on Saturday, I rushed from work at 2 to catch the train.

Evaluation by Mrs. Vitásková

I liked it there, but it was influenced by the war. Everywhere there was discipline, checks. It was very strict there. But as I say, much of it was influenced by the war.

From Zlín to Vítkovice

After the war, when I was in Vítkovice, I needed confirmation from Zlín that I went to school there. But they wrote to me that the school had ceased to exist, so they couldn't give me any confirmation. By return, I wrote to the National Committee in Zlín, and imagine that my letter and their reply were handled within one week. Such quickness. When I was dealing with something on the phone in Vítkovice, it took, I don't know how long. But in Zlín it went right immediately. They had a completely different morale there and not only in the company, but it was all over Zlín.

After the war I worked at the Mannesmann's in Ostrava-Svinov. There was such a family, relaxed atmosphere there. Discipline was missing there. My husband who also worked there often said that they roasted rabbits and cooked dog stews at the workshops. In Zlín, it would not have been possible at all. The discipline of Baťa and Vítkovice bore no comparison.

Text authorised by Mrs. Štěpánka Vitásková on 25.05.2016 in Ostrava.

5.3 Memories by Ing. Anežka Červenáková of Enterprise Social Work

Ing. Anežka Červenáková, (* 1925 in Prague) is a graduate of the University of Social Sciences in Brno, a former member of the teaching staff and teacher of personnel social work at the Prague Secondary Socio-Legal School, a member of the Section of Social Work in Enterprises within the Social Workers' Society, and at the same time an active enterprise social worker at the Tesla Hloubětín Enterprise in Prague in the 1950s. At the end of her professional life, she devoted herself to parents and children with hearing disabilities in the civic association EPHATA, which she also founded. She died in 2019.

Beginning in Enterprise Social Work

I worked at Tesla Hloubětín directly after 1945, where I also met my husband who came from Moravia, from Hradiště. I had an advantage because I was living in Hloubětín, a lot of people knew me, but most of all, they started to trust me, and I actually solved their family problems, children and so on.

Implementation of Social Work at the Tesla Enterprise

For example, I was given the task of making tea for those people and so on, just to be able to do the individual work as well. So, they gave me some sort of a "tea princess" nickname, but in these cases, it's not so bad if these people get to know you as an ordinary person. Of course, then the year 1948, that was a quite difficult situation. For my husband, it meant the end of his career. At work, there were so many little things that one could do, which the people did appreciate like: "Oh, she cares about that, too?" So, even today, in terms of pedagogy in relation to you, I would strongly highlight the practical experience of students.

I actually did the individual work mostly with those governing bodies after 1945. I also supplemented my knowledge of such things afterwards, for example, by going abroad. Two colleagues of mine, Mr. Kohout and another elaborated it in writing. And, for example, I added questions from practice to them. Kohout and his colleague, they were like twins, they also wrote the scripts for the University of Economics. De facto, I completed the University of Economics as well.

Enterprises, I personally think that a lot of business is getting into this work today. That's also why a lot of people teach it and give lectures, and I don't know what. And many times, I would find it interesting to really talk to the people, so that it's not just a political cliché.

Literature as to Enterprise Social Work

As regards printed materials, I wrote scripts on enterprise social work together with Mr. Prchal. And Ms. Věra Novotná – but we called her 'the old Věra Novotná' – wrote with Mrs. Schimmerlingová about social work. She was single, and she virtually didn't really carry out the enterprise work. So, if there was a passage on it, it's rather that Schimmerlingová got her teeth into it. Enterprise social work also depended on the size of the enterprise or the unit which it was supposed to manage, and whether it was the management function of people in the field, that is, in the factories. And also, how far, for example, trade union organisations were reflected in it.

Teaching at the Secondary Socio-Legal School in Prague

Well, to tell you the truth, I did it my way. First, it was a school of pedagogy and then of social law, if you know. I taught the subject of care for workers from a psychological point of view, and to a certain extent, I actually prepared the content based on how the students themselves perceived it.

Figure No. 1 – Photograph of teachers of the Secondary Socio-Legal School in Prague of the school year 1966/1967 from the left: Mrs. Dana Charvátová, Mrs. Ludmila Vávrová, Mrs. Anežka Červenáková.

Source: Městková, 2014

Text authorised by Ing. Anežka Červenáková on 21.06.2016 in Prague.

5.4 Memories by Ing. Helena Šálková of Enterprise Social Work

Ing. Helena Šálková (born 1933 in Prague) completed her specialised education at the Higher Socio-Legal School in Prague in 1952, graduated from the University of Economics in Prague in 1980 (postgraduate course focusing on management of social processes and planning of social development in enterprises) and completed a course in social psychology at the Faculty of Arts of the Charles University in Prague. Between 1952-1965 she worked as a social worker at the enterprise Elektropřístroj Modřany n.p. (formerly a branch plant of ČKD Prague, a state-owned enterprise, manufacturer in the field of low voltage switchgears and control gears). From 1965 to 1968 she worked at a higher management unit – Závody silnoproudé elektrotechniky

179

(High Voltage Electrical Engineering Plants), the General Directorate, and after its dissolution at the end of 1968, she moved to the newly established Federal Ministry of Labour and Social Affairs of the Czechoslovak Socialist Republic to the Department of Work Conditions, where she stayed until its liquidation at the end of 1992. After a short break, she joined the Department of Socio-Legal Protection of Children of the Municipal Authority in Prague 12 as a social worker, for a period of about 9 years. She deserves credit for renewal of the Social Workers' Society and its transfer to the Czech Medical Society. She was an initiator of the establishment of the Section of Enterprise Social Work at SWS, where she had been actively involved in development of social work throughout its existence. She was present at the inception of university education in social work in the 1990s.

Professional Activity in the Field of Enterprise Social Work

In the field of enterprise social policy and especially its important part, i.e. social work, I had been acting at various management levels for almost 50 years, and in the relatively short time of our interview, I will probably not be able to evaluate and briefly summarise my professional career.

After completing the Higher Socio-Legal School, in 1952, I joined the company ČKD Modřany, which was soon renamed Elektropřístroj, n.p. Modřany with several subordinate plants in the Czech Republic with about 50000 workers. At that time, about 1300 workers were employed at the Modřany plant, of which about 800 were in workshops, half of them women. In accordance with the regulations in force, I was assigned to the position of "social clerk" and later I performed the function of the Head of the Social Department. However, for everybody, I was a social worker. The beginnings weren't easy for me, there had been no social worker in this company, so I had nothing to build on. I didn't receive any information or materials. My boss was a sales assistant director. But I was very lucky. Throughout my studies, my leading teacher was JUDr. Marie Machačová (*1902), a graduated educator and social worker doyenne. She didn't only prepare us professionally, but also educated us to understand the importance of social work for needy individuals and groups of citizens. She taught us to understand that we must maintain absolute confidentiality about our clients' intimate problems, but in particular, that we can't expect great appreciation for our work success from our superiors, and often not even from the clients whose difficult life situation we have helped to solve with great effort. Another great benefit for my work in practice and especially for my beginnings was the profile of my studies. I started secondary school in 1948, at a time of great confusion which affected the school system as well. For example, the state Masaryk School of Social and Health Care, the College of Social and Political Sciences and others were discontinued. At the Higher Social-Health School, the curriculum was reworked in two years and the school was renamed the Higher Social-Educational, and I completed my fourth year at the Higher Socio-Legal School. From the names of schools, it is clear which subjects were preferred in the given year, i.e. besides social work, first of all health sciences, then psychology and pedagogy, and finally law. This was extremely useful when I started working in practice. Nobody was managing me in the company, and nobody was barging in my work, either. I was young, full of energy and ideals of how I would help people. I had to rest on the general theory of social work and its methods. I didn't learn much about the specification of enterprise practice during my schooling. There was no literature on this topic, and I don't even know how I got to the model and practice of care for workers of the Baťa company in Zlín. That was my model example. The disadvantage was that from 1952 until 1968, there was no professional association of social workers. But I'll tell you later about it.

Methods of Work with Employees

When I said that nobody directly managed me when I came to Elektropřístroj Modřany, don't take it absolutely. What I mean is that no one commanded me directly like "today, deal with this or that problem". As far as I can remember, the job description was very universal and general: focusing on measures, special socially justified needs of workers, preventing their adverse situations as far as possible, and assistance in solving problems which have already arisen. Very general, isn't it? I could go on and the result would be an old-fashioned methodical aid again. You certainly don't want that.

Cooperation with Other Divisions, Professionals or Territorial Authorities

At the beginning, when I started my work, I got a task, i.e. to detect problematic individuals and groups endangered by negative phenomena, to analyse their situation and to find possibilities of solutions. Such a task requires a wide cooperation with certain enterprise departments, experts acting in them, as well as with institutions outside the enterprise, but especially with foremen of the individual workshops. I cooperated particularly closely with the company physician, mainly in promoting the optimisation of working conditions and working hours for people with reduced working capacity, pregnant women or workers with health problems, etc., when the given work did not allow for early recovery or could harm the worker healthwise or otherwise. The doctor was my support in frequent conflicting negotiations with the relevant manager. We had a shift work system, incl. night shifts which I occasionally attended to get closer to the workers, so that they could contact me in case of a problem. I also had my office – for the same reasons – next to the workshops and not in the administrative building. Once I found out that underage girls were working on the night shift. I warned the foreman that in our country there had been a ban on working at night for minors since 1918, that they can work for, at most, an afternoon shift. He almost 'killed' me because he had a shortage of machine operators and had to follow the production plan. The next day, he went to complain to the company director, and I was called to come, too. The foreman accused me of sabotaging the production plan, requesting the director to ban me from such requirements. Fortunately, the director was wise and listened to my quotation of the relevant sections of the law, and on the contrary, he ordered the foreman to exclude all minor girls from his workshop from work at night. Here you can see that in this case, I used the legal knowledge from my school time.

Content of Enterprise Social Work

I dealt with countless issues, especially in favour of women, who represented a half of the plant employees. Perhaps most of all in calming family relationships, when they turned to me for help, e.g. I wrote suggestions to determine or enforce child maintenance for them, suggested and discussed financial aid for them when in need, I tried to help improve their housing, working time arrangement, etc. At that time, due to a lack of workforce, enterprises refused to allow women with small children to work only part-time in a one-shift system or to postpone the beginning of their shifts. Work normally started at 6 or 7 a.m., so they had to take children to preschool facilities incommensurately early in the morning. I also took care of the placement of children in nurseries and kindergartens, promoted construction of these enterprise facilities, or together with local authorities I searched for a piece of land for construction of a children's holiday camp. I managed to secure four hectares of meadow in a beautiful place at the Blanice River near Mirotice. I negotiated together with the Administration of Buildings and the Trade Union representatives (RTUM), to obtain financial means from the then Central Trade Union Council (CTUO). In the late 1950s, we managed to obtain 10 million CSK for the construction of the holiday camp. That was a huge sum of money. The capacity of the camp was 250 people. Until I left the enterprise, I prepared the camp every year, looked for a head of the section, organised it and was the managing head of the camp. Before I joined the company, I had organised summer and winter recreation for children, always for a maximum of 30 to 50 children in enterprise recreational facilities in Harrachov and Polubné in the Jizera Mountains.

I introduced work with pensioners, former workers, at the enterprise. For example, discussions, meetings with managers, factory catering, trips, recreation, socio-legal and other assistance, etc. I also paid attention to working conditions of older employees.

Individual Social Work

Since the beginning of my activity in practice, social-legal counselling and assistance had prevailed, i.e. the use of classical methods of social work and knowledge of sciences concerning people such as sociology, psychology, social psychology, demography, law, health science, economics, social pathology, psychiatry etc. Our generation of social workers was educated by Dr. Machačová to help people, to put emphasis on prevention, to estimate people, not to manipulate them, to lead them so that they could solve their problem themselves – not to do it for them. The basis of my work was searching for employees for whom I could help. As for the interest of employees in my help, as in all fields of social work, one came to me with a problem asking for help, the other recommended me to a manager or a co-worker, and the last group where the work was most difficult and often also unsuccessful, these were the ones who weren't interested in me noticing them at all, let alone dealing with them, i.e. alcoholics, prostitutes, violent criminals, absentees, debtors, former prisoners, etc. I don't need to tell you that working with these people was very demanding both professionally and in terms of time.

Cooperation with National Committees and Specialised Workplaces

Without broad collaboration with other professionals such as doctors, lawyers, psychologists, state administration bodies and institutions, alcohol and marriage counselling centres, superiors, the collective in which the person was working, my efforts would have been in vain. Just an example to illustrate it. An alcoholic, a very good designer and musician. His attempts at outpatient treatment failed and his wife applied for a divorce. I managed to get her to cooperate. At that time, the company, and in particular the trade union movement, had great powers to impose compulsory alcohol treatment, of course, on the basis of an expert opinion of the alcohol counselling centre and company physician. It was not easy for me, but especially not for the employee. The treatment in Lojovice near Pilsen lasted 11 months at that time! I was in constant contact both with my client and his wife all the time. He managed to abstain from alcohol for five years before I left the enterprise. He then tragically died in a car accident. He wrote me nice letters from the hospital. It's a pity that I threw them away. And another story. A young twenty-year-old employee with a two-year-old child, she came from a children's home without family background and resources. I managed, in cooperation with many others, to arrange allocation of a bedsit for her, to place her child in a nursery, and especially to equip the flat with furniture and necessary household items. Contribution for the equipment was provided by the company, too, but above all, it was my colleagues and me who furnished the flat with furniture and the necessary items.

Cooperation with Local Authorities

You may be interested to know that I have been living in the place of the company that we're talking about since my childhood. Until the mid-sixties, Modřany was a township, and only later it joined Prague. They were only 16,000 inhabitants, many of whom worked in Elektropřístroj, so I knew quite a lot of employees before I started with this company, as well as citizens working in the territorial state administration. I believe that because of my socio-legal expertise, I had always been encouraged to volunteer for this or that commission. So, a membership in the Housing and Social Commission in Modřany was a matter of course. So, don't be surprised that I could, for example, influence the allocation of a flat to a young woman endangered by prostitution. The District National Committee of Prague West was responsible for socio-legal protection of children in Modřany at that time. And what do you think I did in the interest of my clients? I succumbed to the persuasion and became a member of the Social Commission of this DNC. I don't have words for that. I had a small child myself and my husband and I took turns in shifts, he didn't have parents and my mother died when my daughter was still a small. It was extremely difficult for me. Maternity leave was only 18 weeks.

Cooperation with Non-Enterprise Institutions

Of course, I cooperated with all which could help the employees and they always contacted me when they needed something from the company or me. Let me give just an example. I initiated a patronage contract with a nearby children's home. The enterprise provided this facility with smaller technical help or handed over gifts for children e.g. for Christmas etc. I was responsible for contact with the home, and about a year or two before I left Elektropřístroj, every Saturday I arranged a takeover of six children who were taken over for a weekend by our employees, duly inquired and approved for contact with these children by the Department of Care for Children of DNC. Today, human rights defenders would probably not praise us. However, the children benefited from the stays in families because they could get to know better the objective world, animals, family relationships, trips, means of transport, etc., which was impossible in the home conditions. Four children were adopted by families, to which we took them in a Tatra 603 car at weekends.

Next Stage of Life after Leaving the Company in Modřany

I will try to give you just abridged information. After a long time of persuasion, I left Elektropřístroj for a higher management unit, the General Directorate of the High Voltage Electrical Engineering Plants in Prague 2. Its management was interested in the development of social policy and social work in about 22 companies across Czechoslovakia with almost 120,000 workers. Here, alone or with other experts, I prepared several methodological brochures for enterprise on social work and, in particular, on the mission and methods of enterprise social workers' activities. I visited enterprises and discussed the issues of social policy and social work with relevant managers and especially social workers. For social workers, there were 33 of them, I organised seminars in Prague or at an enterprise in both the Czech Republic and Slovakia, as a rule twice a year, with lectures by experts, e.g. on new legal regulations in the social field and other methods and procedures in the sphere of their activities. I worked at the aforementioned General Directorate for a short time, because at the end of 1968, these middle units were abolished, and I moved to the Department of Working Conditions at the Federal Ministry of Labour and Social Affairs of CSSR, to the position of a senior professional officer focusing on working conditions. This is the period from 1968 until 1992, when the Ministry of Labour and Social Affairs was discontinued in the autumn. I retired and after a short break, I was working as a social worker at the Department of Socio-Legal protection of Children at the Municipal Authority in Prague 12 for almost 9 years. But we won't talk about it today.

Working at the FMLSA

Again, I am at a loss from where to start to be able to inform you objectively, systematically and briefly about the broad scope of my work at this central body of state administration. Apparently, I won't manage. I'm sorry for that. It was a significant stage for me where I could apply my knowledge from my school times, but mainly from the practice of Elektropřístroj Modřany, and the opportunity to promote the procedures and targets of social policy and social work through individual ministries in enterprises and other organisations, to influence social education, promote and strengthen the position of enterprise social workers and to assist them in their demanding work by means of the methodologies issued by the FMLSA. The time of social planning was approaching. Before its introduction, Comprehensive Programmes of Care for Workers, later introduced in all organisations, were being experimented with in selected companies. I elaborated the part of the methodical instruction concerning the general care for workers and the development of social work, especially by increasing the number of qualified enterprise workers and the like. In the next five-year-plan, the programmes changed into plans of social development of enterprises. As for the methodological guideline, I was again responsible for the part concerning social work. Territorial methodologies for social planning – as far as I can remember – were worked out by the Research Institute of Labour and Social Affairs. The plans of social development of enterprises were directed and their fulfilment was evaluated up to the level of ministries and national results, also at FMSLA, as part of my agenda. Summary reports for CSSR were submitted to the Federal Government. At that time – in the second half of the 1980s, the profession of "social worker" was successfully re-included into wage regulations. Significant work was done by experts from the Research Institute of Labour and Social Affairs and especially from the Technical and Economic Research Institute of Iron Metallurgy, there in particular by prof. Doc. JUDr. Igor Tomeš, CSc.

Literature on Enterprise Social Work and the Role of the Social Workers' Society

Already at our previous meeting, I expressed my gratitude for your dedication to the history of enterprise social policy and social work. Especially when it was significantly reduced or abolished in the 1990s. Regarding the literature on enterprise social work and the function of enterprise social workers, I didn't have many theoretical or methodical publications except those published by Dr. Purkyňová, who was my predecessor at the Ministry of Social Affairs after the war. Findings implemented for people from the Baťa company in Zlín represented a significant help and inspiration for social policy, and social work within its framework.

I found both theoretical and practical support in the doyennes of social work, especially my teacher during my studies JUDr. Marie Machačová and Ing. Věra Novotná, who worked at FMLSA with a focus on seniors and the disabled. As a part of their inheritance, I received their professional publications and materials, I deposited them in the Prague City Archives and I handed over the literature to the library of the Faculty of Arts of the Charles University. I recommend finding them to you. They were really great personalities in the field of general social work. I was building on my cooperation with them, on their treatises and suggestions throughout the entire duration of my activities, even though neither of them focused on enterprise social work. As you know, I'm a co-founder of the Social Workers' Society, whose first organisation was founded in 1921, was dissolved during the World War II after which it was renewed and then discontinued again in 1948. After 1968, it was again threatened by dissolution after the chairwoman of the Society emigrated. Thanks to thr extraordinary activities of JUDr. Machačová and other female members, its transfer under the wings of the Czech Medical Association of J. E. Purkyně in 1972 was successful. I was present at negotiations at various offices. At that time, the Social Workers' Society had 600 qualified members. In 1989, a Social Workers' Forum was established and already on 2nd June 1990, a constituent meeting of the independent Social Workers Society of the Czech Republic, which has been active up to now, was held.

A section of 70 enterprise social workers was created. I digressed from the topic a bit, but I can't imagine the growth of social work expertise without the activities of this professional association. Every year, the Society organised at least one two-day conference and two working days with expert papers by members from various fields and by non-member invited experts. With the support of MLSA CR, a member – the conference administrator – always prepared proceedings with the presented papers and handed them over to the members as a source of their further education to assist in their difficult work. I'll now return to the second doyenne of social work, Ing. Věra Novotná. It was exactly her who supported me in promoting the renewal of university studies for social workers. After several years and numerous meetings at the Ministry of Education and at universities, I managed to carry through the opening of a specialised study course of social work within the Department of Adult Education at the Charles University in Prague starting from the school year 1989/1990. Today, the Department has been independent for over 20 years. The field of social work can also be studied at other universities. This is a great success.

Termination of Enterprise Social Work

In my opinion, the milestone is around the years 1991-92. Big changes occurred which I write about in Social Policy. Enterprise facilities began to be sold off: kindergartens, nurseries, children's holiday camps… For example, Elektropřístroj has only 80 employees today. There are 20 other companies within the enterprise compound. It was bought by private individuals who made from the original facilities something with a completely different purpose. Social care is expensive, that's why it's no longer done. It's all about finance. And then, it was also affected by restitutions. Our department was dissolved in 1992. Once the state shifted care to enterprises, so now it has turned about and enterprises have returned it to the state.

Thanks for your work in the restoration and development of enterprise social work and the position of social workers in this field.

Text authorised by Ing. Helena Šálková on 24.06.2016 in Prague.

6. SUMMARISING THE FINDINGS

The aim of the treatise was, based on the study of primary sources of written nature in particular, to describe and analyse enterprise social policies of selected entities from the territory of Bohemia and Moravia implemented mainly in the twentieth century. Furthermore, its aim was to describe the areas of enterprise social welfare including institutions and social services offered to employees, and to identify the applied methods of social work, with regard to constitution of enterprise social work as one of the areas of social work performance.

The treatise objective was divided into the following research questions:

1. What did the development and implementation of enterprise social policy of Vítkovice Ironworks look like in the years 1876-1954, and which social institutions and social services were offered to employees?
2. What did the development and implementation of enterprise social policy of the Baťa company look like in the years 1900-1945, and which social institutions and social services were offered to employees?
3. What did the development and implementation of enterprise social policy in the period 1969-1989, carried out through comprehensive programmes of care for workers, look like?
4. Which areas of interest were included in enterprise social policies and comprehensive programmes of care for workers in selected entities in the defined territory and in the period under review?
5. How, if at all, did the development and implementation of enterprise social work of the selected entities take place in the defined territory and monitored period?
6. What did social work, performed in enterprises in the context of the prevalent paradigm of social policy, look like?

The subchapters below provide structurally ordered answers to these research questions.

6.1 Development and Implementation of Enterprise Social Policy of Vítkovice Ironworks between 1876-1954

Some studies positively commented on the social "programme" of the ironworks, while supporting and appreciating the social activities of the company management. Other theses expressed the opposite opinion, most often in the sense of Marxist theories, comparing the social system to "throwing a gnawed bone", as a means of labourers' exploitation. Contemporary specialised texts (Jemelka, Ševeček, Bernhardt) present the Vítkovice phenomenon as a typical example of a corporate town or even a modern-day settlement. This comparison deserves a follow-up analysis by other researchers.

Vítkovice Ironworks had been building social facilities almost since the beginning of its existence. The greatest share of development in the social area is connected with the year 1876 and the start of Ing. P. Kupelwieser as a new director general. A new entrepreneurial strategy aimed at building a sophisticated and structured form of assistance was implemented, using the employee social policy as its instrument. Kupelwieser had gained experience in managing a company in several previous jobs. As stated by Myška (2007), he applied Austrian, German, English and Belgian managerial models of company management.

In a primary document by the author Schwenger, the social policy of VI is depicted positively. The factory is compared to a social community. The factory's social measures and the social services provided in enterprise institutions met almost all employees' needs and, above all, covered the gaps which threatened the standard of living of the company employees. The extensive system of enterprise social support served as a supplementary and additional system to wages. Social services played a role in profit sharing. The VI management used the enterprise profit to implement and finance social measures, social services and institutions. The enterprise owners and managers considered this cycle as employee participation in the enterprise profit.

The implementation of social policy was probably taking place without any plan, although some authors refer to the term "social programme of VI". From the preserved materials I have not identified anything which would suggest the nature of enterprise social policy planning in the ironworks.

At the time of the foundation of the ironworks in the 1830s, Vítkovice was a village with less than two hundred inhabitants. Their predominant work was agricultural activities aimed at securing a livelihood for themselves and their families. The start of industrial activity meant a large influx of new workers from both near and far surroundings. First of all, it was necessary to accommodate the labourers with their families. Therefore, the owners of the ironworks primarily tried to ensure housing construction. Ševeček (2011) considers Baťa's housing policy to have been a very important socio-political instrument, stabilising the number of employees in the factory. Individuals were accommodated in barracks and dormitories, whole families in houses with their own farmland. Housing construction steadily continued in the years to come, but it was never enough for the large influx of labourers and their families. Having ones own flat was not only an attraction for newcomers, but also an obligation or bond to prevent labourers from leaving for other work. This could justify why the care for employees' housing was the most important part of the social "programme" of VI.

The nature of metallurgical production required continuous operation by labourers without any interruption. Stopping the production (extinguishing of the furnaces) would mean major financial losses for ironworks owners. It was therefore necessary to keep the labourers in their jobs. One of the options to make them stay was social benefits such as secured housing, stable income, health care and education for their children.

Iron production was feasible in individual technological steps only with the help of appropriately qualified workers. Each procedure required specific knowledge. The owners approached this fact in two ways. On the one hand, they attracted specialists in the field and retained them by means of higher wages and various differentiated benefits, or they qualified labourers using their own educational system. The differentiation of benefits appeared not only in wages, but it was also reflected in housing care and other areas.

In the early days of VI, the assistance focused on support in the event of incapacity for work and an accident. For this purpose, a Fraternal Treasury was established, consisting of a sickness fund and a maintenance institute. However, the Fraternal Treasury ceased to exist in 1895 in this form. After that, an enterprise health insurance fund, with reference to a legislative requirement, and a general maintenance institute managing several social funds were established. The Pension Institute dates back to the 1840s. However, financial security for old age was also linked to qualification. Only supervisors, foremen and lower officials received pensions from the pension institution. A pension treasury was established for other employees.

In the area of upbringing and education of children and youth, it is worth mentioning the financing of almost all schools in the municipality of Vítkovice, as well as the establishment of the VMIC Orphanage Foundation, children's shelter, and later nurseries and kindergartens. An important part of care for children was recreational holiday care for school children. Due to the need to ensure a supply of qualified labourers, the VI owners proceeded to apprenticeship training. The apprentices were provided with free meals, accommodation and the training included working at workshops.

At the turn of the 19th and 20th century, German was still the official language at the ironworks and at the same time the language of instruction at the Vítkovice Schools. This factor seems to be a way in which the thinking of the emerging generation at schools could be influenced, as Myška states. The ironworks management and the majority of the office staff were Germans. In the 1940s, exclusively Czech was spoken at the factory school.

Care for the labourers' health was an integral part of the extensive social 'programme', including the provision of catering, construction of a hospital, expert counselling facilities and a shelter for convalescents. A psychotechnical laboratory was used to prevent injuries. Job applicants (both labourers and apprentices) who were tested at the laboratory were then placed in adequate positions which matched their capabilities and abilities. Care for seniors involved the establishment of a foundation providing free flats for deserving workers. Generally, there were two old people's homes in Vítkovice, the so-called almshouses. In 1927, the VI management opened workshops for employees who became "disabled" due to an accident in the ironworks. After the World War II, the workshops were used to retrain healthy employees to a new, more demanded line of work. Today we would say that it was a form of retraining.

During the time of Mr. Kupelwieser's activity as director general, health care concentrated on the functioning and development of the hospital, in care for children, emphasis was put on the establishment and operation of a children's shelter, an orphanage and a nursery, and the establishment of primary schools. The field of catering focused on opening the marketplace, a grocery and canteens directly in the factory. After 1900, health care began to develop into other areas as well. Specific counselling centres were opened, employees after an endured illness were allowed to stay in convalescence, institutionalised care for seniors was created, education expanded to the level of apprenticeship training, and employees were served meals in factory canteens. It can be stated that under the leadership of Director Kupelwieser, the social measures only covered the most urgent and pressing problems, while in the later period, following the withdrawal of Director Kupelwieser, social care extended to include the field of care for seniors, people with disabilities, care for apprentice youth, health services were expanded, etc.

The Ironworks also attended to charitable activities supporting charitable organisations. For example, starting from 1901, they actively participated in the financial support of the Public Vocational School for Women's Occupations in Vítkovice, managed by the Dobromila association. Foundation and association activities were not alien to the VI owners. In addition to the orphanage or poorhouse foundation, they also established a foundation for the municipal poor and war survivors.

Thanks to the activities of social nature, the ironworks became in many ways a pioneering enterprise in the field of modern business methods with reference to the construction of Nové Vítkovice not only in the Czech lands, but also in the entire Habsburg monarchy. But even such a developed social policy was faced with the general problems of that time, and there were abandoned and orphaned children, old and helpless people, hunger and illness in Vítkovice. However, as the authors point out, there were far more satisfied people with a secure future. Influencing the local politics can be considered an important circumstance. The sophisticated personnel policy and electoral system were the reason for a repeated success of VI representatives in gaining positions in the administration of Vítkovice, thus strengthening the influence on the promotion of the company's interests.

In the archives of Vítkovice, more primary materials with a date of origin after 1945 have been preserved. Archive materials with a date of origin until 1931 are found in the archives of Vítkovice, mainly in German, which could complicate the implementation of research to some researchers. In addition to the above-mentioned activities of social nature which were preserved after 1945, social work itself, activities of the social department, the social workers' functions and roles, including the possibility of their training and involvement of VI in social research, were newly emerging. At the meeting of the Social Section in December 1949, the catalysing role of the activity of social agents in the work process was recalled. The reasoning was based on the acceleration of positive creative forces and the reduction or elimination of all negative forces which might jeopardise productive work in any way. Cultural activity of the ironworks newly came into existence, with the establishment of an enterprise club including theatre, chess and music sections, establishment of a factory library or regular film screenings.

The differentiation of social benefits continued after 1945, too. The only difference was the selection of whom would benefit from them. While before 1945 the benefits were dependent on qualifications and the number of years worked, after 1945 social benefits applied to those who "deserved it", whether they were affected by illness, accident or their family members' misfortune.

Based on a secondary analysis (thematic analysis and identification of contextual topics), the VI enterprise social policy can be virtually divided into three periods with prevalent elements of social policy. On this basis, the predominant paradigm of the VI enterprise social policy was termed in the given periods.

Table No. 19 – Paradigm of enterprise social policy of Vítkovice Ironworks

Time period	Prevalent elements of enterprise social policy	Prevalent paradigm of enterprise social policy
Period of P. Kupelwieser's management between 1876-1893 and the project of Nové Vítkovice	— Accommodating a large number of incoming employees — "Attaching" the employees to the enterprise — Care or health (hospital) — Care for children (children's shelter, basic schools, orphanage) — Catering (grocery store, canteens, marketplace) — Application of German and Austrian models, Germanization – German language as a priority (schools, official language at the enterprise) — Sufficient number of employees to secure metallurgical production — Investing in people	Targeted investment paternalistic policy of a private entity in order to ensure continuous metallurgical production = to ATTRACT employees
Interval between 1894-1945	— Reducing/suppressing reasons for strikes and forms of resistance — Preventing formation of a labour movement — Reduction of labourers' fluctuation — Increased owners' profit — Health care (almshouse, counselling centres, shelter for convalescents) — Intensive housing construction — Apprenticeship education	Tactical paternalistic policy of a private entity in order to reduce fluctuation and forms of labourers' resistance = to KEEP employees

Time period	Prevalent elements of enterprise social policy	Prevalent paradigm of enterprise social policy
Interval between 1945-1954	— Meritoriousness of social benefits — Increasing labour productivity — Increasing care for people in line with their needs — Preventing adverse social situations — Introduction of professional social workers — Social planning — Identifying the workers' needs	State directive social policy with preventive and caring elements = to CARE for employees

Source: Špiláčková, own construct

6.2 Development and Implementation of Enterprise Social Policy of the Baťa Enterprise between 1900-1945

The Baťa concern is considered by many authors (Matějček, Ševeček, Jemelka) as an example of a corporate town, the same way as Vítkovice. The only difference is that the authors add here the adjective "extraordinary". Zlín is compared to a successor of Nové Vítkovice. The stated similarity also appears in the analysis of the social policy of both private entities.

The quality of the resulting text about the Baťa company corresponds to the richness of content and quantitatively higher number of preserved primary documents, than was the case with Vítkovice Ironworks.

Tomáš Baťa drew his experience and innovative ideas from his foreign travel. He lived in Germany and visited the USA twice. The system of production and care for employees, especially in the Ford company, fascinated him so much that he decided to implement new methods of business management in Zlín as well. The most important link was the social rationalisation consisting in a system of profit participation and self-management of workshops. This created a moral bond between the company and its employees. The labourers were learning new work ethics. The employees became co-shareholders of the company with a corresponding level of profit, success and responsibility for results. Tomáš Baťa thus expressed respect for his colleagues and gave them confidence. The employees were not just common subordinates of the company owner. Baťa respected them, which was also contributed to by his way of addressing them – "co-workers". This fact was very strictly observed in all preserved documents.

Baťa's thought processes are compared to socio-economic pedagogy. He managed to combine individual benefits with the company profit. The Baťa concern became an independent state within a state. It was a functional organism containing many separate departments such as purchasing, production, sales and ancillary plants. Each department had a separate economic account with a weekly accounting. The department profit was dependent on the collective effort of all the employees at the workshop. The prosperity of the company depended on the prosperity of departments, workshops and individuals. According to Gruber (1921), however, the involvement of employees in enterprise management was nothing new, but a historically proven method of public care.

Planning was also carried out in the Baťa concern for a short time. This is evidenced by a three-year plan from 1939, which was created under the leadership of Antonín Baťa. One of the subgroups of this plan, namely the sixth, was enterprise social policy.

The Baťa company did not stay only in its home town of Zlín, but soon expanded to many cities in the then Czechoslovak Republic, abroad within Europe, but also to Asia and America. According to secondary literature, the model of Baťa's management took root very well after the World War II in Japan and Germany.

In its beginnings, the social policy system was built on the same foundations as Vítkovice. Zlín was also a small town (in 1900 only less than three thousand inhabitants), which grew very quickly thanks to the Baťa enterprise. In the first year of the company's existence, 50 labourers were working for Baťa, after twenty years the number multiplied by 1000%. The priority objective was to provide housing to a large number of new employees as the shoe workshops expanded and production increased. Baťa built satellite towns with typical single-family houses made of red brick (the same way as in Vítkovice), homes for single people, boarding schools for young men and girls. Social measures pursued the basic aims of providing housing for employees, offering possibilities of catering and ensure health care.

Baťa was very particular about the upbringing and education of young people. He did not want them to experience misery and distress as he himself had. He was of the opinion that it was better to educate professionals from the beginning of their lives in line with their needs than to "collect them on the street" later in their lives. In this regard, the Baťa School of Labour and the Young man and Young Woman movements are most frequently mentioned.

As for health care, he emphasised prevention. The main medical facility was the Baťa Hospital, which served not only the company employees, but also citizens of Zlín. As part of the hospital, specific counselling centres were established, as was the case in Vítkovice. An interesting achievement was the establishment of a Social-Health Institute within the hospital, where also institutions of social-health care such as the Cs. Red Cross, and Masaryk League against TB and District Youth Care were housed.

Children received care from the maternity hospital onwards. It was not only about health care, but each new-born child also receieved a financial gift from Baťa of 1000 CSK. Upbringing and education started in nurseries, continued in a company kindergarten, followed by a sophisticated system of primary, secondary and vocational schools. Baťa devoted extraordinary care to upbringing and education.

Care for co-workers was thought through from new-born up to senior age. Homes for old people, for people with mental or physical disabilities were established with the help of the Baťa Support Fund.

The company ensured catering in common factory canteens or through a grocery store at the Department Store and its branches. The company system was not negligent of the organisation of leisure time and recreation, either. The centre of entertainment was a Community House, and the following facilities offered entertainment and relaxation: cinema, swimming pool, sports grounds, library, various hobby groups and other leisure activities. Rented boarding houses in Moravia were used for employee recreation.

Both Tomáš Baťa and his half-brother Jan Antonín attached importance to company branding. Therefore, most institutions, funds, schools, and newly created towns bear the word Baťa in their names: Baťa Hospital, Baťa School of Labour, Baťa Support Fund, Baťov, Batawa, Batizovce and others. The public, including co-workers, were constantly reminded of who was behind their way of life, who cared for them, where their children went to school, to whom they should be grateful. Was it a way of strengthening the dependence on the employer?

Just as with lending his name to buildings etc., Baťa was also fond of short mottos and slogans, which concisely presented his thoughts, opinions, and ideas. Based on documents and witness testimony, the slogans appeared everywhere in the plant, in the workshops, on fences, in the Young Women's yearbooks, in every free space – so that the co-workers would permanently keep in mind the main principles of the company management.

All analysed archival documents are written in a comprehensible language and contain a large amount of textual information detailing historical facts. The authors of the materials paid attention to document their work duly. Obviously, it was a duty to thoroughly document and subsequently archive all activities carried out at each position of the enterprise. Only thanks to their discipline is it now possible to analyse the facts taking place in the recent past. The discipline was present not only in making written records, but it also appears in Mrs. Vitásková's memories. In the interview, she stressed that discipline was especially characteristic of Baťa, being noticeable throughout the day at the workshops, at school, in dining halls, and during leisure time.

The analysed period of social policy of the Baťa company is described as a whole, without division into specific sub-periods. After Tomáš Baťa's death in 1932, the same directors Čipera and Vavrečka were primarily responsible for running the company, which means that the social policy was not significantly changed after his death. For this reason, I consider the enterprise social policy, with its important elements in the period 1900 – 1945, to be continuous. Based on a secondary analysis (thematic analysis and identification of contextual topics), I created a description of the given period with prevalent elements of social policy. On this basis, the predominant paradigm of the enterprise social policy was termed in the given period. For the sake of clarity, the findings are presented in the form of a table below.

Table No. 20 – Paradigm of enterprise social policy of the Baťa company

Time period	Prevalent elements of enterprise social policy	Prevalent paradigm of enterprise social policy
Foundation of the Baťa company 1900-1945 (company nationalisation)	Zlín – modern town following overseas experience	Rational business policy with educational elements = to EDUCATE employees
	Triad of priorities Housing – nourishment – health (care for housing, catering and health)	
	Investing in youth	
	Care from new-born up to senior age	
	Involvement of social work	
	Participation in both profit and loss	
	Enhancing an entrepreneurial spirit	
	Activities throughout the whole day – spending of leisure time	
	Functioning of individual parts = functioning of the whole	

Source: Špiláčková, own construct

6.3 Development and Implementation of Enterprise Social Policy between 1969-1989 through Comprehensive Programmes of Care for Workers

Enterprise social policy after 1969 was implemented in practice by comprehensive programmes of care for workers. Legislatively, the main principles and tasks of care for workers were laid down in a resolution of the Government of CSSR in 1973.

For the first time, programmes in selected enterprises appeared as early as 1971 by way of experiment, from which a methodology for social development of work collectives was elaborated.

Implementing the provision of care for workers by the hands of employers meant in practice a transfer of responsibility for provision of social services from the state to lower systems, i.e. enterprises. It was not only a delegation of responsibility for the actual implementation of social plans, but also their financial coverage from the enterprise funds.

Social planning was applied not only within enterprises but was generally a basis of the socialist economy practice. The UN Commission or Social Development was also involved in the preparation of social programmes in enterprises. At its meeting in New York in 1969, it laid the foundations for a comprehensive plans of care for workers by launching a project entitled "Social Aspects of Industrialisation". In point (c), it assigned the member states a task to report on the implementation of social care in enterprises in the years 1969-1970 as a priority. The report for Czechoslovakia was submitted by Ing. Šálková at a seminar held in Moscow in 1971. Here she could already boldly report on the implementation of comprehensive plans in enterprises included in the Czechoslovak experiment. Given the political situation in the then CSSR, examples of social policy in Soviet enterprises were mainly used in practice. In specialised literature, planning successes in the Leningrad region were most frequently mentioned. Models from the domestic environment, for example from Vítkovice or Zlín, were ignored.

Comprehensive programmes of care included general care with social services for employees, as well as individual and group social care. As part of individual and group care, social workers applied methods of social work. Group social care was described as care for selected groups of employees. However, no specific methodologies of social work with a group of clients could be identified in the analysed materials.

The system of care for people was complementarily implemented at two levels. Firstly, it was the state system of social and health care ensured by National Committees in the place of residence and, at the same time, the enterprise care which plants provided for their employees. In both theory and practice of enterprise social policy, there was active cooperation between the participating agents, which was also confirmed by Ing. Šálková.

Social workers, too, were an active part in introducing comprehensive programmes into enterprise social policies. They used methods of social work, whereas individual social work and specifically socio-legal counselling clearly dominated. In relation to each other, the social worker was described as an agent and the client as a subject of enterprise social work, which is also confirmed by the then valid agent-subject paradigm applied in individual social work. University education qualification prerequisites were required for a social worker. The Social Workers'

Society responded flexibly to the need for the development of social work in enterprise practice, when the Section of Enterprise Social Work was founded through initiators around Ing. Šálková. By organising conferences and working days, social workers became acquainted with the specific performance of enterprise social work, with methods of social work, positives or negatives presented by enterprise representatives. Apart from studies at the Social-Legal School, it was, after 1969, the only way to meet the qualification requirements laid down by the MLSA.

Social work in enterprises was of a significantly preventive nature. This fact is mentioned not only in the literature of the time, Mrs. Šálková also emphasised it strongly in her interview. She said: "You as a social worker must foresee that this person is at risk. Not only when he's in trouble, then it's too late."

The positives and negatives of comprehensive programmes of care were reported in the results of experimental verification between 1974-1975. The strengths included: reduced staff fluctuation, increased number of boarders in enterprise catering, establishment of enterprise standards based on an analysis in the enterprise, introduction of a unified information system, declining accident tendency, improving the working environment, reducing the sickness rate, improving advisory care or workers and variegation of possibilities for leisure activities and recreation. Weaknesses were seen in a reduced number of workers in the production section in favour of the personnel and social sections, insufficient staffing of social care, insufficient financial coverage of activities by the enterprise and insufficient professional education of workers in care for employees.

At the legislative level, the social development of working collectives was last modified in 1988, with economic and social development plans being the main instrument. The actual end of social work in enterprise practice occurred in the 1990s, when the Department of Working Conditions of FMLSA, methodically shielding the work of social workers, was dissolved. Other factors were privatisation of companies, restructuring of companies and restitution.

The analysis of comprehensive programmes of care for workers created after 1969 consisted in an analysis of primary literature on the topic, without focusing on a particular enterprise. We can talk about general elements of enterprise social policy which the comprehensive programmes focused on. For the sake of clarity, the results of the thematic analysis are presented in the form of a table below.

Table No. 21 – Paradigm of comprehensive programmes of care for workers between 1969-1989

Time period	Prevalent elements of comprehensive programmes of care for workers	Prevalent paradigm of comprehensive programmes of care for workers
1969-1989	Social planning	Policy directed and enforced by the state based on social planning and identification of needs = to SATISFY the employees' needs
	Need of programmes and planning emphasised by UN	
	Social aspects of industrialisation	
	Agent-subject paradigm between the employer and employee	
	Transfer of responsibility and financial coverage of activities from the state to the enterprise	
	Social analyses as a tool to identify workers' needs	
	Implementation of experience from USSR	
	Satisfying the workers' needs	
	Ensuring socially balanced workers	
	Socio-legal counselling	

Source: Špiláčková, own construct

6.4 Areas of Interest Contained in Enterprise Social Policies and Comprehensive Programmes of Care for Workers in Selected Entities

The analysed social policies of Vítkovice Ironworks, the Baťa Company and the comprehensive programmes of care for workers contained identical areas of interest. They correspond to the definition of enterprise social policy according to Hilger (1996). Equally, they prioritised the following: housing, catering, health, education, recreation and convalescence, leisure time, insurance and work hygiene. Targeted care was directed especially to children and youth, women, seniors, ill people, people who had suffered work accidents, and people with disabilities. The comprehensive programmes of care after 1969 also included: care for workers in extraordinary life situations, care for lone men caring for small children, care for those on probation, for workers of Roma origin, for people released from serving a prison sentence, care for survivors, for workers dismissed due to structural changes, care for transport, socio-legal protection and counselling. The newly emerging areas of interest in enterprise social policy reflected the preventive nature of social work and its professional level attributable to its development. For the sake of clarity, a table was compiled, containing the list of areas of interest and activities of a social nature targeted at specific subjects in selected entities.

Table No. 22 – Areas of interest included in enterprise social policies of the selected entities

Entity / Area of interest	Vítkovice Ironworks	Baťa Concern	Comprehensive programmes of care for employees of FMLSA
Housing	barracks, labourers' settlements, flats or officials, foremen and labourers, factory hotel	boarding schools, homes or single people, family houses	housing care, company flats
Catering	eating houses, marketplace, canteens, factory hotel, dietary dining hall	factory canteens, Department Store, market hall, cafeterias	care or nourishment
Health	factory hospital, rescue service, Institute for Mothers and Infants, Dental Institute, hospital for infectious diseases, specific outpatient departments, psychotechnical laboratory, House of Rest	Baťa Hospital, dental care, specific departments of BN, Scientific Institute for the Study of Foot and Shoe, Social-Health-Institute of BN, Scientific Institute for Industrial Health Care, psychotechnical laboratories	care for the social and health needs of workers and their families

Area of interest \ Entity	Vítkovice Ironworks	Baťa Concern	Comprehensive programmes of care for employees of FMLSA
Education	nurseries, kindergartens, secondary modern and basic schools, workshops or apprentices, language course for Vítkovice officials	nurseries, kindergartens, Baťa School of Labour, basic schools, vocational schools, secondary modern schools, Study Institute, Higher People's School, Export School	company nurseries, kindergartens, apprenticeship education
Insurance	Fraternal Treasury, company health insurance funds, General Maintenance Institute, Pension Institution	Baťa Support Fund	-
Care for children and youth	children's shelter, orphanage, shelter for apprentices, apprentices' homes, counselling centre for infants, nurseries, kindergartens	girls' and boys' boarding schools, gift to new-borns, nurseries, kindergartens, Young Man, Young Woman	group care of workers' children, care for adolescents
Care for seniors	almshouse in Vítkovice and settlement in Rožnov pod Radhoštěm	Baťa's homes for the elderly	care for workers in senior age or just before retirement, care for pensioners
Care for handicapped people	invalids' workshop, rehabilitation workshops	employment of persons with physical disadvantage	care or employees with disabilities
Recreation, convalescence	holiday homes and settlements for children, shelter for convalescents, holiday homes for recreational purposes	rented boarding houses, spas	care for workers' recreational needs

Entity / Area of interest	Vítkovice Ironworks	Baťa Concern	Comprehensive programmes of care for employees of FMLSA
Hygiene at work	grassing of areas, planting trees, dust-free environment, lighting, bathrooms, washrooms, harmless workplaces	factory hygiene and occupational health care as a department of the Baťa Hospital, environmental culture	care for working conditions
Leisure time	swimming pools, sports hall, factory clubs, screening of films, factory broadcasting, factory magazines, library	school leavers of BSL, Community House, library, cinema, magazines, sports club, playgrounds, open-air swimming pool, hobby groups, music school, singers' group, factory broadcasting	care for workers' cultural needs
Newly			care for transport, socio-legal protection and counselling, care for workers in extraordinary life situations, care for women, care for lone men caring for small children, care for conditionally convicted, for workers of Roma origin, for people released from serving a prison sentence, care for survivors, for workers dismissed due to structural changes

Source: Špiláčková, own construct

6.5 Development and Implementation of Enterprise Social Work of the Selected Entities in the Defined Territory and Observed Period

Primary documents evidence the position of a social worker in Vítkovice Ironworks in 1945 in connection with the defined content of social care and the definition of a social worker's tasks. The notions of social worker and socio-health worker are synonymously varied, which corresponds to the concept of social work in the defined territory. Hromada (1942) describes the work of social workers in industrial plants as a practical implementation of socio-health care for workers' health and well-being. According to Hromada, social work understood in this way was already carried out in 1904 in German factories and later also in our country.

The Social Department of VI had already been in operation in 1937, as evidenced by archive sources, but they do not explicitly include the position of a social clerk or social worker. The only observation is that social care was led by inspector Langfort with six other employees. However, this historical fact does not exclude the position of a social clerk in VI before 1945.

The Ironworks operated several facilities, including kindergartens and a shelter for children. In 1937, the materials stated that the kindergartens and shelter operated under the guidance of two inspectors. In 1945, i.e. eight years later, the data are more specific. The shelter was led by a social worker of VI and a social worker also supervised the socio-health aspects of factory kindergartens. From this we can conclude that if there had already been a social department in 1937, the mentioned inspectors could be social workers.

Vostřebalová (1933) clarifies the term "inspector/female inspector" with a view to its correct understanding. It was not inspection in the true sense of the word, but performance of social work. I find it interesting that the author felt the need to explain the contradiction in the dual understanding of the term in 1933. Apparently, already at that time the designation was misleading and alluded to checking, supervision and surveillance, but in fact, this was not the right connotation.

From the methods of social work used, individual social work in the form of counselling is particularly ascertained, and the period literature further refers to the method of clerical intervention in the family. Unfortunately, this method is not specified in more detail. In addition, social workers gave educational lectures from the socio-health field and promoted social work through broadcasting and press.

The VI management was not indifferent to the number of social workers in the enterprise and their professional training. Professional in-service training courses for enterprise social clerks were organised by the Institute of National Health in Ostrava in 1946 and a year later by the Central Council of Trade Unions in cooperation with the Ministry of Social Welfare. In 1946, two qualified social workers and three administrative employees were working in the plant. A year later, there were already three qualified social workers and three trainees. After the World War II, the ironworks were also involved in research activities in the social field. The VI works union council was approached with a request to participate in national social research in metallurgy, the results of which were to be used for subsequent planning in the economy.

Social work in VI was at a high level after 1945, as evidenced by numerous excursions and visits from abroad. The ironworks were visited by Belgian social workers, Mrs. Hana Benešová (consort of the then President of the Republic), social workers from the Škoda Works or students from the Masaryk State School of Health and Social Work.

The Social Department of VI developed cooperation with the Czechoslovak Red Cross, the District Youth Care, the Masaryk League against Tuberculosis, the Social Assistance, the Charity, Municipal Social Care Authority, the Provincial Holiday and Convalescent Care, the Ludmila Association, the Labour Protection Office and other social-health institutions.

The existence of a social department at Baťa dates back to 1924. The main task was to provide supportive care for co-workers and their family members. A key position belonged to social clerks. In 1938 the position was named as a social inspector. A social inspectorate was established to supervise compliance with the standards and employees' labour and social rights. As a social clerk, the social worker was a confessor, confidant, advisor, friend and supporter of all weaker co-workers, as stated in the documents.

Based on the preserved work content, it was the responsibility of social clerks to report all new social cases to the company management and to inform them of the solution plan. This corresponds to the dual status of social workers according to Hromada (1942), being both confidants of labourers and confidants of the company management. Furthermore, ssocial clerks submitted proposals for aids from the Baťa Support Fund for employees who had grown old working at the enterprise, fell ill or needed "deserved" assistance.

As for social work methods, primary sources only mention individual social work and, as in VI, counselling. Part of the work was the necessary keeping of records and filing cabinets.

Management of the Baťa company also took care of improving the quality of social work and the exchange of experience, which is evidenced by a conference of Baťa company social workers held in Napajedla in 1945. This piece of information was published in the Zlín press as well.

The following table was created from the analysed work contents of social clerks at VI and Baťa. In the case of comprehensive programmes of care for workers, no specific work content of social clerks was subjected to an analysis, therefore this agent is not included in the table.

Table No. 23 – Work content of social clerks at VI and Baťa

Area of interest	Social clerk/social worker at VI	Social clerk at the Baťa company
Catering	Initiative collaboration on organising factory catering, on educating to a culture of nutrition.	Social clerks checked the quality of meals.
Housing	Caring for improving the standard of housing, cooperation with construction experts in implementing the enterprise housing programme. Active monitoring of the operation of company flats, youth homes and educating to a culture of housing.	The social worker's agenda included care for accommodation, complaints about accommodation. Social clerk carried out housing interventions at the accommodation department. Social department co-decided on allocation of flats.
Women	Caring for working women, especially during maternity, paying attention to social conditions of their work in enterprises, as well as living conditions in their homes, organising neighbourhood aid events and voluntary enterprise social service. Watching over the proper operation of children's homes – nurseries, kindergartens, shelters, after-school clubs and other facilities.	Employed mothers and women were supported by social workers. Their mission was to care for good functioning of household where the woman was employed or ill and where it was necessary to take care of children, cooking and cleaning.
Adolescents	Caring for juvenile workers in as for social aspects, especially for their housing, catering, recreation, physical and mental health, cooperation in their guidance, education and thus defending their social interests.	Social clerk took care of the morale of young employees.

Area of interest	Social clerk/social worker at VI	Social clerk at the Baťa company
Children	Caring for employees' children, organising or cooperation in short and long-term recreation.	Social clerk established and maintained sanatoriums, established holiday convalescent homes.
Adult recreation	Organising and caring for recreation of adult employees and their families.	*This field was not found in the social clerk's job description in primary materials.*
Hiring new employees	Allowing for social considerations in the distribution of workforce, in recruitment, relocation or dismissal.	Social care for employees included complaints about dismissal, relocation, superiors, co-workers, and wage complaints. Handling requests based on social reasons such as job applications, applications for job change.
Workers with reduced working capacity	Taking care of workers with reduced working capacity, cooperation in their appropriate work integration of in both subjective and objective terms.	*This field was not found in the social clerk's job description in primary materials.*
Individual work	Carrying out individual care for employees and their family members, investigating the social justification of their applications and social assistance of all kinds, and providing their assessments to relevant officials.	Social clerk dealt with issues of a social nature, handled with employees' wishes and complaints, gave advice to all who were faced with personal problems and asked for advice. Solving discrepancies in marriage, giving consultations in divorce proceedings, paying visits to families. Suggestions for improving the working environment of employees were concentrated at the social clerk.

Area of interest	Social clerk/social worker at VI	Social clerk at the Baťa company
		Informing sick employees of their claims against the health insurance fund or the Central Social Insurance Agency.
		Giving information on claims under social insurance.
		Caring for a happy family life of employees. Frequently acting as a magistrate in families or helping with both advice and deed in cases of indebtedness.
Cooperation, record keeping, health	Cooperation with the works council, trade union organisation, participation in the fight against social diseases, cooperation in re-education of social subverters, establishing and managing the social file of employees. Providing first aid in case of accidents in the absence of a physician or relevant medical staff.	Social clerk kept an alphabetical index of social cases, which was part of the family filing cabinet or aid filing cabinet, illness records, death records, new-born filing cabinet or filing cabinet for large families. Social clerk watched over the employees' health, cooperated with other departments to ensure that the working environment complied with safety and health regulations.
Contact with institutions	Mediation of contacts between the company and other institutions with regard to performance of social work.	Founding and management of various support funds, mediation of contacts with social institutions such as pension institutions and health insurance companies.

Source: Špiláčková, own construct

Implementation of enterprise social work depended on the personal prerequisites for the position of social worker. In practice, until 1969 there were no methodological procedures or instructions on how to do social work. It was necessary to lean towards one's own intuition on how to deal with situations, to build on the experience and skills acquired from school years. Mrs. Šálková also referred to this when she recalled her teacher from the socio-legal college: "Our generation of social workers was educated by Dr. Machačová to help people, to put emphasis on prevention, to estimate people, not to manipulate them, to lead them so that they could solve their problem themselves – not to do it for them." It follows from the interviews conducted with Mrs. Červenáková and Mrs. Šálková that it was necessary to be personally committed and to search for clients in enterprises. Making contacts after working hours, in private life and even in leisure activities also paid off, for example, as people approached both respondents just because they had known them from their place of residence and knew they were "helpful people". Living in the same place where the enterprise was located was considered an advantage. According to the respondents, another important condition for the performance of social work was gaining people's trust in the social worker.

Sociological surveys conducted after 1945 were an important tool for implementation of enterprise social policy and social work in practice. Examples include the involvement of VI in social research, or the presence of sociologists in enterprises in order to analyse the workers' needs. Social research in a plant/workshop also appeared as a form of social work in a document from 1969.

As part of comprehensive programmes of care, social workers were considered to be agents, specialists in the field, actively participating in formulating the company's social policy. They were members of the enterprise team and maintained constant contact with managers. A minimum qualification for holding the position of a social clerk was completed secondary professional education with specialisation in a social-legal field, together with at least three years of professional experience.

The major milestones in the development of enterprise social work are marked in the timeline below. The findings are results of an analysis of available sources of both primary and secondary nature.

Diagram No. 8 – Timeline of the development of social work in the defined territory[18]

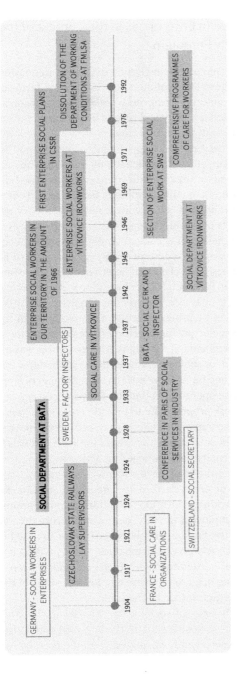

Source: Špiláčková, own construct

---

18 Explanatory notes to the diagram: activities in the defined territory are marked with a grey background and for the sake of illustration, found data of examples from abroad are marked with a frame.

6.6 Social Work Performed in Enterprises in the Context of the Prevalent Social Policy Paradigm

The thesis deals with a defined time period beginning in the fourth quarter of the 19th century. In Europe, the industrial revolution was underway, factories were introducing new technologies, working conditions were changing, production organisation was changing. Traditional society had turned into modern society, sociology was beginning to interfere with theoretical concepts.

Enterprise owners or their managers tried to maximize their profits. The purpose was to make production more efficient, which meant ensuring the necessary number of employees, who, based on their qualifications, were assigned different positions. In VI there were labourers, qualified workers, technicians, foremen and supervisors. It was a vertical stratification in line with sociological theory, as stated by Keller (2005). Representatives of the individual positions were duly evaluated not only financially, but also by means of accompanying services and benefits. At Vítkovice the stratification was emphasised more visibly, in the types of housing (officials', foremen's and labourers'), ten classes of health insurance depending on the wage amount, old age pension for officials after long time in service and others. At Baťa, however, all "co-workers" of Tomáš Baťa and his successor were taken into account. Naturally, a stratification by professions was also necessary in the Baťa company, but the benefits for specific positions arising from the company's social policy are not obvious in the documents at first sight. The exception was a higher percentage of profit participation for senior employees in the given department.

Both in the case of Vítkovice and Baťa, the need for a large number of employees at the beginning of the enterprise operation is evident. It was necessary to recruit workers, to motivate them to work properly and to provide them with "something extra" to make them stay in the company. In effect, they had adequate wages for their work, and then, based on the set criteria, they could progress towards factory housing and other benefits. The enterprises launched an active and progressive social policy, which offered meeting the basic needs: focused on housing, insurance against risks arising from work or life cycle (old age, maternity, childhood, widowhood), ensuring catering, providing education for children, youth, apprentices. The police also focused on the employees directly, organising leisure time and the opportunity to use organised recreation or convalescence. In the analysed period, VI and the Baťa company were largely private companies, while in 1969 it was an introduction of programmes into state enterprises, which had already been operating and functioning. There was no need to motivate employees to stay in the company. "Working somewhere" was guaranteed by the state.

In accordance with the dichotomy of sociological theories in the context of Czech historiography, as stated by Rákosník (2010), the analysed enterprise social policies of VI and Baťa can be viewed from two angles: from the perspective of sociological theories of consensus or conflict. The consensus theory views enterprise as an abstract system, a social organism in which a balance of parts is necessary for the functioning of the whole. Individual workers and the enterprise take pride in symbiosis, in equal coexistence with the aim of gaining benefits for all involved, while avoiding disputes. Mr. Stojeba also had the intention of reducing conflict situations in mind, when he made a demand at the meeting of the Social Section of VI that social agents should act as a catalyst in the work process and reduce or eliminate all negative forces which would hamper or threaten productive work.

As for maximizing profits for all, the following can be identified for employers (both VI and Baťa): financial profit, competitiveness, company prestige, sufficient employees to ensure production, obtaining new orders domestically and abroad, share in municipal policy. As for employees, it included the following potential benefits: financial security for themselves and their family, security in the area of housing, health care, nourishment, qualifications, gaining status, belonging to the company, acquiring collective identity, belonging to a social group. The well-being of the whole was conditioned by the well-being of all its parts, as Bláha says (1931). Likewise, Matějček and Vytiska (1978) write that the sophisticated social policy of VI paid off for everyone. In the 1930s, a social department with its workers could be found both at VI and Baťa. In this situation, a social worker could be a mediator between employees and employers, ensuring enhanced symbiosis between the agents, and integrating the participants. They took care to adhere to the determined rules so as to enable mutual coexistence in the company.

At Baťa, a pedagogical element can be additionally found. Tomáš Baťa did not only want to increase the company's performance, but also to cultivate and educate his labourers. The tool was profit participation, participation in the company success. It was important for Baťa to elevate the labouring class both materially and morally. And he started his intention with young people, as evidenced by the Young Men and Young Women societies. From their belonging to the company and all the related responsibilities and benefits, young people developed a sense of responsibility and perspective for the future. The definition of social policy by Engliš from 1916, too, refers to a distribution of the fruits of material and spiritual culture in a fair way among the various layers of society, while deepening and intensifying the life of possibly all members towards a qualitatively ideal, healthy, educated and moral human. An ideal human model was set, a standard which a person was supposed to meet in order to reach for the mentioned "fruits".

The labourers' satisfaction was not only based on meeting the material needs, social policy should was also intended to satisfy their spiritual needs. It was not just about wages, but also about culture and entertainment, as Arnošt Bláha suggested in 1930. He encouraged scientific research into the lives of labourers both in home and work environment. At Baťa, social clerks were encouraged to work in line with methods which were deemed scientifically correct.

The other sociological point of view, the theory of conflict, understands an enterprise as a social institution whose owners or managers exercise power through their policies. Policy tools maintain discipline and ensure supervision and control. The aim is to neutralise danger, prevent riots and weaken social tensions. It is worth mentioning the catalytic function of social clerks or social workers at VI in this passage as well. Again, using social policy instruments, it was about eliminating and diminishing the negative effects which would make workers manifest their dissatisfaction. Social workers acted as a catalyst and could contribute to the elimination of manifestations of labourers' displeasure.

According to Keller (2005), factories were used for exerting discipline. Through discipline, according to Foucault (2000), the power of a standard emerged which easily worked within a system of formal equality. Normalising power forces towards homogeneity, but at the same time it allows for measuring deviations from the given standard. Foucault states that in society, there are judges of normality all around us. Social workers monitored and ensured the implementation of a universal normative as well. They were part of a checking mechanism. They checked intensively and continuously. The Baťa company established a social inspectorate in 1938, in which the social inspector had the task of "supervising compliance with the laws and employees' labour and social rights". He even participated in checking the served meals. In VI, the social inspector supervised the operation of social facilities or supervised the allocation of flats.

Foucault (2005) described biopolitics of the human species as the promotion of biopower, which, on the pretext of improving the individual's life, seeks to strengthen the established order. Biopolitics deals with manifestations of deviations from the norm, such as anomalies, problems, abnormalities or injuries. According to Foucault, professional social work in the 20th century became the exercise of this power. By applying this theory, social workers in an enterprise (and not only in it) supervise and monitor norms through their work and solve manifestations of deviations from normality. If we accept this thesis about the supervision of standards and solving the already "pre-packaged" problems, an important element of social work is missing and this is avoidance of difficulties, i.e. prevention. Prevention forms part of the social workers' goals. As Šálková writes, the objective of a social worker in enterprise practice was to prevent and solve social problems of people in their connection with the environment.

A link between biopolitics and enterprise practice can also be found in contemporary literature. Holubec comments on linking the Tomáš Baťa's company with M. Foucault, which can serve as an example. According to Holubec (2009), at Baťa, an obsession with biopower can be identified in many places. The human body is compared to a machine or an engine. According to Baťa, a worker without certain care is like a machine without oil and without spare parts. Body regulation is associated with a great interest of biopower in human purity, in proper functioning of body organs, in the birth of children in maternity hospitals and, last but not least, in regulating human sexuality. Baťa encouraged his employees to practice hygiene, to have rational lifestyles and to plan their lives. The cult of youth promoted by Baťa was also closely related to biopolitics. Young people seemed to be the easiest to form and naturally most dissatisfied as a social group. The most common terms in Baťa's discourse are the words "life", "struggle", "strength", "machine", and "youth" (Holubec, 2009). Based on the performed analysis, the word "education" can be added to the list.

After 1969, specialised literature on the topic of enterprise social policy evinces a link to the management of socialist enterprises with reference to K. Marx. Social structure of enterprises was conceived as part of the social structure of society as a whole. The result should be, according to Kohout (1976), an enterprise as an integral part of society in which a substantial part of the workers' lives takes place. It means that on the basis of a conducted analysis of employees' needs, all their requirements should be met so as to make their life in the company as pleasant for them as possible. This fact emerged both in the social policy of VI after 1945 and in comprehensive programmes of care for workers.

Through comprehensive programmes of care for workers, the state transferred responsibility and the actual implementation, including funding, from the state level to the enterprise level. Enterprises were supposed to become autonomous within the planned economy in order to facilitate enterprise social policy. These factors are mentioned as one of the processes important for achieving the third type of welfare state of industrial society, as stated by Mishra (in Rákosník, 2010).

Provision for individuals as an important part of social programmes of enterprises emerged within the concept of corporate towns and later also in the business policy of "human relations". By changing the environment, including educational influences on employees, their promoters tried to ennoble humans as early as in the 19th century, as stated in literature (Kohout, 1976, Ševeček, 2009) in the case of entrepreneur Robert Owen in New Lanark, which had factory settlements as a first social experiment in the industrial era. The continuity is evident at Baťa, where the pedagogical element in rational activities of social nature was emphasised. The concepts of providing for employees to create belonging to a common enterprise, awareness of collective identity, a sense of togetherness in relation to the company were evident both at VI and Baťa.

Based on a thematic analysis of the development and implementation of enterprise social policy of the selected entities, their predominant models or schemes of social policy were described, which I consider as paradigms of social policy (see chapters 6.1, 6.2, 6.3) in accordance with Kuhn (1997: 35). Subsequently, the development of social work was described in line with the time periods and paradigms (see chapter 6.5). From both partial concepts, a picture of social work was created in the context of the prevalent paradigm of VI, the Baťa company and comprehensive programmes of care for workers. For the sake of clarity, the findings are presented in the form of a table below.

Table No. 24 – Social work in the context of the prevalent paradigm

Analysed entity and period	Prevalent paradigm of social policy	Roles/functions/methods of social work
Vítkovice Ironworks 1876-1893	Targeted investment paternalistic policy of a private entity in order to ensure continuous metallurgical production = to ATTRACT employees	*Social work not found in primary and secondary sources.*
Vítkovice Ironworks 1894 – 1945	Tactical paternalistic policy of a private entity in order to reduce fluctuation and forms of labourers' resistance = to KEEP employees	*Social work not found in primary and secondary sources.* However, its existence can be deduced from partial indications. Social worker acted as a social inspector. Social work fulfilled the function of supervision and surveillance.
Vítkovice Ironworks 1945-1954	State directive social policy with preventive (prophylactic) and caring elements = to CARE for employees	Social work was presented as a tool for making the life of workers in the company "more pleasant" and for satisfying their needs. Social worker was an official, an administrative employee. The term clerical intervention is used. Social worker was a social-health worker. The method of individual social work was used.
Baťa 1900-1945	Rational business policy with educational elements = to EDUCATE employees	Social worker was presented as a confessor, advisor, supporter of the weak, inspector, supervisor of meals.

Analysed entity and period	Prevalent paradigm of social policy	Roles/functions/methods of social work
		Social worker acted as a social inspector in 1938, later as a social clerk.
		Social worker provided supportive care for co-workers. The method of individual social work was used.
Comprehensive programmes of care for workers 1969-1989	Policy directed by the state based on social planning and identification of needs = to SATISFY the employees' needs	Social work fulfilled the function of professional assistance in preventing adverse life situations and eliminating their causes and consequences.
		Cooperation with UN, with Social Workers' Society. The term social worker was used.
		The method of individual social work was used. Social work with groups is only implied.

Source: Špiláčková, own construct

Social work is an applied tool of social policy. It has been the case in its history and today, too. In the monitored period, social work was carried out in enterprise practice in an environment where it was necessary to care for employees, participate in their education or satisfy their needs. When the policy was aimed at attracting a sufficient number of employees, social work did not appear at all. When the aim consisted in keeping employees, the position of social worker appeared only covertly in the role of a social inspector.

Based on the performed analysis, it can be stated that social work was described in the contemporary literature as a socially educational and facilitating tool for securing mentally and socially balanced employees without any significant social problems. It served to "maintain" and regenerate the workforce, including participation in the prevention of problematic situations.

CONCLUSION

The topic of this treatise was a reconstruction of the development of social work in enterprises implemented as part of enterprise social policy in the territory of Bohemia and Moravia between the years 1876-1989.

Its aim was, based on the study of primary sources of written nature in particular, to describe and analyse enterprise social policies of selected entities from the territory of Bohemia and Moravia implemented mainly in the twentieth century, to describe the areas of enterprise social welfare including institutions and social services offered to employees, and to identify the applied methods of social work, with regard to constitution of enterprise social work as one of the areas of social work performance.

As was relevant to the topic, the treatise was anchored on a background of textual hermeneutics through historical research. The approach of social and economic history, with the method of hermeneutic-classificatory content analysis, according to Plichtová (1996), and koral history as a triangulation method were chosen. Subsequently, a thematic analysis in the role of a "secondary analysis" was applied to the collected findings, whose output was contextual themes pursuing the fulfilment of the defined aim of the treatise.

The result is a synthesis of findings about the constitution of enterprise social work, implemented in the enterprise social policy environment of three intentionally selected entities in the history of the defined territory and the monitored period, elaborated on scientific foundations. There is no author dealing with this topic comprehensively in the current specialised literature, therefore, I can state, on the basis of the conducted historical research, that the work is unique in its content and contains historical facts unpublished so far.

The ambition of the treatise is to fill the gaps in the development of Czech social work in the enterprise environment, to provide relevant knowledge to the professional public, to support the identity of social workers with their profession and the collective consciousness at the same time, while contributing to the development of thinking about social work history. It can also motivate or inspire researchers to further follow-up work.

Enterprise social policy of the VI, the Baťa company, or policy implemented through comprehensive programmes of care for workers created a motivating environment for the constitution and development of expert social work.

Social work was understood as a professional activity based on theoretical foundations utilising knowledge from other scientific disciplines. Its role in enterprises was conditioned upon the professional having completed education in a relevant social field. In this sense, it appealed to the need for the renewal of university education in social work, but this appeal was not heard until 1990.

Social work was a socially educational and facilitating tool of enterprise social policy to ensure mentally and socially balanced employees without significant social problems. It served to "maintain" and regenerate the workforce, including participation in the prevention of problematic situations, including prevention of disease, an issue especially noted after 1969.

Using the described methodological key, a timeline of the development of enterprise social work was created. Its constitution in the Czech territory did not lag behind development abroad. This is evidenced by ascertained findings, especially from the magazines Social Worker and Social Review. The first mentions of social work performance appear in German enterprises in 1904. Social workers cared for the social and health aspects of the enterprise workers and their families. This is followed by examples of a social secretary in a Swiss factory of 1924, female factory inspectors in Sweden of 1933, and even legislatively regulated social and health care at workplaces in France in 1942. In Czechoslovak territory, we find the first mention of the existence of lay supervisors at the Czechoslovak State Railways in 1921. In the Baťa enterprise, a social department with the function of social inspectors was established in 1924. In 1937, social care was proven in VI with the presence of social clerks.

Enterprise social work did not escape the notice of the professional public. Already in 1928, an International Conference in Paris was held with the theme of Social Services in Industry. This conference was also attended by Marie Krakešová, Helena Radlinska and other doyennes of the history of both national and international social work. The study of social work contributed to raising the importance of the profession. Firstly, by participating in social research, as indicated in materials from VI, and also by organising a conference of social workers, e.g. of the Baťa company in 1945 in Napajedla. An important contribution was the involvement of Czechoslovakia in the UN Commission for Social Development. Within this framework, a task to practically implement plans of care for workers in enterprises was assigned. As a result, comprehensive programmes of care for workers were compiled and implemented after 1973.

The fate of social work and its professional development was dependent upon enthusiastic individuals engaged in the re-establishment of the Social Workers' Society and its section for enterprise social workers. Important personalities of enterprise social work in the country include Ing. Helena Šálková and Ing. Anežka Červenáková, with whom I had the honour to speak in person and, at least to the extent possible, to capture their memories of their personal life mission – helping people.

I consider the inclusion of memories of direct participants of the topic under study as a great positive of the treatise. After all, it would not have been possible to trace some facts without their memories. An example is the acquisition of materials from the UN Commission for Social Development. I could only study these documents because Mrs. Šálková found her travel order to Moscow for a Commission seminar in her personal archive, to which, thanks to her precise approach, she noted the number of the minutes of the UN meeting. As a consequence, I could address the UN administration with a targeted request for the specific document. Many thanks!

The recollections of the interviews serve as an illustration of the times in which the witnesses lived and touched on the topic of the treatise in a way. Capturing oral history means an enrichment of the whole work, it is a source of historical knowledge, which reflects individual experiences and the dimensions of everyday life. During the interview, Mrs. Vitásková repeatedly returned to the experience of the bombardment of the Baťa company in Zlín. It is obvious that the wartime period had left indelible marks on her memory. I am aware of the fact that these memories do not specifically relate to the analysed topic, yet I left this passage in the treatise, because all memories are rare and we can use in the future. Mr. Heczko also recalled the events of the war, having experienced them in Vítkovice. He even mentioned the specific number of bombs which hit Vítkovice. In general, Mr. and Mrs. Heczko commended their work in VI. The reason for their positive relationship was not exactly the social policy of the ironworks, but the "ordinary" human advantage, represented by the workplace proximity and acquisition of suitable and affordable housing. Another important factor was the tradition of work in VI, which has been kept in the Heczko family to this day. The family tradition, workplace proximity and acquired housing was more important for them than the social services offered. Mrs. Vitásková recalled the period of her secondary school years at Baťa in terms of the omnipresent discipline, obedience, checks and order. She described this period positively, although it was significantly influenced by the war, too. Coincidentally, after the war, she also worked in VI. When we encountered this fact unintentionally during the interview, she herself stated that the discipline at Baťa and at Vítkovice bore no comparison. According to her, the morale was more relaxed in Vítkovice. Mr. and Mrs. Heczko had the same experience with a relatively lower level of checking in favour of employees as well. I believe that the described memories of witnesses completed the picture of the bygone times, in which enterprise social policy and social work at the analysed entities was taking place.

Social work is described as a practical professional activity. Its genesis and continuous development would not have been possible without its anchoring in theoretical concepts available to the professional public in the given period. Enterprise social work did not deviate from the level of knowledge available in the defined territory and observed period. It copied the theoretical discourse of social work as it was developing in other areas of social care (Špiláčková, 2014). Primarily, the diagnostic model of social work prevailed, which was also reflected in the actual work of social workers in determining the client's diagnosis, ascertaining their medical history and creating a social therapy plan. As for social work methods, individual social work was used to correspond to enterprise practice and, after 1969, partly also group social work. Socio-legal counselling prevailed, for instance, I noted the term "clerical intervention in a family" in the practices of VI as a new piece of information.

In line with the agent-subject paradigm applied in individual social work, a company employee acts as the subject of social worker's work. This corresponds to the historical discourse of social work, when the agent-subject paradigm continued to be applied in Czech practice even in the 1980s.

Documents after 1945 state that the beginnings of enterprise social work date to the time after the nationalisation of enterprises. This piece of information contradicts my findings, as examples of the existence of enterprise social work in practice can be found already during the period of the First Czechoslovak Republic, for instance through articles in the magazine Social Worker. However, these contradictions are understandable in light of the obligatory "ideological padding", which sought to ascribe all successes to the then ruling party in a directive way.

In all three analysed entities, I have found three significant links. (1) Application of experience from abroad. Through their directors, directors general and owners, VI applied experience from Germany, Austria and England. Tomáš Baťa took pride mainly in American practice and the Federal Ministry of Labour and Social Affairs of the CSSR very often referred to examples from the USSR. Another common element is (2) similar areas of social policy interest. All three entities have the same "target groups", which the enterprises took account of when planning their social system, namely housing, education, health, care for children, seniors, people with disabilities, catering, recreational activities, insurance and funds. The last common element is (3) the establishment of a social department and the need to create a position of social inspector/clerk/worker in an effort to prevent or solve problems of the company employees.

After 1945, literature on the topic existed only to a limited extent. Sporadically, professional articles by the authors Hromada a Purkyňová appeared in the journal Social Workers. New impulses for practice are then brought by Helena Šálková in the 1960s, whose publications on enterprise social policy and social work are based on her own experience from work in enterprises.

After World War II, state policy was implemented mainly in the form of planning. The social sphere falling within the realm of social policy was part of state plans for a specific legislative period. Five-year planning periods were practically applied, from which the term five-year plan became popular. The five-year plans also determined the economic and social development of territorial units, which included the social development of enterprises through enterprise social plans or comprehensive programmes of care for workers. Part of enterprise social policy and social plans was social work as a professional social activity performed in a competent way. It clearly follows from the archival materials that enterprise social workers played an important role in the enterprise social system. They offered advisory, consulting and operational assistance to all company employees and their families or immediate relatives (Špiláčková, 2015).

Social work in enterprises represented a precursor to the development of social care for all other target groups, especially in the 1970s. On the basis of enterprise social work, the area of care for seniors, for children, youth and families, for people with reduced working capacity and care for citizens of Roma origin developed (Špiláčková, 2014). After 1989, when changes in the country took place leading to the democratisation of society, enterprise social work was gradually suppressed to the background. At present, there are no social workers present in enterprises at all. Although enterprise social work was fully developed and successfully implemented in practice, the year 1989 brought its existence gradually to an end. Nevertheless, enterprise social work played an important role in the history of social work in the territory of today's Czech Republic (Špiláčková, 2015).

Finally, I will now return to reflect on the importance of studying history for the present and future generations, on which I premised the treatise introduction. For many centuries, the idea expressed in the Latin phrase *Historia est Magistra Vitae* was accepted – history is life's teacher. The question is how much the statement has maintained its validity in contemporary society. It is not only about our willingness to be influenced by historical experience. Contemporary society is changing very dynamically, thus moving away from its past, while becoming increasingly different. Therefore, it is problematic to assert the idea that we should learn from the past. Some lessons are of a more permanent nature, others become outdated over time (Šubrt, Vinopal et al., 2013). However, according to Hroch (2010), everyone can find a lesson which suits them in the endless breadth of history, because we will never reach any consensual interpretation of history anyway.

An acclaimed Czech philosopher Karel Kosík (1966: 97-103) shows that in relation to the past, human history is a continuous totalisation, i.e. a revival in which human practice incorporates moments of the past and only revives them through this integration. In this sense, human reality is not only a production of the new, but also a critical and dialectical reproduction of the past. In human memory, the past becomes present, thus overcoming the temporary, as the past itself is for humans something which is not left behind as an unnecessary thing, but something which constitutively enters their presence, as a creating and developing human nature. The past is an integral part of human existence.

It can be stated, from the results of the conducted research, that the practice of enterprise social policy in the territory of Bohemia and Moravia during the 20th century was a dignified and inspiring place for the development of practical social work. It created a suitable environment for the constitution of social work in enterprises as a distinct area of its development. With reference to Karel Kosík, I believe that the analysed texts have helped to revive the history of enterprise social work, which have become part of our present in a positive way.

RESUMÉ

The topic of the work was reconstruction of the development of social work in enterprises implemented as part of enterprise social policy in the territory of Bohemia and Moravia between the years 1876-1989. Since its professional beginnings, social work has been a major actor and instrument of social policy. Social policy created an environment for establishment of professional social work. In current specialised literature, enterprise social work is described only in fragments, without any link to the content of social policy realised in individual enterprises and to the way of its implementation. Selected subjects of implementation of enterprise social policy are the Vítkovice Ironworks, the Baťa company, the state or more precisely the Federal Ministry of Labour and Social Affairs, centrally shielding social policy of state-owned enterprises starting from the 1970s in terms of methodology. The methodology is hermeneutical, based on historical research which is an approach of qualitative research strategy. The selected research design corresponds to the concept of social and economic history exploring the transformation of societal institutions, communities and structures. Research methods are represented by hermeneutic – classificatory content analysis, methods of oral history and a thematic analysis applied to the collected findings. The work result is a synthesis of findings about the constitution of enterprise social work elaborated on scientific foundations. The enterprise social policy of the Vítkovice Ironworks, the Baťa company, or policy implemented through comprehensive programmes of care for workers created a motivating environment for the constitution and development of expert social work. Social work was a social-educational and facilitating instrument of enterprise social policy, aimed at ensuring mentally and socially balanced employees without any significant social problems. It served as the basis for "maintenance" and regeneration of the workforce, including participation in prevention of problematic situations. It can be concluded from the results of the conducted research that the practice of enterprise social policy in the territory of Bohemia and Moravia during the twentieth century provided a respectable and inspiring space for development of practical social work. It created an expedient environment for the constitution of social work in enterprises as a distinct field of its development.

REFERENCES

ABBOTT, C., ADLER, S. Historical Analysis as a Planning Tool. *Journal of the American Planning Association,* Autumn 1989. Vol. 55, No. 4/1989, pp. 467-473.

BARCUCH, A., ROHLOVÁ, E. *Místopis starých Vítkovic.* In *Ostrava.* 20. Příspěvky k dějinám a současnosti Ostravy a Ostravska. Ostrava: Tilia, 2001. s. 270-303. (BARCUCH, A., ROHLOVÁ, E. *Topography of Old* Vítkovice. In *Ostrava.* 20. Contributions to the History and Present Age of Ostrava and the Ostrava Region. Ostrava: Tilia, 2001. pp. 270-303.)

BAUEROVÁ, J., KOLÁŘ, J., RŮŽIČKA, J. *O sociálním plánování.* Praha: Práce, 1972. (BAUEROVÁ, J., KOLÁŘ, J., RŮŽIČKA, J. *About Social Planning.* Prague: Práce, 1972.)

BEK, P. *Podnikový pojišťovací systém na železnici.* In HLAVAČKA, M., CIBULKA, P., POKORNÝ, J., FEJTOVÁ, O., BEK, P. *Sociální myšlení a sociální praxe v Českých zemích 1781-1939. Ideje, legislativa, instituce.* Praha: Historický ústav, 2015. s. 416-580. (BEK, P. *Company Insurance System of the Railways.* In HLAVAČKA, M., CIBULKA, P., POKORNÝ, J., FEJTOVÁ, O., BEK, P. *Social Thinking and Social Practice in the Czech Lands 1781-1939. Ideas, Legislative, Institutions.* Prague: Institute of History, 2015. pp. 416-580.)

BERKA, J., ŠÁLKOVÁ, H., TOMEŠ, I. Úvod do podnikové sociální politiky. *Sociální/ Sociálna politika,* 1987, roč. 13, číslo 6/1987. Teoretická příloha. (BERKA, J., ŠÁLKOVÁ, H., TOMEŠ, I. Introduction to Enterprise Social Policy. *Social Policy,* 1987, vol. 13, No. 6/1987. Theoretical Appendix.)

BERNHARDT, Ch. *The Place of Company Town in 20th Century Urban History.* Paper presented at an international conference "Company Towns of the Baťa Concern": 24-25th March 2011, Prague. Available at file:///C:/Users/oem/Downloads/BernhardtAbstract%20(1).pdf

BLÁHA, A. Výzkumný ústav dělnický. *Sociologická revue,* 1931, roč. II., svazek 3/1931, s. 310-316. (BLÁHA, A. Research Institute of Labourers. *Sociological Review,* 1931, year II., vol. 3/1931, pp. 310-316.)

BRNULA, P, KUSIN, V. *Fenomén pomoci v sociálnom myslení.* Bratislava: Iris, 2013. ISBN 978-80-89238-81-1. (BRNULA, P, KUSIN, V. *Phenomenon of Help in Social Thinking.* Bratislava: Iris, 2013. ISBN 978-80-89238-81-1.)

CEKOTA, A. Baťa – myšlenky, činy, život, práce. Knihovna Baťovy služby veřejnosti. Svazek IV. Praha: 1929. (CEKOTA, A. Baťa – Thoughts, Deeds, Life, Work. Library of Baťa Service for the Public. Volume IV. Prague: 1929.)

Commission for Social Development. Report on the Twentieth Session 17. 2.- 5. 3. 1969. E/CN.5/441. New York: United Nations, 1969. Available at www. un.org

DAVIDOVÁ GLOGAROVÁ, J. Křiky a pláče jako historický pramen. *HISTORICA – RE-VUE PRO HISTORII A PŘÍBUZNÉ VĚDY*, 2015, roč. 6, č. 1/2015. s. 43-57. (DAVI-DOVÁ GLOGAROVÁ, J. Shouting and Crying as a Historical Source. *HISTORICA – REVIEW FOR HISTORY AND RELATED SCIENCES*, 2015, vol. 6, No. 1/2015. pp. 43-57.)

DVOŘÁK, T., FASORA, L., CHOCHOLÁČ, B., MALÝ, T., NEČASOVÁ, D., STOKLÁSKOVÁ, Z., WIHODA, M. Úvod do studia dějepisu 1. Brno: Masarykova univerzita, 2014. ISBN 978-80-210-7012-7. (DVOŘÁK, T., FASORA, L., CHOCHOLÁČ, B., MALÝ, T., NEČASOVÁ, D., STOKLÁSKOVÁ, Z., WIHODA, M. *Introduction to the Study of History 1*. Brno: Masaryk University, 2014. ISBN 978-80-210-7012-7.)

EFMERTOVÁ, M. C. České země v letech 1848-1918. Praha: Libri, 1998. (EFMER-TOVÁ, M. C. *The Czech Lands Between 1848-1918*. Prague: Libri, 1998.)

ENGLIŠ, K. *Sociální politika*. Praha: Topič, 1916. (ENGLIŠ, K. *Social Policy*. Prague: Topič, 1916.)

ENGLIŠ, K. *Věčné ideály lidstva*. Edice Cesty. Praha: Vyšehrad, 1992. (ENGLIŠ, K. *Eternal Ideals of Humanity*. Edition of Ways. Prague: Vyšehrad, 1992.)

ERDÉLY, E. *Baťa švec, který dobyl světa*. Praha: Dobrovský, 2013. ISBN 978-80-7390-037-3. (ERDÉLY, E. *Baťa, the Shoemaker who Conquered the World*. Prague: Dobrovský, 2013. ISBN 978-80-7390-037-3.)

FOUCAULT, M. *Archeologie vědění*. Z franc. originálu přeložil Čestmír Pelikán. Herrmann & synové, 2002. (FOUCAULT, M. *Archaeology of Knowledge*. Translated from French original by Čestmír Pelikán. Herrmann & synové, 2002.)

FOUCAULT, M. *Dohlížet a trestat. Kniha o zrodu vězení*. Z franc. originálu přeložil Čestmír Pelikán. Praha: Dauphin, 2000. (FOUCAULT, M. *Discipline and Punish. The Birth of the Prison*. Translated from French original by Čestmír Pelikán. Praha: Dauphin, 2000.)

FOUCAULT, M. *Je třeba bránit společnost*. Z franc. originálu přeložil Petr Horák. Praha: Filosofia, 2005. ISBN 80-7007-221-0. (FOUCAULT, M. *Society Must Be Defended*. Translated from French original by Petr Horák. Prague: Filosofia, 2005. ISBN 80-7007-221-0.)

GÖPPNER, H. J. & HÄMÄLÄINEN, J. *Debatte um Sozialarbeitswissenschaft. Auf der Suche nach Elementen für eine Programmatik*. Lambertus. 2004. (GÖPPNER, H. J. & HÄMÄLÄINEN, J. *Debate about the Social Work Science. Looking for Elements for an Aim*. Lambertus. 2004.)

GRUBER, J. Ministerstvo sociální péče a přehled dosavadní sociální politiky československé republiky. *Sociální revue,* 1921, roč. II., číslo 2/1921. s. 217-232. (GRUBER, J. Ministry of Social Welfare and an Overview of the Social Policy of the Czechoslovak Republic up to Now. *Social Review,* 1921, vol. II., No. 2/1921. pp. 217-232.)

HECZKOVI, A. a S.. *Osobní archiv k Vítkovickým železárnám*. Ostrava: 2016. (HEC-ZKOVI, A. a S. *Personal archive as to Vítkovice Ironworks*. Ostrava: 2016.)

HENDL, J. *Kvalitativní výzkum. Základní metody a aplikace*. Praha: Portál, 2005. (HENDL, J. *Qualitative Research. Basic Methods and Application*. Prague: Portál, 2005.)

HILGER, S. *Sozialpolitik und Organisation. Formen betrieblicher Sozialpolitik in der rheinisch-westfalischen Eisen- und Stahlindustrie seit der Mitte des 19. Jahrhunderts bis 1933*. Stuttgart: Franz Steiner Verlag, 1996. (HILGER, S. *Social Policy and Organization. Forms of Enterprise Social Policy in the Rhineland-Westphalian Iron and Steel Industry from the mid-19th Century until 1933*. Stuttgart: Franz Steiner Publishing House, 1996.)

HLAVAČKA, M. *Boj proti chudobě, sociální otázka a sociální politika v českých zemích v 19. a na začátku 20. století: definice, ideje a instituce*. In HLAVAČKA, M., CIBULKA, P., POKORNÝ, J., FEJTOVÁ, O., BEK, P. *Sociální myšlení a sociální praxe v Českých zemích 1781-1939. Ideje, legislativa, instituce*. Praha: Historický ústav, 2015. s. 11-107. (HLAVAČKA, M. *The Fight against Poverty, Social Issue and Social Policy in the Czech Lands in the 19th and early 20th century: Definitions, Ideas and Institutions*. In HLAVAČKA, M., CIBULKA, P., POKORNÝ, J., FEJTOVÁ, O., BEK, P. *Social Thinking and Social Practice in the Czech Lands 1781-1939. Ideas, Legislation, Institutions*. Prague: Institute of History, 2015. pp. 11-107.)

HLAVAČKA, M., CIBULKA, P. et alii. *Chudinství a chudoba jako sociálně historický fenomén: ambivalence dobových perspektiv, individuální a kolektivní strategie chudých a instrumentária řešení*. Praha: Historický ústav, 2013. ISBN 978-80-7286-225-2. (HLAVAČKA, M., CIBULKA, P. et al. *Poorness and Poverty as a Socio-Historical Phenomenon: Ambivalence of Contemporary Perspectives, Individual and Collective Strategies of the Poor and Apparatus of Solutions*. Prague: Institute of History, 2013. ISBN 978-80-7286-225-2.)

HLAVAČKA, M., CIBULKA, P., POKORNÝ, J., FEJTOVÁ, O., BEK, P. *Sociální myšlení a sociální praxe v Českých zemích 1781-1939. Ideje, legislativa, instituce*. Praha: Historický ústav, 2015. (HLAVAČKA, M., CIBULKA, P., POKORNÝ, J., FEJTOVÁ, O., BEK, P. *Social Thinking and Social Practice in the Czech Lands 1781-1939. Ideas, Legislation, Institutions*. Prague: Institute of History, 2015.)

HLAVAČKA, M., ŘEPA, M. *Devatenácté století: historiografický přehled*. In ČECHUROVÁ, J., RANDÁK, J. a kol. *Základní problémy studia moderních a soudobých dějin*. Praha: Lidové noviny a FF UK, 2014. s. 17-44. (HLAVAČKA, M., ŘEPA, M. *The Nineteenth Century: Historiographic Overview*. In ČECHUROVÁ, J., RANDÁK, J. et al. *Basic Problems of Studying Modern and Contemporary History*. Prague: Lidové noviny and FF UK, 2014. pp. 17-44.)

HODEK, A. Dva modely sociální politiky. *Sociologický časopis*, 1978, roč. 14, č. 3/1978. s. 241-247. (HODEK, A. Two Models of Social Policy. *Sociological Journal*, 1978, vol. 14, No. 3/1978. pp. 241-247.)

HOLUBEC, S. Silní milují život. Utopie, ideologie a biopolitika Baťovského Zlína. In *Kuděj*, 2009, č. 2/2009. s. 30-55. (HOLUBEC, S. The Strong Ones Love Life.

Utopia, Ideology and Biopolitics of Baťa's Zlín. In *Kuděj*, 2009, No. 2/2009. pp. 30-55.)

HROCH, M. *Historické vědomí a potíže s jeho výzkumem dříve a nyní.* In ŠUBRT, J. (ed.) *Historické vědomí jako předmět badatelského zájmu: teorie a výzkum.* Kolín: Nezávislé centrum pro studium politiky, 2010. s. 31-46. ISBN 978-80-86879-25-3. (HROCH, M. *Historical Awareness and Difficulties with its Research Before and Now.* In ŠUBRT, J. (ed.) *Historical Awareness as a Subject of Research Interest: Theory and Research.* Kolín: Independent Centre for Political Studies, 2010. pp. 31-46. ISBN 978-80-86879-25-3.)

HROMADA, J. Sociální pracovnice v průmyslových závodech. *Sociální pracovnice,* 1942 roč. 11, číslo 7/1942. s. 89-93. (HROMADA, J. Social Worker in Industrial Enterprises. *Social Worker,* 1942 year. 11, No. 7/1942. pp. 89-93.)

JEMELKA, M. *Lidé z kolonií vyprávějí své dějiny.* Ostrava: FF OU, 2009. ISBN 978-80-7329-229-4. (JEMELKA, M. *People from Settlements Narrate their History.* Ostrava: FF OU, 2009. ISBN 978-80-7329-229-4.)

JEMELKA, M. a kol. (ed.) *Ostravské dělnické kolonie III: Závodní kolonie Vítkovických železáren a dalších průmyslových podniků.* Ostrava: Ostravská univerzita v Ostravě, 2015. ISBN 978-80-7464-754-3. (JEMELKA, M. et al. (ed.) *Ostrava Labourers' Settlements III: Factory Settlements of Vítkovice Ironworks and other Industrial Enterprises.* Ostrava: University of Ostrava in Ostrava, 2015. ISBN 978-80-7464-754-3.)

JIŘÍK, K. *Hutní úřednické a dělnické kolonie a kasárna v Ostrava.* In *Ostrava.* 20. Příspěvky k dějinám a současnosti Ostravy a Ostravska. Ostrava: Tilia, 2001. s. 304-344. (JIŘÍK, K. *Metallurgical Officials' and Labourers' Settlements and Barracks in Ostrava.* In *Ostrava.* 20. Contributions to the History and Present Age of Ostrava and the Ostrava Region. Ostrava: Tilia, 2001. pp. 304-344.)

JURNEČKOVÁ, M., Úkoly sociální péče v sociální politice. *Sociální pracovnice,* 1935, roč. 4., číslo 5/1935. s. 70-73. (JURNEČKOVÁ, M., Tasks of Social Care in Social Policy. *Social Worker,* 1935, vol. 4, No. 5/1935. pp. 70-73.)

KELLER, J. *Dějiny klasické sociologie.* 2. vydání. Praha: Slon, 2005. (KELLER, J. *History of Classical Sociology.* 2nd edition. Prague: Slon, 2005.)

KELLER, F., CHARVÁTOVÁ, D. *Péče o pracovníky.* Praha: SPN, 1977. (KELLER, F., CHARVÁTOVÁ, D. *Care for Workers.* Prague: SPN, 1977.)

KLADIWA, P. *Starosta.* In MYŠKA, M., ZÁŘICKÝ, A. (eds.) *Člověk v Ostravě v XIX. století.* Ostrava: Ostravská univerzita, 2007. s. 123-134. (KLADIWA, P. *The Mayor.* In MYŠKA, M., ZÁŘICKÝ, A. (eds.) *Human in Ostrava in XIX. Century.* Ostrava: Faculty of Arts of the University of Ostrava in Ostrava, 2007. pp. 123-134.)

KLADIWA, P., POKLUDOVÁ, A., KAFKOVÁ, R. *Lesk a bída obecních samospráv Moravy a Slezska.* 1850-1914. II. díl, 2. svazek. Finance a infrastruktura. Ostrava: Ostravská univerzita, 2009. (KLADIWA, P., POKLUDOVÁ, A., KAFKOVÁ, R. *The Shine and Misery of the Municipal Self-Governments of Moravia and Silesia.*

1850-1914. Part II, 2nd vol. Finance and Infrastructure. Ostrava: University of Ostrava, 2009.)

KLÍMA, J. V. Sociální a zdravotní péče a jejich vztahy k pedagogice. *Pedagogické rozhledy,* 1931, roč. XLI. s. 30-34. (KLÍMA, J. V. Social and Health Care and their Relationships to Pedagogy. *Pedagogical Horizons,* 1931, vol. XLI. pp. 30-34.)

KOHOUT, J. *Sociální analýza a řízení socialistického podniku.* Praha: Práce, 1976. (KOHOUT, J. *Social Analysis and Management of a Socialist Enterprise.* Prague: Práce, 1976.)

KOHOUT, J., KOLÁŘ, J. K metodologii sociální analýzy pracovních kolektivů. *Sociologický časopis,* 1978, roč. 14, č. 3/1978. s. 228-240. (KOHOUT, J., KOLÁŘ, J. On the Methodology of Social Analysis of Working Groups. *Sociological Journal,* 1978, vol. 14, No. 3/1978. pp. 228-240.)

Koncepce sociální politiky Národního výboru města Ostravy do roku 1980. Ostrava: Odbor sociálních věcí Národního výboru města Ostravy, 1973. *(Concept of Social Policy of the National Committee of Ostrava City until 1980.* Ostrava: Department of Social Affairs Policy of the National Committee of Ostrava City, 1973.)

Kolektiv autorů. *110 let strojírenství ve Zlíně od roku 1903.* Zlín: Tajmac-ZPS, 2013. (Collective of authors. *110 Years of Mechanical Engineering in Zlín since 1903.* Zlín: Tajmac-ZPS, 2013.)

KOSÍK, K. *Dialektika konkrétního. Studie o problematice člověka a světa.* 3.vyd. Praha: Academia, 1966. (KOSÍK, K. *Dialectics of the Concrete. Study on Human and World Issues.* 3rd edition. Prague: Academia, 1966.)

KOTEK, J. Mezinárodní sjezdy, pořádané v rámci „Čtrnáct dní mezinárodní sociální péče" v Paříži v r. 1928. *Sociální revue,* 1928, roč. IX. s. 368-376. (KOTEK, J. International congresses, held within "Fourteen days of International Social Care" in Paris in 1928. *Social Review,* 1928, vol. IX. pp. 368-376.)

KOTOUS, J. MUNKOVÁ, G., PEŘINA, P. Úvod do sociální politiky. Praha: ES PF UK, 2003. (KOTOUS, J. MUNKOVÁ, G., PEŘINA, P. *Introduction to Social Policy.* Prague: ES PF UK, 2003)

KOTOUS, J. MUNKOVÁ, G., RYS, V., ŠTEFKO, M. *Velké osobnosti české školy sociální politiky.* Praha: PF UK, 2014. (KOTOUS, J. MUNKOVÁ, G., RYS, V., ŠTEFKO, M. *Great Personalities of the Czech School of Social Policy.* Prague: PF UK, 2014)

KRAUS, F. *Sociální plán 5LP.* Praha: Ministerstvo informací a osvěty, 1948. (KRAUS, F. *Social Plan for 5LP.* Prague: Ministry of Information and Public Awareness, 1948.)

KRAKEŠ, J. KRAKEŠOVÁ, M. *Sociální případ.* Praha: Organizace sociálních pracovnic, 1934. (KRAKEŠ, J., KRAKEŠOVÁ, M. *Social Case.* Prague: Organization of Social Workers, 1934.)

KREBS, V. a kol. *Sociální politika.* Praha: Aspi, 2007. (KREBS, V. et al. *Social Policy.* Prague: Aspi, 2007.)

KUHN, T. S. *Struktura vědeckých revolucí.* Praha: OIKOYMENH, 1997. (KUHN, T. S. *Structure of Scientific Revolutions.* Prague: OIKOYMENH, 1997.)

Kurs sociální práce. *Sociální pracovnice,* 1934, roč. 3., číslo 8/1934. s. 113-114. (Social Work Course. *Social Worker,* 1934, vol. 3, No. 8/1934. pp. 113-114.)

Kurs sociální práce. *Sociální pracovnice,* 1935, roč. 4., číslo 5/1935. s. 80. (Social Work Course. *Social Worker,* 1935, vol. 4, No. 5/1935. p. 80.)

KUTTA, F. a kol. *Sociální plánování a programování.* Praha: VŠ politická, 1980a. (KUTTA, F. et al. *Social Planning and Programming.* Prague: University of Politics, 1980a.)

KUTTA, F. a kol. *Teorie a praxe sociálního plánování a programování v ČSSR.* Praha: Svoboda, 1980b. (KUTTA, F. et al. *Theory and Practice of Social Planning and Programming in CSSR.* Prague: Svoboda, 1980b.)

LEHÁR, B. *Dějiny Baťova koncernu (1894-1945).* Praha: Státní nakladatelství politické literatury, 1960. (LEHÁR, B. *History of the Baťa Concern (1894-1945).* Prague: Státní nakladatelství politické literatury, 1960.)

LUND, H. Hranice působnosti laiků a pracovníků z povolání. *Sociální pracovnice,* 1935, roč. 8., číslo 5/1939. s. 73-77. (LUND, H. Limits of the Activities of Lay and Professional Workers. *Social Worker,* 1935, vol. 8, No. 5/1939. pp. 73-77)

MACEK, J. *Základy sociální politiky.* Praha: Antonín Svěcený, 1925. (MACEK, J. *Basics of Social Policy.* Prague: Antonín Svěcený, 1925.)

MACEK, J. Co je sociální politika? *Sociální revue,* 1923, roč. IV. s. 1-10. (MACEK, J. What is Social Policy? *Social Review,* 1923, vol. IV. pp. 1-10.)

MATĚJ, M., KORBELÁŘOVÁ, I., LEVÁ, P. *Nové Vítkovice. 1876-1914.* Ostrava: Památkový ústav, 1992. ISBN 80-85034-07-7. (MATĚJ, M., KORBELÁŘOVÁ, I., LEVÁ, P. *New Vítkovice. 1876-1914.* Ostrava: Heritage Institute, 1992. ISBN 80-85034-07-7.)

MATĚJ, M., KORBELÁŘOVÁ, I., TEJZR, L. *Kulturní dědictví Vítkovických železáren.* Ostrava: Národní památkový ústav, 2014. (MATĚJ, M., KORBELÁŘOVÁ, I., TEJZR, L. *Cultural Heritage of Vítkovice Ironworks.* Ostrava: National Heritage Institute, 2014.)

MATĚJČEK, J. *Sociální politika Vítkovických železáren od 70. let 19. století do 1. světové války.* In SULDOVSKÝ, A. a kol. (ed). *Ostrava. Sborník příspěvků k dějinám a výstavbě města, 9.* Ostrava: Profil, 1977. s. 236-249. (MATĚJČEK, J. *Social Policy of Vítkovice Ironworks from 1870s until World War I.* In SULDOVSKÝ, A. et al. (ed). *Ostrava. Anthology Papers on History and Construction of the City, 9.* Ostrava: Profil, 1977. pp. 236-249.)

MATĚJČEK, J., VYTISKA, J. *Vítkovice. Železárny a strojírny Klementa Gottwalda.* Praha: Práce, 1978. (MATĚJČEK, J., VYTISKA, J. *Vítkovice. Klement Gottwald Ironworks and Engineering Plants.* Prague: Práce, 1978.)

MENČÍK, F. *Poskokem u Jana Bati.* Praha: Victoria Publishing, 1993. (MENČÍK, F. *Henchman at Jan Baťa.* Prague: Victoria Publishing, 1993.)

MĚSTKOVÁ, J. *Osobní archiv ke vzdělávání na sociálně právní škole v Praze*. Praha: 2014. (MĚSTKOVÁ, J. *Personal archive as to education at the Socio-Legal School in Prague*. Praha: 2014.)

MORAVČÍKOVÁ, H. Social and Architectural Phenomenon of the Bataism in Slovakia. *Sociológia – Slovak Sociological Review*. Vol. 36, No. 6. 2004. pp. 519-543.

MYŠKA, M. *Generální ředitel*. In MYŠKA, M., ZÁŘICKÝ, A. (eds.) Člověk v Ostravě v XIX. století. Ostrava: Ostravská univerzita, 2007. s. 95-104. (MYŠKA, M. *Director General*. In MYŠKA, M., ZÁŘICKÝ, A. (eds.) *Human in Ostrava in XIX. Century*. Ostrava: University of Ostrava, 2007. pp. 95-104.)

MYŠKA, M. *Založení a počátky Vítkovických železáren 1828-1880*. Ostrava: Krajské nakladatelství, 1960. (MYŠKA, M. *Foundation and Beginnings of Vítkovice Ironworks 1828-1880*. Ostrava: Krajské nakladatelství, 1960.)

MYŠKA, M., ZÁŘICKÝ, A. a kol. Člověk v Ostravě v XIX. století. Ostrava: Filozofická fakulta Ostravské univerzity v Ostravě, 2007. (MYŠKA, M., ZÁŘICKÝ, A. et al. *Human in Ostrava in XIX. Century*. Ostrava: Faculty of Arts of the University of Ostrava in Ostrava, 2007.)

NOVOTNÁ, V., SCHIMMERLINGOVÁ, V. *Sociální práce, její vývoj a metodické postupy*. Praha: Karolinum, 1992. (NOVOTNÁ, V., SCHIMMERLINGOVÁ, V. *Social Work, its Development and Methodical Procedures*. Prague: Karolinum, 1992.)

OLÁH, M., SCHAVEL, M., ONDRUŠOVÁ, Z., NAVRÁTIL, P. *Sociálna práca: vybrané kapitoly z dejín, teorie a metód sociálnej práce*. Bratislava: Vysoká škola zdravotnictva a sociálnej práce sv. Alžbety, 2009. ISBN 80-969449-6-7. (OLÁH, M., SCHAVEL, M., ONDRUŠOVÁ, Z., NAVRÁTIL, P. *Social Work: Selected Chapters from History, Theory and Methods of Social Work*. Bratislava: St. Elisabeth University of Health Care and Social Work, 2009. ISBN 80-969449-6-7.)

PALÁT, J. *Dělnické dynastie z Vítkovic (1828-1988)*. Ostrava: VŽSKG, 1989. (PALÁT, J. *Labourers' Dynasties from* Vítkovice *(1828-1988)*. Ostrava: VŽSKG, 1989.)

PLICHTOVÁ, J. Obsahová analýza a jej možnosti využitia v psychológii. Čs. Psychologie, 1996, vol. 4, 40/1996. s. 304-314. (PLICHTOVÁ, J. Content Analysis and Possibilities of its Use in Psychology. *Cs. Psychology*, 1996, vol. 4, 40/1996. pp. 304-314.)

POCHYLÝ, J. *Baťova průmyslová demokracie*. Praha: Utrin, 1990. (POCHYLÝ, J. *Baťa's Industrial Democracy*. Prague: Utrin, 1990.)

POKLUDA, Z. *Ze Zlína do světa. Příběh Tomáše Bati*. Zlín: Tigris, 2004. (POKLUDA, Z. *From Zlín to the World. The Story of Tomáš Baťa*. Zlín: Tigris, 2004.)

POKLUDA, Z. Člověk a práce. Z ekonomických principů a vizí Tomáše Bati. Zlín: Nadace Tomáše Bati a Univerzita Tomáše Bati ve Zlíně, 2014. (POKLUDA, Z. *Human and Work. Of Tomáš Baťa's Economic Principles and Visions*. Zlín: Tomáš Baťa Foundation and Tomáš Baťa University in Zlín, 2014.)

POKLUDOVÁ, A. *Formování technické inteligence v Moravské Ostravě na konci 19. a počátkem 20. století*. In *Ostrava. 20. Příspěvky k dějinám a současnosti Ostravy a Ostravska*. Ostrava: Tilia, 2001. s. 28-59. (POKLUDOVÁ, A. *Formation of*

Technical Intelligence in Moravská *Ostrava at the End of 19th and the Beginning of 20th Century.* In *Ostrava.* 20. Contributions to the History and Present Age of Ostrava and the Ostrava Region. Ostrava: Tilia, 2001. pp. 28-59.)

POLÁŠEK, J., KELLER, F., ŠÁLKOVÁ, H. *Péče o pracovníky v průmyslových podnicích v nové soustavě řízení.* Praha: Práce, 1969. (POLÁŠEK, J., KELLER, F., ŠÁLKOVÁ, H. *Care for Workers in Industrial Enterprises in the New Management System.* Prague: Práce, 1969.)

POTŮČEK, M. *Sociální politika.* Praha: SLON, 1995. (POTŮČEK, M. *Social Policy.* Prague: SLON, 1995.)

PRŮCHA, M. a kolektiv. *Sborník materiálů k otázkám sociální politiky v ČSSR.* Praha: Horizont, 1983. (PRŮCHA, M. et al. *Anthology of Materials as to Social Policy Issues in CSSR.* Prague: Horizont, 1983.)

PURKYŇOVÁ, M. Péče o zaměstnance v podnicích. *Sociální pracovnice,* 1946, roč. 15., číslo 5-6/1946. s. 75-83. (PURKYŇOVÁ, M. Care for Workers in Enterprises. *Social Worker,* 1946, vol. 15, No. 5-6/1946. pp. 75-83.)

PURKYŇOVÁ, M. Organisační zapojení závodní sociální pracovnice. *Sociální pracovnice,* 1947, roč. 16., č. 1/1947. s. 1-7. (PURKYŇOVÁ, M. Organizational Involvement of Enterprise Social Worker. *Social Worker,* 1947, vol. 16, No. 1/1947. pp. 1-7.)

RÁKOSNÍK, J. *Sociální politika jako předmět historického zkoumání.* In ČECHUROVÁ, J., ŠTAIF, J. (eds.) *K novověkým sociálním dějinám Českých zemí VI. Sociální dějiny dnes.* Praha: Karolinum, 2004. s. 179 – 192. (RÁKOSNÍK, J. *Social Policy as a Subject of Historical Exploration.* In ČECHUROVÁ, J., ŠTAIF, J. (eds.) *To the Modern Social History of the Czech Lands VI. Social History Today.* Prague: Karolinum, 2004. pp. 179 – 192.)

RÁKOSNÍK, J. *Sovětizace sociálního státu – Lidově demokratický režim a sociální práva občanů v letech 1945-1960.* Praha: FF UK. Fontes, sv. 2, 2010. (RÁKOSNÍK, J. *Sovietization of the Welfare State – People's Democratic Regime and Social Rights of Citizens in the Years 1945-1960.* Prague: FF UK. Fontes, vol. 2, 2010.)

RÁKOSNÍK, J., TOMEŠ, I, BISKUP, J., KOLDINSKÁ, K., TKÁČ, V., NOVÁK, D. *Sociální stát v Československu.* Praha: Auditorium, 2012. ISBN 978-80-87284-30-8. (RÁKOSNÍK, J., TOMEŠ, I, BISKUP, J., KOLDINSKÁ, K., TKÁČ, V., NOVÁK, D. *The Welfare State in Czechoslovakia.* Prague: Auditorium, 2012. ISBN 978-80-87284-30-8.)

REISCH, M. The Use of History in Teaching Social Work. *Journal of Teaching in Social Work.* The Haworth Press, 1988, vol. 2, 1/1988. pp. 3-16.

RICHMOND, M. Definice sociální práce případové. *Sociální pracovnice,* 1942, roč. 11., č. 8-9/1942. s. 112-117. (RICHMOND, M. Definition of Social Casework. *Social Worker,* 1942, vol. 11, No. 8-9/1942. pp. 112-117.)

ROHÁČKOVÁ, H. Sociální a zdravotní péče o dělníky ve Francii. *Sociální pracovnice,* 1947, roč. 16., č. 1/1947. s. 8-10. (ROHÁČKOVÁ, H. Social and Health Care for Workers in France. *Social Worker,* 1947, vol. 16, No. 1/1947. pp. 8-10.)

ROHEL, J. *Vítkovice, odbory, století 1870-1970.* Ostrava: Podnikový výbor ROH VŽKG, 1970. (ROHEL, J. *Vítkovice, Trade Unions, Century 1870-1970.* Ostrava: Enterprise Committee of RTUM of KGVI, 1970.)

RŮŽIČKA, J., ŠÁLKOVÁ, H. *Sociální pracovník v individuální a skupinové péči o pracovníky v podniku. Podniková péče o pracovníky- část II.* Praha: Ministerstvo práce a sociálních věcí ČSSR, odbor práce, 1971. (RŮŽIČKA, J., ŠÁLKOVÁ, H. *Social Worker in Individual and Group Care for Workers in an Enterprise. Enterprise Care for Workers – Part II.* Prague: Ministry of Labour and Social Affairs of CSSR, Division of Work, 1971.)

Sborník referátů a přednesených diskuzních příspěvků z celostátního aktivu ke komplexním programům péče o pracovníky konaného v Praze dne 2. září 1976. Praha: Ústřední rada odborů, 1976. (*Anthology of Papers and Discussion Contributions from a Nationwide Event on Comprehensive Programmes of Care for Workers held in Prague on 2nd September 1976.* Prague: Central Trade Union Council, 1976.)

Sociální péče československých státních drah. *Sociální revue.* 1923, roč. IV., č.4/1923. s. 298-306. (Social Care of Czechoslovak State Railways. *Social Review.* 1923, vol. IV., No. 4/1923. pp. 298-306.)

SOVA, V. Životní úroveň a její plánování. Praha: Svoboda, 1978. (SOVA, V. *The Living Standard and its Planning.* Prague: Svoboda, 1978.)

ŠÁLKOVÁ, H. *Informace pro podnikové sociální pracovníky.* Sekce sociálních pracovníků v podnicích při Společnosti sociálních pracovníků. Praha: Společnost sociálních pracovníků, 1969. Osobní archiv Ing. Heleny Šálkové. (ŠÁLKOVÁ, H. *Information for Enterprise Social Workers.* Section of Social Workers in Enterprises at the Social Workers' Society. Prague: Social Workers' Society, 1969. Personal archive of Ing. Helena Šálková.)

ŠÁLKOVÁ, H. *Optimální model péče o pracovníky v socialistickém podniku.* Ostrava: Institut hutního průmyslu, 1973. (ŠÁLKOVÁ, H. *An Optimum Model of Care for Workers in a Socialist Enterprise.* Ostrava: Institute of Metallurgical Industry, 1973.)

ŠÁLKOVÁ, H. *Podniková péče o pracovníky. Metodická pomůcka I.* Praha: Ministerstvo práce a sociálních věcí ČSSR, odbor práce, 1971. (ŠÁLKOVÁ, H. *Enterprise Care for Workers. Methodological Aid I.* Prague: Ministry of Labour and Social Affairs of CSSR, Division of Work, 1971.)

ŠÁLKOVÁ, H. Podniková sociální péče. *Zdravotnická pracovnice.* 1970, roč. XX., č.12/1970. s. 656-659. (ŠÁLKOVÁ, H. Enterprise Social Care. *Health Worker.* 1970, year XX., No.12/1970. pp. 656-659.)

ŠÁLKOVÁ, H. Předpokládané změny v podnikové sociální politice. *Sociální/Sociálna politika,* 1991, roč. 17, č. 5/1991. str. 6-20. (ŠÁLKOVÁ, H. Presupposed Changes in Enterprise Social Policy. *Social Policy,* 1991, vol. 17, No. 5/1991. pp. 6-20)

ŠÁLKOVÁ, H. *Sociální politika organizací a sociálně-právní činnosti. Svazek 4.* Pardubice: Dům techniky ČSVTS, 1981. (ŠÁLKOVÁ, H. *Social Policy of Organizations and Socio-Legal Activities. Volume 4.* Pardubice: House of Technology of the Czech Association of Scientific and Technical Societies, 1981.)

ŠÁLKOVÁ, H. *Sociální politika organizací, její řízení a diferencovaná péče o pracovníky.* Pardubice: Dům techniky ČSVTS, 1980. (ŠÁLKOVÁ, H. *Social Policy of Organizations, its Management and Differentiated Care for Workers.* Pardubice: House of Technology of the Czech Association of Scientific and Technical Societies, 1980.)

ŠÁLKOVÁ, H. *Sociální pracovník v průmyslovém podniku.* Praha: Závody silnoproudé elektrotechniky, 1968. Osobní archiv Ing. Heleny Šálkové. (ŠÁLKOVÁ, H. *Social Worker in an Industrial Enterprise.* Prague: High Voltage Electrical Engineering Plants, 1968. Personal archive of Ing. Helena Šálková.)

ŠÁLKOVÁ, H. TOMEŠ, I. *Podniková sociální politika.* Pardubice: Vysoká škola chemicko-technologická, 1983. (ŠÁLKOVÁ, H. TOMEŠ, I. *Enterprise Social Policy.* Pardubice: University of Chemical Technology, 1983.)

ŠÁLKOVÁ, H. *Osobní archiv materiálů k podnikové sociální práci.* Praha: 2016. (ŠÁLKOVÁ, H. *Personal archive of enterprise social work materials.* Prague: 2016.)

ŠÁLKOVÁ, H. *Zaměření práce sociálních pracovníků v podnikové praxi.* Materiál pro kolegium FMPSV konaného 4. 9. 1989. Praha: FMPSV Odbor práce, 1989. Osobní archiv Ing. Heleny Šálkové. (ŠÁLKOVÁ, H. *Focus of Social Workers' Work in Enterprise Practice.* Material for FMLSA Body held on 4. 9. 1989. Prague: FMLSA Division of Work, 1989. Personal archive of Ing. Helena Šálková.)

ŠÁLKOVÁ, H., SVOBODOVÁ, L. Plánování sociálního rozvoje v organizacích a přestavba hospodářského mechanismu. *Ekonomika práce*, 1988, č. 5, roč. 5/1988. s. 7-16. (ŠÁLKOVÁ, H., SVOBODOVÁ, L. Planning of Social Development in Organizations and Reconstruction of the Economic Mechanism. *Economy of Work*, 1988, vol. 5, year 5/1988. pp. 7-16.)

ŠEVEČEK, O. *Zrození Baťovy průmyslové metropole.* Ostrava: Ostravská univerzita v Ostravě, 2009. ISBN 978-80-7368-678-9. (ŠEVEČEK, O. *Inception of Baťa's Industrial Metropolis.* Ostrava: University of Ostrava in Ostrava, 2009. ISBN 978-80-7368-678-9.)

ŠEVEČEK, O. *Company Towns of the Baťa Concern. Introductory remarks.* Paper presented at an international conference "Company Towns of the Baťa Concern": 24-25th March 2011, Prague. Available at file:///C:/Users/oem/Downloads/Prednaska_EN_WEB%20(1).pdf

ŠILHÁNOVÁ, H. Dobrovolná sociální péče v období první republiky. *Sociální politika*, 1992, č. 8/1992, s. 9. (ŠILHÁNOVÁ, H. Voluntary Social Care in the Period of the First Republic. *Social Policy*, 1992, vol. 8/1992, p. 9.)

ŠLACHTA, E. *Od starého Zlína k dnešnímu Gottwaldovu.* Gottwaldov: Oblastní muzeum jihovýchodní Moravy, 1986. (ŠLACHTA, E. *Fromold Zlín to Today's Gottwaldov.* Gottwaldov: Regional Museum of South-Eastern Moravia, 1986.)

ŠMÝD, B. *Sociální služby.* In SCHIMMERLINGOVÁ, V. *Metody sociální práce se starými lidmi.* Praha: MPSV ČSR, 1972. s. 112-113. (ŠMÝD, B. *Social Services.* In SCHIMMERLINGOVÁ, V. *Methods of Social Work with Old People.* Prague: MLSA CSR, 1972. pp. 112-113.)

ŠPILÁČKOVÁ, M. *Soziale Arbeit im Sozialismus: Ein Beispiel aus der Tschechoslowakei (1968-1989).* Research, XXIV. Wiesbaden: Springer VS, 2014. ISBN 978-3-658-04721-4. (ŠPILÁČKOVÁ, M. *Social Work in Socialism: An Example from Czechoslovakia (1968-1989).* Research, XXIV. Wiesbaden: Springer VS, 2014. ISBN 978-3-658-04721-4.)

ŠPILÁČKOVÁ, M. Social Policy and Social Planning in Czechoslovakia and the Role of Social work in enterprises. *Journal of Education & Social Policy,* 2015, year 2, vol. 6/2015, pp. 76-84.

ŠPILÁČKOVÁ, M. The Importance of Historical Knowledge for Social Work as a Science, Profession and Academic Discipline – Experiences from the Czech Republic. *ERIS Journal – Summer 2016.* English edition of Sociální práce/Sociálna práce/Czech and Slovak Social Work, 2016, vol. 16, No. 4/2016, pp. 66-78.

ŠTERN, E. Sociální podnikatel. *Sociální revue,* 1925, roč. IV., s. 1-7. (ŠTERN, E. Social Entrepreneur. *Social Review,* 1925, year IV., pp. 1-7.)

ŠUBRT, J. (ed.) *Historické vědomí jako předmět badatelského zájmu: teorie a výzkum.* Kolín: Nezávislé centrum pro studium politiky, 2010. ISBN 978-80-86879-25-3. (ŠUBRT, J. (ed.) *Historical Awareness as a Subject of Research Interest: Theory and Research.* Kolín: Independent Centre for Political Studies, 2010. ISBN 978-80-86879-25-3.)

ŠUBRT, J., VINOPAL, J. a kol. *Historické vědomí obyvatel České republiky perspektivou sociologického výzkumu.* Praha: Karolinum, 2013. (ŠUBRT, J., VINOPAL, J. et al. *Historical Awareness of the Population of the Czech Republic from the Perspective of Sociological Research.* Prague: Karolinum, 2013.)

ŠUBRT, J. *Historické vědomí a kolektivní paměť.* In ŠUBRT, J., VINOPAL, J. a kol. *Historické vědomí obyvatel České republiky perspektivou sociologického výzkumu.* Praha: Karolinum, 2013. s. 13-25. (ŠUBRT, J. *Historical Awareness and Collective Memory.* In ŠUBRT, J., VINOPAL, J. et al. *Historical Awareness of the Population of the Czech Republic from the Perspective of Sociological Research.* Prague: Karolinum, 2013. pp. 13-25.)

ŠÚSTKOVÁ, H. *Sociální systém VHHT: Rafinovaný způsob vykořisťování zaměstnanců anebo ukázka sociálního kapitalismu? Pohledem historiků v posledních 100 letech. (Social System of VMIC: A Refined Way of Employee Exploitation or Demonstration of Social Capitalism? Through the Eyes of Historians in the Last 100 Years.)* Paper presented at an international conference "Company Towns of the Baťa Concern": 24-25th March 2011, Prague. Available at file:///C:/Users/oem/Downloads/Sustkova_abstract%20(1).pdf

TOMEŠ, I. *Sociální politika: teorie a mezinárodní zkušenost.* Praha: Sociopress, 1996. (TOMEŠ, I. *Social Policy: Theory and International Experience.* Praha: Sociopress, 1996.)

TOMEŠ, I. Úvod do teorie a metodologie sociální politiky. Praha: Portál, 2010. (TOMEŠ, I. *Introduction to Theory and Methodology of Social Policy.* Prague: Portál, 2010.)

TOMEŠ, I. Metamorfózy sociální státu v Československu v letech 1956-1989. *Soudobé dějiny,* 2013, č. 1-2/2013. s. 65-89. (TOMEŠ, I. Metamorphoses of the Welfare State in Czechoslovakia in the Years 1956-1989. *Contemporary History,* 2013, vol. 1-2/2013. pp. 65-89.)

TOULOTTE, S. *The Social Service in the Workplace: An Agent in Change.* Paper presented at the 8th year of International Spring School of Social Work between 8th-11th April 2014 in Ostrava. European Research Institute of Social Work, 2014. Available at http://evis.osu.cz/index.php?kategorie=35844&id=12154

VALACH, F. *Fenomén Baťa.* Praha: Práce, 1990. ISBN 80-208-0025-5. (VALACH, F. *The Baťa Phenomenon.* Prague: Práce, 1990. ISBN 80-208-0025-5.)

VAVREČKA, H. *Předmluva.* In ERDÉLY, E. *Baťa švec, který dobyl světa.* Praha: Dobrovský, 2013. s. 5-11. (VAVREČKA, H. *Preface.* In ERDÉLY, E. *Baťa, the Shoemaker who Conquered the World.* Prague: Dobrovský, 2013. pp. 5-11.)

VITÁSKOVÁ, Š. *Osobní archiv k firmě Baťa.* Ostrava: 2016. (VITÁSKOVÁ, Š. *Personal archive as to Baťa company.* Ostrava: 2016.)

Vítkovice a dělnictvo. *Moravsko – Slezský Duch Času,* 1900, roč. 1, číslo 1/20. červenec 1900, s. 1. (Vítkovice and Labourers *Moravian-Silesian Spirit of Time,* 1900, year 1, vol. 1/20. July 1900, p. 1.)

VOSTŘEBALOVÁ, V. Švédské tovární inspektorky. *Sociální pracovnice,* 1933, roč. II., číslo 7/1933. s. 40-41. (VOSTŘEBALOVÁ, V. Swedish Factory Inspectors. *Social Worker,* 1933, year II., vol. 7/1933. pp. 40-41.)

ZAHRADNÍK, S. *Třinecké železárny. Období báňské a hutní společnosti 1906-1938.* Praha: Práce, 1969. (ZAHRADNÍK, S. *Třinec Iron and Steel Works. Period of Mining and Metallurgical Company 1906-1938.* Prague: Práce, 1969.)

Závodní sociální pracovnice. *Sociální pracovnice,* 1943, roč. 12., č. 2/1943. s. 36. (Factory Social Workers. *Social Worker,* 1943, year 12., vol. 2/1943. p. 36.)

ZAPLETALOVÁ, L., ZAPLETAL, P. *Sociologie v kádrové a personální praxi. In Kolektiv autorů. Vědy o člověku v kádrové a personální praxi.* Ostrava: Hutnický institut, 1972. s. 83-200. (ZAPLETALOVÁ, L., ZAPLETAL, P. *Sociology in Personal Screening and Personnel Practice. In Collective of authors. Human Sciences in Personal Screening and Personnel Practice.* Ostrava: Institute of Metallurgy, 1972. pp. 83-200.)

Z historie prvního Českého spolku v Moravské Ostravě. *Polední deník*, 1940, ročník XLI, číslo 18/23.1.1940, str. 2. (From History of the First Czech Association in Moravská Ostrava. *Midday Daily*, 1940, year XLI, volume 18/23.1.1940, p. 2.)

ZWETTLER, O., VACULÍK, J., ČAPKA, F. Úvod do studia dějepisu a technika historikovy práce. Brno: Pedagogická fakulta, Masarykova univerzita v Brně. 1996. (ZWETTLER, O., VACULÍK, J., ČAPKA, F. *Introduction to the Study of History and Techniques of Historian's Work*. Brno: Faculty of Education, Masaryk University in Brno. 1996.

LIST OF ARCHIVAL SOURCES

1. Moravian Land Archives in Brno, State District Archives of Zlín, Archives of Zlín – Klečůvka[19].

Baťa Archival Fonds

sign. I.   **Company Management**

sign. II. **Personnel Department**

sign. II/8   **Cutting Service – collection of newspaper articles**
                    inv. No. 34. Care or employees, c. No. 191-194
                    inv. No. 35. Saving and Employees' Savings Balance, c. No. 195
                    inv. No. 37. School system and education, c. No. 206
                    inv. No. 38. Housing, c. No. 212
                    inv. No. 45. Social care, donations, c. No. 239, 241, 244

sign. II/9   **Accommodation Department**
                    inv. No. 8., c. No. 1331, fol. č. 0-68

sign. II/10   **Social Department** (allowances, filing cabinets, visits, illnesses,
                    weddings, social institute, enterprise catering)
                    inv. No. 1. c. No. 1331, fol. 1-10
                    inv. No. 4, c. No. 1332
                    inv. No. 5, c. No. 1333
                    inv. No. 29, c. No. 1338
                    inv. No. 30, c. No. 1338
                    inv. No. 31, c. No. 1339
                    inv. No. 34, c. No. 1339

Archival fonds sign. X – Selling v in CSR, inv. No. 87

Archival fonds sign. 035 BH – Baťa Hospital
                    inv. No. 74. fol. 16 – Baťa's "House of Health"
                    inv. No. 131. fol. 131 – Baťa Social-Health and Medical Institute

---

19 In 2012 the Zlín workplace of the Moravian Land Archives in Brno was closed down. The fonds
of the enterprise archives of Svit jsc. Zlín which had been deposited there were transferred to the
State District Archives in Zlín, as follows from the Annual Report on the Activities of the Moravian Land Archives in Brno for 2012.

Archival fonds sign. 036 BSF – Baťa Support Fund
inv. No. 1 Original Company Statutes – c. No. 1
inv. No. 7 Record of activity of BSF in 1945 – c. No. 2
inv. No. 19 Information report on the BSF mission – c. No. 5
inv. No. 25 Social activity of BSF for 1944 – c. No. 6
inv. No. 205 Brief history of the enterprise and BSF – c. No. 48

Baťa Archival fonds, sign. II/2, c. No. 1026, inv. No. 14, serial Mo. 80 – Jabůrek

2. Archives of Vítkovice jsc

VMIC Fonds – 10

Inv. No. 149, reg. No. 14	Book of records and commands of Director Kupelwieser 1882-1886.
Inv. No. 151, reg. No. 16	Book of proceedings and conferences of Department Heads (in German)
Inv. No. 1064, reg. No. 180	Overview of the history, situation and economic management and technology of VMIC – participation in companies. 1942.

VMIC Fonds – 11

Inv. No. 1383, reg. No. 248	Applications of the women's charitable Association Dobromila for support of the Public Vocational School for Women's Occupations in Vítkovice. 1901-1902, 1924-1939.
Inv. No. 1610, reg. No. 302	Annual reports of the Department of Social Facilities of VMIC from years 1935-1944 and overviews of social facilities of VMIC from years 1911-1944.
Inv. No. 1623, reg. No. 304	Writings reading the almshouse, apprentices' home and nursery of VMIC, years 1926-37.
Inv. No. 1636, reg. No. 309	Descriptions of W. Gutmann Almshouse, Orphanage Foundation of VMIC, shelter or children and kindergartens of VMIC, year 1937.

VMIC Fonds – 17

Inv. No. 6099, reg. No. 1405	Study on work and social policy of VI (Dr. R. Schwenger, German text).

Fonds – General Maintenance Institute No. 35

Inv. No. 28, reg. No. 12	A brief overview of the history of the GMI for the enterprise chronicle 1946.

RTUM Fonds 1945-54

Inv. No. 53, reg. No. 14	Social section – minutes of meetings, activity reports, 1945-49.
Inv. No. 78, reg. No. 15	Care for workers – credit event "Radio receiver for employees". 1947-49.
Inv. No. 189, reg. No. 26	Czechoslovak Institute of Labour organises social research in metallurgy, 1949.
Inv. No. 232, reg. No. 28	Activity of enterprise social service – monthly reports for the attention of the Social Committee, 1952.

Fonds of Enterprise Sickness Fund

Inv. No. 10, reg. No. 1	A brief overview of the history of the sickness insurance fund for the enterprise chronicle, 1946.

VMIC Fonds – n.a.

Inv. No. 423, reg. No. 29	Reports on Social Activities in the Ironworks, 1945.
Inv. No. 184, reg. No. 23	Activity report of the Social Group for October 1945.

Fonds Vítkovice 1946-1954

Inv. No. 898, reg. No. 153	Change in organization of the Employee Department 1949-51.
Inv. No. 900, reg. No. 153	Socio-Political Department, names and functions of managers, 1946.
Inv. No. 901, reg. No. 153	Socio-Political Department, scope and personnel costs, 1947.
Inv. No. 1070, reg. No. 167	Annual report of the Social Department for the year 1946.
Inv. No. 1072, reg. No. 167	Preliminary report on social service of VI, s.o.e. in 1947.
Inv. No. 1078, reg. No. 167	Overview of activities of the Sh department – economic matters from 1948, report of the social section for 1952.
Inv. No. 1082, reg. No. 167	Social policy in year 1948.
Inv. No. 1087, reg. No. 168	Enterprise social workers, 1946-47, 49.
Inv. No. 1115, reg. No. 169	Overview of social buildings, 1947.
Inv. No. 1684, reg. No. 218	How s.o.e. VI cares for its employees and what social benefits it provides to its employees, 1947.

3. Ostrava City Archives

Fonds – Higher School of Health Care in Vítkovice NAD 490

File 6, inv. No. 125   Final examinations of social workers and sick-nurses, 1947-1950.

LIST OF ARCHIVAL AIDS

Fond Baťa, akciová společnost Zlín. 1894-1945. Inventář. Osobní oddělení II/9-II/13, III., IV., V. Zlín: Podnikový archiv Svit a.s., Zlín. 2004. *(Fonds of Baťa, joint stock company Zlín. 1894-1945. Inventory.* Personnel Department II/9-II/13, III., IV., V. Zlín: Company Archives of Svit jsc, Zlín. 2004.)

Fond Baťa, akciová společnost Zlín. 1894-1945. Inventář. Osobní oddělení II/8. Zlín: Podnikový archiv Svit a.s., Zlín. 2004. *(Fonds of Baťa, joint stock company Zlín. 1894-1945. Inventory.* Personnel Department II/8. Zlín: Company Archives of Svit jsc, Zlín. 2004.)

KLEPÁČ, J., PROKEŠ, F. *Fond Baťův podpůrný fond. Inventář. 1872-1960.* Zlín: Podnikový archiv Svit a.s. Zlín, 1961. (KLEPÁČ, J., PROKEŠ, F. *Fonds of Baťa Support Fund. Inventory. 1872-1960.* Zlín: Company Archives of Svit jsc, Zlín. 1961.)

KOCKOVÁ, R. *Odborné školy v Ostravě, Vítkovicích, Zábřehu. Inventář.* Ostrava: AMO, 1962. číslo pomůcky 8. (KOCKOVÁ, R. *Vocational Schools in Ostrava, Vítkovice, Zábřeh. Inventory.* Ostrava: OCA, 1962. Aid No. 8.)

Kolektiv podnikového archivu VŽKG n.p. *Vítkovické horní a hutní těžířstvo (1756) 1828-1945 (1951).* Inventární seznam. Ostrava: Podnikový archiv Vítkovic – železáren a strojíren Klementa Gottwalda, 1973-1974. (Collective of the Company Archives KGVI s.o.e. *Vítkovice Mining and Iron Corporation (1756) 1828-1945 (1951).* Inventory list. Ostrava: Company Archives of Vítkovice – Klement Gottwald Ironworks, 1973-1974.)

MACHOTKOVÁ, J. *Bratrská pokladna Vítkovických železáren. 1883-1893.* Inventář č. 12. Ostrava: Sdružený archiv Vítkovice a.s., 2000a. (MACHOTKOVÁ, J. *Fraternal Treasury of Vítkovice Ironworks. 1883-1893.* Inventory No. 12. Ostrava: Associated Archives of Vítkovice jsc, 2000a.)

MACHOTKOVÁ, J. *Pensijní ústav I. VHHT 1897-1941. Pensijní ústav II. VHHT 1904-1941.* Sdružený inventář č. 28. Ostrava: Sdružený archiv Vítkovice a.s., 2000b. (MACHOTKOVÁ, J. *Pension Institute I. VMIC 1897-1941. Pension Institute II. VMIC 1904-1941.* Associated Inventory No. 28. Ostrava: Associated Archives of Vítkovice jsc, 2000b)

MACHOTKOVÁ, J. *Všeobecný zaopatřovací ústav Vítkovických železáren n.p. 1895-1954.* Inventář č. 10. Ostrava: Sdružený archiv Vítkovice a.s., 2000c. (MACHOTKOVÁ, J. *General Maintenance Institute of Vítkovice Ironworks s.o.e. 1895-1954.* Inventory No. 10. Ostrava: Associated Archives of Vítkovice jsc, 2000c.)

MACHOTKOVÁ, J. *Závodní nemocenská pojišťovna Vítkovických železáren n.p. 1895-1948.* Inventář č. 11. Ostrava: Sdružený archiv Vítkovice a.s., 2000d.

(MACHOTKOVÁ, J. *Company Health Insurance Funds of* Vítkovice *Ironworks s.o.e. 1895-1948.* Inventory No. 11. Ostrava: Associated Archives of Vítkovice jsc, 2000d.)

ROH – podnikový výbor VÍTKOVICE s. p. Ostrava, časová vrstva (1917) 1945-1954. Pořádací schéma k archivnímu fondu. (*RTUM – Enterprise Committee of VÍTKO-VICE s.o.e. Ostrava, time layer (1917) 1945-1954.* Arrangement scheme for archival fonds.)

VHHT, n. s. Časová vrstva 1945-1946. Inventární seznam a.s. Vítkovice. Ostrava, 1993. (*VMIC, n.a. Time layer 1945-1946.* Inventory list of jsc Vítkovice. Ostrava, 1993.)

LIST OF USED ABBREVIATIONS

ABŠ	School leaver of the Baťa School of Labour (abbreviated from Czech 'Absolventi Baťovy školy práce')
AV	Archives of Vítkovice jsc
BH	Baťa Hospital
BSF	Baťa Support Fund
BSL	Baťa School of Labour
c. No.	carton number
Cs.	Czechoslovak
CSK	Czechoslovak crown
CSR	Czechoslovak Republic
CSSR	Czechoslovak Socialist Republic
FMLSA	Federal Ministry of Labour and Social Affairs
fol.	folium (archival identification data)
inv. No.	inventory number
jsc	joint stock company
KGVI	Klement Gottwald Vítkovice Ironworks
MLSA	Ministry of Labour and Social Affairs
n.a.	national administrator
OCA	Ostrava City Archives
reg. No.	registration number
RTUM	Revolutionary Trade Union Movement
SDAZ	State District Archives of Zlín
s.o.e.	state-owned enterprise
SUY	Socialist Union of Youth
SWS	Social Workers' Society
UN	United Nations
USSR	Union of Soviet Socialist Republics
VI	Vítkovice Ironworks
VMIC	Vítkovice Mining and Iron Corporation

LIST OF DIAGRAMS AND FIGURES

LIST OF TABLES

INDEX